Gold and the Modern World Economy

Gold is not merely an element, it has become a byword for preciousness and has been inextricably linked to currency since the long period of economic history which saw the commodity used as the main means of transaction all over the world.

This book, a comprehensive guide to the role of gold in the modern world economy, contains contributions from a wide range of leading experts in economics. *Gold and the Modern World Economy* examines such themes as:

- the role of gold throughout the history of economics
- gold as a commitment measurement
- the price of gold and the exchange rate

This important topic is addressed with style and rigour, and the book will interest students and academics involved in financial, international and industrial economics.

MoonJoong Tcha is a Senior Lecturer at the University of Western Australia.

Routledge Studies in the Modern World Economy

To Sooyoung, Kyungchae (Estelle) and Dongyoung,
who are more precious than gold to me

Gold and the Modern World Economy

Edited by
MoonJoong Tcha

LONDON AND NEW YORK

First published 2003
by Routledge
11 New Fetter Lane, London EC4P 4EE

Simultaneously published in the USA and Canada
by Routledge
29 West 35th Street, New York, NY 10001

Routledge is an imprint of the Taylor & Francis Group

Typeset in Times by
Prepress Projects Ltd, Perth, Scotland
Printed and bound in Great Britain by
Antony Rowe Ltd, Chippenham, Wiltshire

British Library Cataloguing in Publication Data
A catalogue record for this book is available from the British Library

Library of Congress Cataloging in Publication Data
A catalog record for this book has been requested

ISBN 0–415–27561–X

Contents

Figures

Tables

Contributors

Chris Allen, Taron Brearley, Antony Clarke, Julie Harman and **Peter Berry** are economists in the Australian Bureau of Agricultural and Resource Economics.

Michael D. Bordo is a Professor in the Department of Economics, Rutgers University, New Jersey.

Andrew Feltenstein is a Professor in the Department of Economics, Virginia Polytechnic.

Izan H. Y. Izan is a Professor in the Graduate School of Management, University of Western Australia.

Duane Rockerbie is a Professor in the Department of Economics, University of Lethbridge.

Fabio Scacciavillani is an economist with the European Central Bank.

E. A. Selvanathan is a Professor in the School of International Business, Griffith University.

Saroja Selvanathan is an Associate Professor in the School of Economics, Griffith University.

Larry Sjaastad is a Professor in the Department of Economics, University of Chicago.

MoonJoong Tcha is a Senior Lecturer in the Department of Economics, University of Western Australia.

Ernst Juerg Weber is a Senior Lecturer in the Department of Economics, University of Western Australia.

Chris Wiggins is a non-executive director for N M Rothschild & Sons (Australia) Limited.

Jeffrey Wong is a former graduate student of the Department of Accounting and Finance, University of Western Australia.

Foreword

Even after the formal demonetarization of gold in the early 1970s, with the break-down of the Bretton Woods system of fixed exchange rates, gold still retains its fascination to economists for several reasons:

- The price of gold acts as an early-warning signal of future turmoil in the world economy, be it a major slump in economic activity in the large industrialized countries, war, an increase in inflation, or disruptions to other global commodity or currency markets.
- Gold still occupies a substantial share in the portfolios of many central banks. Does this represent a good investment for taxpayers in terms of risk and return?
- Gold's unique properties of durability mean that its price is governed by forward-looking considerations, such as those emphasized in asset-pricing models of modern financial economics. This perspective highlights the role of the overall outstanding stock of gold, and the key role played by expectations regarding future developments. Interestingly, the gold industry tends to emphasize a completely different set of factors that determine gold prices, viz. the flow supply of gold from current and future mines and the flow demand for jewellery and industrial uses, and for investment purposes. Is it possible to reconcile these two approaches, or are they basically incompatible? To put it another way, can the variability of gold prices be decomposed into an expectations component and a flow component?
- Gold is an important export for some countries, Australia and South Africa in particular. In Australia, there has been a major surge in gold production and exports over the last two decades, which has had a substantial impact on the national and regional economies. What is the fundamental source of this surge, and what can other industries learn from this success story?
- There are interesting public finance issues associated with gold. Although many economists favor a resource rent tax, whereby economic profits (or rents) are subject to taxation, with the distortionary impacts minimized, in practice, such a system is rarely employed. Interestingly, until the late 1980s, gold mining was the only industry entirely exempt from income taxation in Australia. And in Western Australia, the major gold-producing state of Australia, gold was

royalty free until the late 1990s. It is a challenge to economists to understand these unusual taxation arrangements pertaining to gold, and to devise better approaches.

This book deals with some of these fundamental issues, and several others. The material in the book will be of interest to those working in financial markets, policy makers, researchers, and all students of the world economy.

Kenneth W. Clements,
Department of Economics,
University of Western Australia

Acknowledgements

I have benefited enormously from the contributions made by many people while I was editing this collection. Ken Clements, who contributed the foreword for this book, was always helpful and supportive at every stage of its gestation. The idea to collect papers on the subject of gold and economics was in fact sparked from discussions I had with him. I am indebted to the Department of Economics at the University of Western Australia and to Paul Miller, then head of the department, for generously providing financial support for this project. Patricia Wang's assistance was always excellent, and K. Andrew Semmens provided wonderful editorial assistance. Much gratitude is also owed to two people at Routledge: Robert Langham and Terry Clague. Separated by thousands of miles, we nevertheless shared the joys and sorrows of the 2002 World Cup together, and this book represents the culmination of a real partnership between publisher and author. I was very fortunate to work with both these people and I am grateful for the professionalism and humanity they displayed throughout the project. We can console each other that neither of the teams we support made the final in the World Cup.

I would also like to gratefully acknowledge the following journals and organizations for generously granting permission to reproduce papers: 'Gold as a Commitment Mechanism: Past, Present and Future' (Michael Bordo), *Research Study* No.11, World Gold Council, 1995; 'The Price of Gold and the Exchange Rate' (Larry Sjaastad and Fabio Scacciavillani), *Journal of International Money and Finance*, vol. 15(6), 1996; 'An Analysis of the Implications for the Gold Mining Industry of Alternative Tax Policies: A Regional Disaggregated Model for Australia' (Andrew Feltenstein), *Economic Record*, vol. 73, 1997; 'International Barriers to Gold Trade' (Chris Allen, Taron Brearley, Antony Clarke, Julie Harman and Peter Berry), *ABARE Research report* 99.8, Australian Bureau of Agricultural and Resource Economics, 1999. In addition, 'Gold Production in Western Australia: An Econometric Analysis' (Anthony Selvanathan and Saroja Selvanathan) and 'Output Response to Gold Prices: More Evidence for South Africa' (Duane Rockerbie) are developments of their papers originally published in *Resource Policy* 25 (1999).

If there is any value-added that I have created by editing this book, it is because of my family, my teachers at Seoul National University and the University of Chicago, and my colleagues at the University of Western Australia, all of whom have played such an important role in my personal and professional development. Therefore, I thank all of them.

MoonJoong Tcha

1 Gold and the world economy
Overview

MoonJoong Tcha

We all know that gold is precious. We also have learnt, however, that there is not necessarily a correlation between everything that we regard as being precious and what lies at the centre or at the heart of our real interests. In this sense, gold is unique not simply because of the never-ending demand for gold to make jewellery but also because it is the commodity most closely related to a variety of issues that we face every minute in our lives, especially where economic incentives and reasoning are involved. In addition to the long period when gold was used as an official means of transaction, even after the collapse of the Bretton Woods international monetary system cut the link between gold and money in 1971, gold continues to be used as part of most countries' reserve holdings. In fact, gold is the only commodity held as reserves by monetary authorities. Moreover, gold's role as a financial asset has become increasingly significant as the present system of floating exchange rates struggles to find firm ground in markets and currencies of increasing volatility (Kile, 1991). Bernstein (2000) alludes to the fact that the concept of gold as a certain and risk-free asset has been dormant in humans' behaviour from ancient times, when he states that:

> . . . from poor King Midas who was overwhelmed by it to the Aly Kahn who gave away his weight in gold every year, from the dank mines of South Africa to the antiseptic cellars at Fort Knox, from the gorgeous artworks of the Scythians to the Corichancha of the Incas, from the street markets of Bengal to the financial markets in the City of London, gold reflects the universal quest for eternal life – the ultimate certainty and escape from risk.
>
> (Bernstein, 2000: 5)

The history of gold as the most important part of the monetary system goes back to the sixth century BC, when the country of Lydia created electrum coins, which were an alloy of gold and silver (Mundell, 1997). Since then, gold has been at the centre of monetary systems, in spite of the frequent challenges from another metal, silver. In the modern economy, although gold no longer enjoys the prestigious status of a 'currency', it is still treated as a special commodity for a variety of reasons. Today, gold has a wide variety of uses, and is found in jewellery, electronic products and official coins and medals, as well being used in dentistry and as reserves by the monetary authorities and a principal means of hoarding or investment. Table 1.1 reports a variety of end uses of gold, in addition to its use as reserves.

As gold has a variety of end uses, a large number of studies on various facets of gold have been carried out. In the field of economics, the relationship between gold and currencies has received the widest and the most extensive attention. Although, not surprisingly, two chapters in this book concentrate on this topic, this book goes further and discusses other crucial issues related to gold in the modern economy, such as gold and exchange rates, gold exposures, trade and a range of issues pertaining to gold production.

An encyclopaedic introduction on the place of gold as a unique and important commodity in the modern economy is provided by Wiggins in the next chapter. Examining the characteristics of gold, he introduces a variety of topics related to gold, such as a brief history of gold as a commodity, the supply of and demand for gold, hoarding, investment and financial transactions involving gold. Wiggins's chapter, in particular, discusses timely and relevant topics regarding gold and finance, such as gold loans and hedging, to which extensive attention has been paid in the modern era.

Although gold has been used extensively for a variety of purposes, to economists and policy makers the most important role of gold stems from the unique place it has in the context of monetary systems. Bordo, one of the leading experts in this field, discusses this aspect of gold in Chapter 3. He gives a useful summary of recent advances in the analysis of the gold standard and related monetary regimes. Using an analytic framework jointly developed with Kydland, the author applies the literature on monetary rules vs. discretionary rules to the gold standard. He describes the ways in which gold has historically functioned as a commitment

Table 1.1 World gold absorption by end use (million fine troy ounces)

	1975	1980	1985	1990	1995	1999
Industrial						
Jewellery: advanced countries	10.0	10.7	20.2	28.5	33.1	34.5
Jewellery: developing countries	6.6	6.8	17.3	32.4	53.5	58.3
Electronics	2.2	3.2	3.8	4.2	4.0	4.5
Dentistry	2.0	2.1	1.9	2.0	2.2	2.4
Other industrial	1.9	1.6	1.2	1.5	1.5	1.5
Medals etc.	0.7					
Investment						
Official coins	7.8	7.7	4.8	3.9	2.5	4.0
Hoarding	0					
Speculation and investment	4.4					
Small bars						
Bullion		13.7	3.6	3.9	3.1	6.8
Medallions		1.2	0.4	0.7	0.6	0.8
Total	35.7	47.0	53.2	77.1	94.3	112.8

Source: *Minerals Yearbook* (various issues).

mechanism, and argues that it can still serve as an indirect credibility mechanism in modern conditions. In this respect, his view is, by and large, in accordance with other leading experts in the field, such as Mundell (1997, 2000).

Though the role of gold as a commitment mechanism is almost univocally supported by experts, in Chapter 4 Weber presents a fresh perspective, which is critical of the conventional view of central bank gold holdings. The official relationship between currency and gold has been broken. Nevertheless, gold is still the most popular medium of exchange among policy makers and bankers, and constitutes a large portion of most countries reserves, together with the US dollar and special drawing right (SDR) and, more recently, the euro. Contrary to the popular argument that official gold reserves make a currency more secure (a view that was strengthened by the Washington Agreement in 1999, which defined gold as an important element of global monetary reserves), Weber demonstrates that this argument misses the point as it applies principles that were true under the classical gold standard regime to the modern international monetary system. After an intensive discussion on the role of gold holdings by central banks, the author interestingly concludes that central banks should dispose of their gold holdings because they are an ineffective cover for the currency and potentially detrimental to the conduct of monetary policy; the opportunity cost incurred is also substantial. His argument is instructive in pointing out that gold holdings can be misused by policy makers to increase the money authorities' welfare. As summarized in Table 1.2, in spite of a significant decrease in the amount gold reserves held by some countries, such as the USA and the UK (where a significant decrease occurred only in the early 1970s), there is no evidence that the total amount of gold held as reserves in the world has decreased since 1971. Some countries, including Japan, France, Germany and the Netherlands, have actually maintained or even increased the level of the gold reserves compared with what they held in 1970. Throughout the 1980s, the total amount of gold held by monetary authorities has been stable, ranging from 1,140 to 1,150 million fine troy ounces, an amount that represents about one-third of the total gold in the world, even higher than that in the early 1970s. At that time, the total volume of gold reserves held by central banks reached just over 1,000 million troy ounces. The 1990s witnessed a slight decrease in the level of gold holdings; however, even at the end of the 1999, it amounted to almost 1,100 million fine troy ounces. Even though some of these reserves are used as

Table 1.2 Central bank gold reserves (million fine troy ounces)

	1970	1975	1980	1985	1990	1995	1999
USA	316.3	275.2	264.3	262.7	261.9	261.7	261.7
UK	38.5	21.0	18.8	19.0	18.9	18.4	23.0
Japan	15.2	21.1	24.2	24.2	24.2	24.2	24.2
France	100.9	100.9	81.9	81.9	81.9	81.9	97.0
Germany	113.7	117.6	95.2	95.2	95.2	95.2	111.5
The Netherlands	51.1	54.3	43.9	43.9	43.9	34.8	32.5

Source: *Minerals Yearbook* (various issues).

financial instruments such as gold loans, as Weber points out, the opportunity cost is never negligible.

These last two chapters mentioned certainly provide an excellent review of the role of gold as a commitment mechanism in the era of the floating exchange regime. Moreover, they also raise the importance, and highlight the inherent danger, of central banks' gold holdings, which have been largely ignored previously. The following three chapters in the book deal with very important issues related to gold in the modern economy: first, international barriers to gold trade; second, gold prices and exchange rates; and, third, gold exposures in the stock market. Chapter 5, by Allen *et al.*, reviews international barriers to gold trade and the effects on the world gold price of removing tariffs on gold import. Though gold is traded competitively in an extensive network of global spot and forward markets, the authors indicate that substantial trade barriers are prevailing. For example, import tariff on gold as jewellery is as high as 40 per cent in some countries such as China and Vietnam, but, in contrast, import tariff on gold as bullion is almost negligible. The authors accept the welfare arguments of the mainstream international economics about the effect of free trade on price, consumer welfare and producer welfare, and estimate the effect of tariff removal. With some assumptions on selected parameters such as price elasticity of gold production, they estimate that free trade will result in an increase in world gold price of between 1.7 and 5.4 per cent in the long run, and Australia's gold production could increase by between 4 and 12 per cent.

Chapter 6, co-authored by Sjaastad and Scacciavillani, examines the determination of gold prices influenced by the fluctuation in exchange rates, and Chapter 7, written by Izan and Wong, analyses how the fluctuation in the spot price of gold affects the value of gold mining companies. The topics explored in both of these chapters have not previously been thoroughly researched, in spite of their significant implication for a variety of stakeholders from gold miners to policy makers.

The price of gold had been stable until the early 1970s, and then started to become relatively more volatile after the dissolution of the Bretton Woods system, as shown in Figure 1.1. Sjaastad and Scacciavillani begin by constructing a model of the theoretical relationship between the major exchange rates and the prices of internationally traded commodities. The authors then empirically analyse the case of gold using the model constructed and forecast error data. Among other things, their most crucial finding is that, since the dissolution of the Bretton Woods international monetary system, floating exchange rates among the major currencies have been a major source of price instability in world gold markets. This finding is noteworthy as it contradicts the prevailing view that the price of gold depends on other factors related to demand and supply. Although the breakdown in the official relationship between gold and currencies accelerates the fluctuation of exchange rates, that same fluctuation of exchange rates, in turn, influences the price of gold. The authors also find that appreciations or depreciations of European currencies – such as the Deutschemark – have strong effects on the price of gold in other currencies – such as the US dollar or the Japanese yen. The European currency bloc is found to account for about two-thirds of total market power, and, although gold is usually denominated in US dollars, this bloc has a small influence on the dollar price of

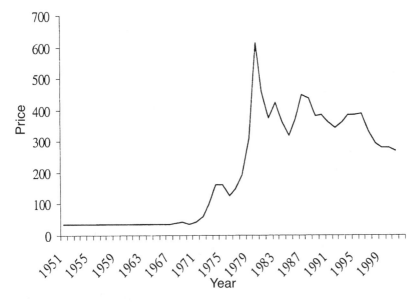

Figure 1.1 Fluctuations of gold prices (in US dollars).

Source: *Minerals Yearbook* (various issues).

gold. The major gold producers such as South Africa, Australia and the former USSR appear not to have a significant influence on the world price of gold.

It is well known that the share price of gold mining companies reacts differently to changes in the spot price of gold. Chapter 7, written by Wong and Izan, investigates why some companies are more sensitive than others to changes in the gold price. In particular, the chapter examines the relationship between gold price exposure (the sensitivity of the share price to changes in the gold price) and the characteristics of the gold companies. Based on the valuation models proposed by Tufano (1998), and using data collected and pooled over the period 1 July 1996 to 30 June 1999, this chapter quantitatively analyses Australia's gold mining companies, and finds that the gold price exposure is greater than 1, but the size of the exposure for individual companies is not always greater than 1. The authors also find that gold prices, production costs and the degree of financial leverage are the only significant determinants of gold price exposure. In contrast, the hedging quantity and the hedging contract price, variables which proxy for the companies' risk management policies, are not found to influence the gold price exposure of the company. These chapters will provide invaluable information to policy makers and investors as well as to gold miners.

As Sjaastad and Scacciavillani demonstrate in Chapter 6, the world gold price is not as significantly affected by the major producers' currencies as by the major consumers' currency. Nonetheless, this finding does not undermine the importance of the topics associated with the production of gold. The analysis of the supply of gold is particularly interesting as gold is not a perishable commodity. Moreover, as Bernstein (2000) pointed out, although gold deposits are widespread, no single deposit has allowed its gold to be easily extracted. For example, each year some 70 million tonnes of earth must be raised and milled in South Africa to produce about 500 tonnes of gold. While it seems clear that the iron law of supply – the positive elasticity of supply with respect to price – applies, it is not clear, especially when we take into consideration the complex and time-consuming process of production, for how long and to what degree fluctuations in price affect gold production. Nor is it clear how, and in what ways, the gold industry affects the economy. The last three chapters of this book explore these topics. The three chapters, using rigorous quantitative analytical methods, are devoted to discussing the effect of changes in gold prices or costs on the production of gold, focusing in particular on two of the world's major gold producers, South Africa and Australia. In Chapter 8, Rockerbie, a specialist in this area, develops a model of gold production that makes use of the relationship between the price of gold and the average mill pay limit, and therefore allows for the possibility of an inverse gold supply curve. Increases in the price of gold, with constant production costs, reduce the average mill pay limit, which provides an incentive for producers to step up production and move into deeper shafts of lower quality ore. If the reduction in the average grade of ore outweighs the increase in the quantity of ore milled, the actual amount of gold produced will fall. His model explicitly considers the feedback from a declining average grade of ore to higher extraction costs. Utilizing an econometric specification of the model based on South African production data, his findings suggest that the necessary conditions for a perversely downward sloping gold supply curve do not hold, but only just so. Although his work is based on South African data, his approach and results may be applied to other gold-producing countries.

In Chapter 9, Selvanathan and Selvanathan intensively analyse the effects of price changes on gold production in Australia, where, in recent years, the production of gold has grown strongly. In 2002, Australia is ranked the world's third largest gold producer, behind only South Africa and the USA. Most of the Australian gold production comes from one of its states, Western Australia. Selvanathan and Selvanathan use recent developments in econometric time series analysis to present an analysis of gold production and prices in this state during the period 1948–94. Their results show that if the price of gold (relative to costs) increases by 10 per cent and the price (in levels) remains the same for the next 5 years, then gold production will rise by 0.3 per cent in the first year; by 2.2 per cent in the second year; by 7.4 per cent in the third year; by 8.9 per cent in the fourth year; and by 10.7 per cent in the fifth year. They conclude, therefore, that the dynamic elasticity almost achieves unity after 5 years, and the long-term steady-state elasticity of value 1.24 is reached after 12 years. They also use Efron's (1979) bootstrap technique to assess the quality of the estimated results and forecasts of gold production.

Chapter 10, written by Feltenstein, uses a computable general equilibrium model to examine the effect on the economy of taxing gold. The author constructs a dynamic model of the Australian economy, which has a regional subsection, to investigate how the taxation of gold exports affects the economy. It is useful to analyse the Australian economy in this regard considering that gold constitutes

Australia's second largest export commodity. Carrying out a simulation in which gold exports are subject to some rate of tax, Feltenstein finds that there is no fiscal improvement at the national level, although the budget of Western Australia, the leading state of gold production, improves. However, he also finds that real income falls both nationally and within the state, as reduced gold sales cause the trade balance to deteriorate, and an increased real interest rate causes investment to fall. The author argues convincingly that taxation on gold exports leads to few measurable benefits, and may have quite negative consequences as well.

As a collection of articles contributed by leading experts in the field, this book will provide precious information regarding various aspects of the economics of gold, from its production to trade and its final uses. It will also contribute to understanding of the role of gold in modern economies, by examining timely issues such as gold and stock markets, and gold reserves and monetary systems. All the chapters that analyse empirical data construct very well-designed models and adopt quantitative analysis methods, which provide good examples to those who intend to investigate the field of how to model related issues to gold and estimate relevant relationships. While some parts are quite advanced and technical, the implications of the results presented will be easily understood by anyone who is interested in the economics of gold.

References

Bernstein, P. (2000) *The Power of Gold*, New York: John Wiley & Sons.

Efron, B. (1979) 'Bootstrap methods: another look at the jacknife', *Annals of Statistics*, 7(1): 1–26.

Kile, M. (1991) *The Case for Gold in the 1990s*, East Perth, WA: Gold Corporation.

Mundell, R. (1997) 'The international monetary system in the twenty first century: could gold make a comeback?', lecture delivered at St. Vincent College, Pennsylvania. Available online at http://www.columbia.edu/~ram15/LBE.htm

——(2000) 'The relationship between currencies and gold', *The Euro, the Dollar and Gold*, London: World Gold Council.

Tufano, P. (1998) 'The determinants of stock price exposure: financial engineering and the gold mining industry', *Journal of Finance*, 53(3): 1015–52.

US Bureau of Mines (various issues) *Minerals Yearbook*, Washington: US Bureau of Mines.

2 Western Australian mineral commodity outlook
Gold

Chris Wiggins

Introduction

Gold is a unique commodity. It is prized for its scarcity and colour. It is malleable, durable and indestructible. It is valued for itself, and has no real substitutes. It differs from other commodities in three essential ways. First, gold exhibits many of the characteristics of a currency. It is a source of savings and wealth, it can be borrowed and lent and it is extensively traded in futures and option contracts. Second, gold is indestructible. Virtually all the gold ever mined remains in circulation as hoarding, jewellery or reserves held by governments. The amount held is equivalent to about 35 years' consumption. Third, the demand for gold is relatively elastic. For most buyers, gold purchase is a non-essential, impulse or speculative activity. Demand depends on price and buyers' perceived view of its future movement.

History and overview

Throughout history gold has been accepted as a store of value and medium of exchange. It has formed an integral part of social and religious customs in the form of jewellery and ornaments. Today its high electrical conductivity and corrosion resistance make it a key material for use in the electronics industry. For the last 400 years, gold has played a key role in currencies and banking. In the sixteenth century, the supply of gold gold and silver increased substantially as a result of the opening of mines in the New World, coinciding with the growth in manufacturing and trade in Europe (see Figure 2.1).

Since then the role played by gold can be divided into the following three periods.

- Gold as the basis for currency (1660–1968). During this period, most currencies were on a gold standard. Inflation was low until the Second World War. Gold was the property of central banks and governments. Private ownership was not permitted.
- The demonetization of gold (1968–81). Gold went through a very turbulent period, resulting in price increases from US$35 per ounce in 1968 to peak at US$850 per ounce in 1980, and dropping back to nearly US$400 per ounce by the end of 1981.

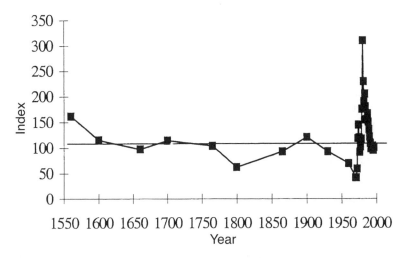

Figure 2.1 Historical gold purchasing power index (1996 = 100).

Source: *Minerals Yearbook* (various issues).

- Free market for gold (1981 to the present). Since 1981, gold has traded at a price in the range US$300–490 per ounce. The price has been less volatile when measured in constant-value special drawing rights (SDRs). Gold does appear to behave in a similar fashion to other commodities. Consumption of gold is quite sensitive to price. Supply and demand were fairly evenly balanced, but demand now appears to be exceeding supply.

The role of gold in each period is more fully reviewed below.

Gold as the basis for currency (1660–1968)

In 1663, England issued the guinea, a gold coin with a nominal face value of 20 silver shillings. This became overvalued in respect of shillings, and in 1717 Sir Isaac Newton, Master of the Royal Mint, set the buying price of gold at L3 17s 10 1/2d per ounce (equivalent to 21 shillings per guinea). The official price of gold remained at this level until 1930.

In the nineteenth century, increasing supplies of gold from California, Russia, Australia and South Africa helped make a worldwide gold standard workable. By the middle of the nineteenth century, most currencies of the world were fully convertible into gold.

Following the outbreak of the First World War, the major countries ended convertibility. However, many of the European nations paid for their supplies from the USA with gold, leading to a doubling of US gold stocks. Most countries embargoed private exports and ownership of gold in order to protect their gold reserves.

There was some return to the gold standard in the 1920s, but the Great Depression ended this, with Britain suspending convertibility in 1931 and the USA in 1933. This officially ended the nexus between money supply and movements in gold which had existed for the previous 200 years.

Following the Second World War, as a result of which US gold reserves again substantially increased, the International Monetary Fund (IMF) was established. The US dollar was defined in gold at US$35 per ounce and became the central monetary reserve unit, supplemented by other major currencies, principally sterling. The Bretton Woods conference set up a central clearing house for international payments. This system worked well until the late 1960s, when the US dollar came under pressure owing to a large deficit in the US balance of payments. By this time, gold accounted for less than one-third of central banks' reserves.

The demonetization of gold (1968–81)

In 1968, the USA repealed the gold cover requirement on the US currency. A two-tier structure was formed, under which official transactions between central banks were conducted at US$35 per ounce, and the price for private transactions was determined by the market. This led to a decline in US gold stocks and, in 1971, the US government ceased selling gold to other central banks at US$35 per ounce. The US dollar was allowed to float. US citizens were permitted to hold gold, with the US government auctioning its gold stocks to stabilize prices.

The USA continued to sell gold from its stock pile until 1980. As a result of these policies and other economic events, the market price rose substantially, peaking in 1974 at US$180 per ounce, declining to US$117 in 1976, and then peaking at US$850 in 1980. Since 1980, the price has generally fluctuated between US$350 and US$450.

The major factors in these fluctuations appear to have been those given below.

Price increases from US$40 to US$180 (to 1974)

The floating of gold price, and granting permission to the private sector to invest in gold in the early 1970s, coincided with a reduction in mine output from South Africa. This, together with the general boom in commodities, led to the first major peak of US$180 per ounce in 1974.

Price falls to US$91 (to 1976)

Following the decision by the USA to auction gold, it followed other commodities in a major decline from 1974 to 1976. This period also saw a major increase in sales by the Eastern Bloc.

Price climbs to US$850 (to 1981)

This peak coincided with a major drop in supply as a result of the actions of the central banks, which sold 550 tonnes in 1979, becoming net buyers, and a sharp decline in Eastern Bloc sales in 1979 and 1980. It also coincided with the second oil shock, and the resulting disruption to the world economies.

Free market, 1981–present

After the peak in 1980, the price fell briefly to US$300 by late 1982. Since then it has generally been fluctuating between US$350 and US$450. Supply and demand have been in reasonable balance. The fluctuations in US dollar price reflect the strong dollar in 1985 and a weak dollar in 1987.

Outlook for gold

Supply side

Mine production

Mine production has been growing very slowly over the 1990s. After rapid growth in the 1980s, the growth rate is now stagnant. South African production, which is high cost, is declining. This is being replaced by growth principally from South America and Asia (Table 2.1).

Mine production is growing at only about 1 per cent per annum, with substantial growth from the emerging producers replacing declines in South African production. Emerging producing countries now account for 26 per cent of production. If one includes the ex-communist countries, this increases to 43 per cent.

Table 2.1 Gold supply 1980–95

	1980	1985	1990	1995	Percentage increase 1990–5
South Africa	675	673	605	522	−14
USA	30	79	294	329	12
Australia	32	93	254	268	14
Canada	51	90	167	150	−10
Emerging					
South Africa	89	172	220	274	25
Asia	36	58	108	187	73
Other Africa	33	54	71	130	83
Europe	12	16	35	28	−20
Ex-communist	90	210	380	382	1
Total mine production	1,048	1,445	2,135	2,272	6
Scrap	482	299	532	602	13
Total supply	1,530	1,744	2,667	2,874	8

Source: *Minerals Yearbook* (various issues).

Production costs

Costs of production in different countries for 1985 and 1995 are shown in Table 2.2.

The average production costs above are important for two reasons. They establish a floor price below which the price of gold is most unlikely to drop. Short-term floor price would be the cash operating cost outside of South Africa, say US$200 (A$300) per ounce. Longer-term floor price is unlikely to ever fall below the third quartile of the cash cost of production, i.e. about US$325 (A$410) per ounce.

It establishes a benchmark against which to compare the viability of mines. Provided a mine has a cost of production below the average cost, preferably in the bottom 50 per cent, it is likely to remain viable in the longer term while others would be forced to close. This represents a cost of US$250 or A$325.

Scrap

Scrap is an important source of gold. This is gold that is recycled from manufacturing processes, processing electronic scrap and recovered jewellery. Supply has been relatively constant at around 500–600 tonnes per year.

Demand side

Jewellery fabrication

World consumption of gold has been rising at about 10 per cent per annum this decade. Jewellery accounts for 66 per cent of demand. Following the large decline in consumption in the period 1974–80, when prices rose, consumption has increased at a rate of 6 per cent per annum (see Table 2.3).

Large increases in demand have come from the developing countries, especially India, Turkey, Saudi Arabia, Taiwan and Hong Kong. Demand in the developed countries has increased at a slower rate. On average, the developed country

Table 2.2 Mine production costs

	1985	US$	1995	US$
South Africa	147	189	323	364
Australia	195	93	254	268
Canada	218	90	167	150
USA	219	302	224	291
Papua New Guinea			169	246
Average cost (including South Africa)	169	214	257	315
Average cost (excluding South Africa)	196	245	235	300

Source: *Minerals Yearbook* (various issues).

Note
The cash costs exclude capital expenditure, depreciation and financing costs.

Table 2.3 Reported gold consumption

	1980	1985	1990	1995	Percentage increase 1990–5
Total supply	1,530	1,744	2,667	2,874	8
Consumption					
Jewellery					
Western	315	535	867	898	4
Asian/Middle East	187	591	1232	1,639	33
Electronics	94	114	148	184	24
Coins	211	119	156	102	–35
Other	127	108	67	103	54
Total mine production	934	1,467	2,676	3,257	22
Reported surplus (shortfall)	596	262	–9	–383	

Source: *Minerals Yearbook* (various issues).

Note
The surplus represents the amount that is taken up by investors/speculators.

consumer purchases only one gram of gold per year (A$20 worth), so the market is a long way from being saturated. The recently established World Gold Council now markets gold in a similar fashion to the industrial organizations for wool and diamonds.

Coins

Gold coins have accounted for an average of 200 tonnes per annum. This amount could increase with the strong marketing programmes such as those implemented by Gold Corp., Australia.

Hoarding and investment

Table 2.4 shows the levels of hoarding and investment for the years 1980 to 1995. As the table shows, there has been a substantial increase in gold hoarding and investment during the period.

Hedging

The hedging of future production, or selling forward of gold by producers, adds to gold supply. The hedging transaction is accomplished by the producers' bankers borrowing gold from a hoarder, normally a central bank, and then selling the gold. The proceeds are placed on deposit, earning interest, which becomes the contango. When the contract matures, the producer gives gold to the bank, in return for the deposit plus contango. The bank gives the gold back to the hoarder.

Table 2.4 World gold position

	1980	1985	1990	1995	Percentage increase 1990–5
Total supply	1,530	1,744	2,667	2,874	8
Total consumption	934	1,467	2,676	3,257	22
Reported gold surplus (shortfall)	596	262	–9	–383	
Identified bar hoarding increase			–202	280	
Forward sales and gold loans (net)			227	438	
Official sector sales			187	201	
Implied net investment			–203	–24	

Source: *Minerals Yearbook* (various issues).

Forward sales have recently added substantial amounts of gold to the market. They are hard to follow closely, as large mining companies are highly secretive about their forward-selling strategies (see Table 2.5).

Central banks are conservative and see it as sound practice to hold a portion of their reserves in gold. This is profitable in times of rapidly rising gold prices but expensive in times of falling prices and high interest rates. Overall, during the last 20 years, an investment gold has appreciated by 1,000 per cent; by comparison, investment in US dollars, with interest compounded, would have increased by 500 per cent. However, it is most unlikely that gold will appreciate at such a high rate in the future. As Table 2.5 indicates, central banks have made almost no changes to their gold holdings. With total holdings of ten times the annual production, any attempt to sell would result in a major decline in the price of gold, which would not be in the interest of the central banks.

Total official holdings are about 30,000 tonnes, representing around 25 per cent of the world's gold holdings. These have been relatively constant. The major holders are the USA, with 8,000 tonnes, and Germany, France, Italy and Britain, with about 2,000–3,000 tonnes each.

There have been indications that some smaller countries have been selling part of their holdings, motivated by a desire to earn greater rates of interest on their reserves.

This is another sector that is very hard to follow until official figures are published, usually about a year behind.

Other holders of gold

The other holdings of gold, consisting of jewellery, coins and gold bullion, are estimated at 65,000 tonnes. Holdings are increasing by the amount of world production, say 1,500 tonnes per annum (including the Eastern Bloc countries). The major demand is for jewellery.

A large part of this demand comes from Middle East and Asian countries. A review of figures for individual countries, published in the Gold Survey report, indicates that net demand from individual countries varies substantially depending

Table 2.5 International reserves

Major holders	Tonnes
USA	8,000
Europe	12,000
Japan	1,000
Australia	245
Others	9,000
Total IMF countries	30,000
IMF	3,000
European monetary community	2,000
Ex-communist countries	5,000
Coins	9,000
Jewellery	60,000
Private hoarders and investors	10,000
Total world gold stocks	119,000

Source: *Minerals Yearbook* (various issues).

Note
Total holdings are equivalent to 35 years' current world production (including communist countries).

on economic conditions. When a country's economy is strong, such as for the Middle East countries during times of high oil prices and the Asian 'tiger' countries (Taiwan, Korea and Hong Kong) plus Japan until 1997, they are major purchasers of gold in all forms. In times of economic decline, they become net sellers, as occurred in Saudi Arabia, Egypt, Iran and Indonesia in 1986 and some East Asian countries in 1997 and 1998. The amount of gold purchased for jewellery and the amount sold as scrap also vary substantially with price, as indicated where the variation of price is given in Figure 2.2.

How to understand gold prices

The physical supply–demand relationship is inherently stable. Producers can always sell all their output on the open market. Production reacts very slowly to price changes. There is historically about a 5-year lag between a major price increase and significant production increases, as in 1980. Now, with prices at about 150 per cent the cost of production, mine production is increasing at only 1 per cent annually, compared with 6 per cent per annum in the 1980s, when the price was 200 per cent of the cost of production. Demand is very price sensitive, and thus adjusts quickly to the supplies available on the market, compared with oil, for which demand is very inelastic with respect to price.

Though the official statistics indicate that demand is only growing at around, there is a lot of evidence to suggest the statistics reported by the Gold Field Mineral Service (GMS) substantially under-report the actual demand. In the 1980s, gold demand was increasing at around 6 per cent per annum, nearly all driven by the growing Asian market. It seams strange that these figures indicate that growth has stopped in the 1990s, when growth in the Asian economies continues unchecked. The increase in production of 6 per cent per annum is roughly in line with increase in real gross national product (GNP) for the world. I believe that demand in the form of gold jewellery, though fluctuating and sensitive to price, appears to be increasing at a similar rate.

Frank Veresco, in a paper he delivered at the Kalgoorlie Gold Conference, estimates that the unreported flows, which are about equal to the gold shortfall, are running in the region of 700–1,400 tonnes. If this is the case, a substantial gold price rise will be required in the future to bring demand back into balance with supply, which is inelastic. Veresco estimates this price to be A$500 per ounce if the shortfall is 700 tonnes per annum and A$600 if the shortfall is over 1000 tonnes per annum.

However, in the meantime there are a number of parties who wish to sell large amounts of gold. These are central banks, including the IMF, gold producers through their forward-selling programme and currently hedge funds, a number of which are long in gold, and cannot wait until the market turns around to liquidate their positions.

Evidence indicates that the private sector buys gold in good times, and sells it in times of financial hardship, or when the price becomes very high. Contrary to some opinions, gold would appear not to be a good hedge against recession. The price and demand move in parallel with the economic cycles. Gold is a good investment in cases in which currencies lose their purchasing power, as happened in Germany between the wars. It is also a relatively safe investment against declining currency values, and when other markets are overheated. However, as gold pays no interest, and normally has little prospect of substantial capital gains, it is used only by conservative investors for long-term investment.

With some 95 per cent of gold investments being in the form of futures and options, the gold market has a highly speculative element in the short term, with the gold trading price being determined by the collective herd instinct of some 10,000 currency and commodity traders, investors and speculators worldwide. However, as discussed above, the physical demand for gold is quite price sensitive, and since 1980 speculative surges have been short-lived.

Major influences on the price of gold are:

- Supply and demand: this looks as if it will stay reasonably in balance. The supply of gold is relatively price inelastic, while demand (mostly jewellery) is quite price elastic, with significant declines in 1980 and 1983.
- Commodity cycles: gold price appears to follow other major commodity movements. The current increase in commodities prices could well lead to a commodities boom, which will probably affect gold as well.
- Currency values: during the last 4 years, currency values have changed as much as, or more than, real gold prices. Speculating in gold also involves currency speculation.
- The Australian economy: the Australian dollar should remain relatively weak until the current account deficit is eliminated (which still leaves A$100 billion

debt to be repaid). Once a significant portion of the deficit burden and the overseas debt are repaid, the value of the Australian dollar is likely to increase by as much as 20–30 per cent, which will impact on the viability of gold mining in Australia.

- International instability: gold is still regarded as a refuge currency in times of political and economic problems. However, the fall in price following the October market crash surprised many people who thought that gold would be a hedge against a stock market collapse.
- The political situation in South Africa: South Africa accounts for 40 per cent of world production. Its production could be interrupted as a result of the current political problems. However, any major interruption of supply would probably be of a temporary nature, and the possible effects would already have been largely discounted by the market.

In summary, it would appear that US$400–50 is a realistic longer-term trading range, with the price fluctuating between US$350 and US$500 over shorter periods.

In the event of some major structural changes occurring, which could be caused by events such as larger than expected increases in mine production and new discoveries, major liquidation of holdings by investor, and/or central banks and major recession, the price could conceivably drop as low as US$250 per ounce. Below this level, mine production would start dropping significantly and demand for jewellery would rapidly increase. Speculative surges could drop the demand lower, but it should be short-lived.

Postscript

This chapter is based on my the paper written in 1996 for presentation to the Curtin University Mineral Economics Program at a seminar on resources in 1996. In the original version, I note that I optimistically forecast a long-term gold price of US$400–50 per ounce, with the proviso that it could drop to as low as US$250 per ounce in the event of greater production or central bank selling. From 1996 onwards, the central banks did start selling substantial quantities of gold. In addition, a strong US dollar, combined with devaluations of the South African rand, has resulted in a substantially lower world average production cost.

In the long run, commodity costs of production drive the price, and gold increasingly seems to behave as a commodity rather than a currency.

The effects of all this can be seen in Figure 2.2. As with most commodities, over the last 6 years gold has exhibited a close relationship between cash cost of production and price.

I have become very cautious in projecting commodity prices, other than to note that the seventieth percentile cash cost of production appears to provide a floor for most commodities.

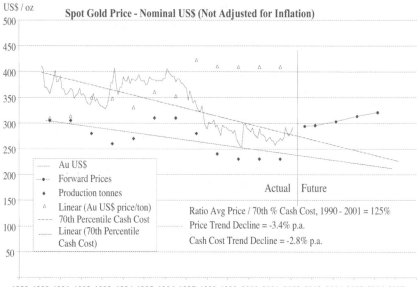

Figure 2.2 Spot gold price.

References

Gold Fields Mineral Services (various years) *Gold Survey*. Available online at http://www.gfms.co.uk/Press_Releases.asp

US Bureau of Mines (various of issues) *Minerals Yearbook*, Washington: US Bureau of Mines.

3 Gold as a commitment mechanism

Past, present and future

Michael D. Bordo

3.1 Historical introduction and an outline of the section headings

Gold has long played a crucial role in the monetary systems of most nations. Traditionally, gold has served as the highest form of commodity money. It was prized for its properties of durability, divisibility, portability and storability. It also served for over 150 years as the base for the monetary systems of major countries (Bordo and Schwartz, 1993). Modern monetary systems evolved in the nineteenth century from pure specie standards to mixed (bank money and fiat) fiduciary and specie standards in order to economize on the scarce resources tied up in the precious metals of a commodity standard. Crucial to this development was adherence by monetary authorities and commercial bankers to convertibility of their fiduciary monetary liabilities to a fixed weight of gold (or other specie coins) defined as the unit of account. Adherence to gold convertibility by a number of countries in turn created a fixed exchange rate international monetary system under which members would settle payments imbalances with gold or gold claims.

Many observers view gold-based national and international monetary systems as having provided the world with unprecedented stability of nominal variables (McKinnon, 1988). Such stability stems from the operation of a commodity money standard which, via the interaction of bullion and money markets, ensures a tendency towards long-term mean reversion of price levels (Barro, 1979). The tendency of a gold-based monetary system to provide long-term price stability meant that gold served as an excellent form of nominal anchor to the international monetary system (Giovannini, 1993).

Finally, adherence to a fixed weight (or price) of the national currency in terms of gold can be viewed as a form of monetary rule to constrain monetary authorities from excessive expansion of their liabilities. In this chapter, we focus on gold's role as part of a rule or a commitment mechanism.

Traditionally, the gold standard (or other specie standards such as silver or bimetallism), by causing a nation's money supply to vary automatically with the balance of payments, was viewed as superior to entrusting policy to the discretion of well-meaning and possibly well-informed monetary authorities (Simons, 1951).[1] In contrast to this traditional view, which stresses both impersonality and automaticity, the approach to rules taken in this chapter follows the literature on the time inconsistency of monetary and fiscal policy (Kydland and Prescott, 1977), which views a rule as a credible commitment mechanism binding policy actions over time.

According to this approach, adherence to the fixed price of gold served as a credible pre-commitment mechanism to prevent governments from following the otherwise time-inconsistent policies of creating surprise fiduciary money issues in order to capture seigniorage revenue, or defaulting on outstanding debt (Bordo and Kydland, 1992; Giovannini, 1993). On this basis, adherence to the gold standard rule before 1914 enabled many countries to avoid the problems of high inflation and stagflation that troubled the late twentieth century.

Moreover, the gold standard that prevailed before 1914 was a contingent rule, or a rule with escape clauses. Under the rule, gold convertibility could be suspended in the event of a well-understood, exogenously produced emergency, such as a war, on the understanding that after the emergency had safely passed convertibility would be restored at the original parity. Market agents would regard successful adherence as evidence of a credible commitment and would allow the authorities access to seigniorage and bond finance at favourable terms.

Section 3.2 discusses the concepts of rules, contingent rules and time inconsistency and applies them to gold. I focus first on the classical gold standard and successive variants of the gold standard – the inter-war gold exchange standard and the Bretton Woods international monetary system. I then consider a possible use of gold as a commitment mechanism under the present-day managed fiduciary standard. Section 3.3 presents a brief historical survey of the role of gold as a commitment mechanism in a number of countries and in the international monetary system. It covers the period from the early nineteenth century until the closing of the gold window by Richard Nixon in August 1971. Section 3.4 presents some empirical evidence for a number of countries, comparing the performance of a number of nominal variables across monetary regimes, which highlights the importance of adherence to the gold convertibility rule. Section 3.5 introduces some empirical evidence on a possible mechanism by which gold may serve as a credibility-enhancing mechanism for present-day policy makers: as a signal of future inflation and future policy actions. Section 3.6 concludes with a discussion of future prospects for gold as a commitment mechanism.

3.2 Gold as a commitment mechanism: concepts

This section explains the theoretical concepts underlying my approach. The simplest example of how a commitment mechanism operates is in a modern, closed economy environment in which monetary authorities use the tools of monetary policy in an attempt to maintain full employment and zero inflation. Assume that the monetary authority has announced at the beginning of the year a rate of monetary growth consistent with zero inflation. Assume further that population believes the announcement and it is incorporated into wage bargaining and other contracts which are binding over the whole year. In this circumstance, the authorities, in the absence of pre-commitment, knowing that the workers believe their stated intentions and have already made their contracts, have an incentive to create a monetary surprise (follow an expansionary monetary policy) to either reduce unemployment (stimulate the economy) or to capture seigniorage revenue. However, workers, with rational expectations, will take account of the government's actions in their behaviour and in the next year, when new contracts are formed, will demand higher wages and prices. This will in turn lead to higher inflation and a return to the original level of employment (and economic activity). In addition, desired real cash balances will decline, reducing the tax base for seigniorage. A credible pre-commitment mechanism, such as a rule that prevents the authorities from altering monetary growth from its pre-announced path, by preventing the government from cheating, can preserve long-term price stability (Barro and Gordon, 1983).

A second relevant example is in the use of fiscal policy. Governments use debt finance to smooth tax revenues over time. When faced with unusual government expenditures, such as in wartime, it is more efficient to sell bonds than to impose higher taxes, which can reduce work effort at the time of greatest need. The debt is issued on the assumption that taxes will be raised once the emergency is passed, in order to service and reduce the debt. In this context, a time-inconsistent fiscal policy would be to impose a capital levy or to default on the debt, once the public has purchased it. Following such a policy would capture additional resources for the government in the *present*, but in the event of a *future* emergency would make it very difficult for the government to sell its bonds at favourable prices. A credible commitment mechanism can force the government to honour its outstanding debt.

The pledge to fix the price of a country's currency in terms of gold represented just such a rule or commitment mechanism to prevent governments from following the previously mentioned practices. The rule involved defining a gold coin as a fixed weight of gold, called, for example, one dollar. The monetary authority was then committed to keep the mint price of gold fixed through the purchase and sale of gold in unlimited amounts. Under the bimetallic system based on gold and silver, which prevailed in most countries until the third quarter of the nineteenth century, the monetary authorities would define the weight of both gold and silver coins, freely buying and selling them. Maintaining the bimetallic ratio fixed is a variant of the basic convertibility rule, as it is the fixed value of the unit of account that is the essence of the rule.[2]

The gold standard rule followed in the century before the First World War can be viewed as a form of contingent rule or rule with escape clauses (Grossman and Van Huyck, 1988; Dekock and Grilli, 1989; Flood and Isard, 1989; Bordo and Kydland, 1992). The monetary authority maintains the standard – keeps the price of the currency in terms of gold fixed – except in the event of a well-understood emergency such as a major war. In wartime it may suspend gold convertibility and issue paper money to finance its expenditures, and it can sell debt issues in terms of the nominal value of its currency, on the understanding that the debt will eventually be paid off in specie. The rule is contingent in the sense that the public understands that the suspension will only last for the duration of the wartime emergency plus some period of adjustment. It assumes that afterwards the government will follow the deflationary policies necessary to resume payments at the original parity.[3] Following such a rule will allow the government to smooth its revenue from different sources of finance: taxation, borrowing and seigniorage (Lucas and Stokey, 1983; Mankiw, 1987).[4]

As we document in section 3.2, the gold standard contingent rule worked successfully for three core countries of the classical gold standard: Britain, France and the USA. In all these countries the monetary authorities adhered faithfully to the fixed price of gold except during major wars. During the Napoleonic War and the First World War for England, the Civil War for the US, and the Franco-Prussian War for France, specie payments were suspended and paper money and debt were issued. But in each case, after the wartime emergency had passed, policies leading to resumption were adopted.[5] Indeed, successful adherence to the rule may have enabled the belligerents to obtain access to debt finance more easily in subsequent wars.[6] In the case of Germany, the fourth 'core' country, no occasions arose for application of the contingent aspect of the rule before 1914. Otherwise, its record of adherence to gold convertibility was similar to that in the other three countries.

Examples of discretion – breaches in the rule – include postponement of resumption after the war and reasonable delay period have passed, and pegging to specie at a devalued parity. In both situations, should there be another war within memory of the previous one, then the public's behaviour in being willing to absorb government debt would be quite different from that in the previous war, even if the situation is otherwise similar and the government claims to subscribe to a reasonable delay rule.

It is crucial that the rule be transparent and simple and that only a limited number of contingencies be included. Transparency and simplicity would avoid the problems of moral hazard and incomplete information (Canzoneri, 1985; Obstfeld, 1991), i.e. prevent the monetary authorities from engaging in discretionary policy under the guise of following the contingent rule. In this respect, a second contingency – a temporary suspension in the face of a financial crisis, which in turn was not the result of the monetary authorities' own actions, may also have been part of the rule. However, because of the greater difficulty of verifying the source of the contingency than in the case of war, invoking the escape clause under conditions of financial crisis, or in the case of a shock to the terms of trade (a third possible contingency), would be more likely to create suspicion that discretion was being followed.

The gold standard rule may have been enforced by reputational considerations. Long-term adherence to the rule was based on the historical evolution itself of the standard; thus, for example, gold was accepted as money because of its intrinsic value and desirable properties. Paper claims, developed to economize on the scarce resources tied up in a commodity money, became acceptable only because they were convertible into gold.

In turn, the reputation of the gold standard would constrain the monetary authorities from breaching convertibility, except under well-understood contingencies. Thus, when an emergency occurred, the abandonment of the standard would be viewed by all to be a temporary event since, from their experience, only gold or gold-backed claims truly served as money. An alternative commitment mechanism was to guarantee gold convertibility in the constitution. This was the case, for example, in Sweden before 1914, when laws pertaining to the gold standard could be changed only by two identical parliamentary decisions with an election in between (Jonung, 1984: 368). Convertibility was also enshrined in the laws of a number of gold standard central banks (Giovannini, 1993).

The international gold standard

The gold standard rule originally evolved as a domestic commitment mechanism, but its enduring fame is as an international rule. The classical gold standard emerged as a true international standard by 1880, following the switch by the majority of countries, from bimetallism, silver monometallism and paper, to gold as the basis of their currencies (Eichengreen, 1985). As an international standard, the key rule was maintenance of gold convertibility at the established par. Maintenance of a fixed price of gold by its adherents in turn ensured fixed exchange rates. The fixed price of domestic currency in terms of gold provided a nominal anchor to the international monetary system.

Recent evidence suggests that, indeed, exchange rates throughout the 1880–1914 period were characterized by a high degree of fixity in the principal countries. Although exchange rates frequently deviated from par, violations of the gold points were rare (Officer, 1986), as were devaluations (Eichengreen, 1985).

According to the game theoretic literature, for an international monetary arrangement to be effective both between countries and within them, a time-consistent credible commitment mechanism is required (Canzoneri and Henderson, 1991). Adherence to the gold convertibility rule provided such a mechanism. Indeed, Giovannini (1993) finds the variation of both exchange rates and short-term interest rates within the limits set by the gold points in the 1899–1909 period to be consistent with market agents' expectations of a credible commitment by the 'core' countries to the gold standard rule in the sense of this paper.[7] In addition to the reputation of the domestic gold standard and constitutional provisions which ensured domestic commitment, adherence to the international gold standard rule may have been enforced by other mechanisms. These include improved access to international capital markets; the operation of the rules of the game; the hegemonic power of England; and central bank cooperation.

Support for the international gold standard probably grew because it provided improved access to the international capital markets of the core countries. Countries were eager to adhere to the standard because they believed that gold convertibility would be a sign to creditors of sound government finance and the future ability to service debt.[8]

This was the case both for developing countries seeking access to long-term capital, such as Austria–Hungary (Yeager, 1984) and Latin America (Fishlow, 1989), and for countries seeking short-term loans, such as Japan, which financed the Russo–Japanese war of 1905–06 with foreign loans 7 years after joining the gold standard (Hayashi, 1989). Once on the gold standard, these countries feared the consequences of suspension (Fishlow, 1987; 1989; Eichengreen, 1992a: 19).

The fact that England, the most successful country of the nineteenth century, as well as other 'progressive' countries, was on the gold standard, was probably a powerful argument for joining (Friedman, 1990; Gallarotti, 1993).

The operation of the 'rules of the game', whereby the monetary authorities were supposed to alter the discount rate to speed up the adjustment to a change in external balance, may also have been an important part played by the commitment mechanism under the international gold standard rule. To the extent that the 'rules' were followed and adjustment facilitated, the commitment to convertibility was strengthened and conditions conducive to abandonment were lessened.

Evidence on the operation of the 'rules of the game' questions their validity. Bloomfield (1959), in a classic study, showed that, with the principal exception of England, the rules were frequently violated in the sense that discount rates were not always changed in the required direction (or by sufficient amounts) and in the sense that changes in domestic credit were often negatively correlated with changes in gold reserves. In addition, a number of countries used gold devices – practices to prevent gold outflows.

One can reconcile the violation of the 'rules of the game' and the use of gold devices with maintenance of credibility in the commitment to gold by viewing the gold points as a form of target zone (Eichengreen, 1994). Belief that intervention would occur at the upper and lower gold points created a honeymoon effect whereby stabilizing capital flows caused the market exchange rate to revert towards parity before reaching the gold points (Krugman, 1991). Within the zone, the monetary authorities could alter discount rates to affect domestic objectives such as stabilizing real activity and smoothing interest rates (Svennson, 1994).[9] Moreover, for the major countries, at least before 1914, such policies were not used extensively enough to threaten the convertibility into gold (Schwartz, 1984).

An additional enforcement mechanism for the international gold standard rule may have been the hegemonic power of England, the most important gold standard country (Eichengreen, 1989). A persistent theme in the literature on the international gold standard is that the classical gold standard of 1880–1914 was a British-managed standard (Bordo, 1984). Because London was the centre for the world's principal gold, commodities and capital markets, because of the extensive outstanding sterling-denominated assets, and because many countries used sterling as an international reserve currency (as a substitute for gold), it is argued that the Bank of England, by manipulating its bank rate, could attract whatever gold it needed and, furthermore, that other central banks would adjust their discount rates accordingly. Thus, the Bank of England could exert a powerful influence on the money supplies and price levels of other gold standard countries.

The evidence suggests that the Bank of England did have some influence on other European central banks (Linder, 1969). Eichengreen (1987) treats the Bank of England as engaged in a leadership role in a Stackelberg strategic game with other central banks as followers. The other central banks accepted a passive role because of the benefits to them of using sterling as a reserve asset. According to this interpretation, the gold standard rule may have been enforced by the Bank of England. Thus, the monetary authorities of many countries may have been constrained from following independent discretionary policies that would have threatened adherence to the gold standard rule.

Indeed, according to Giovannini (1989), the gold standard was an asymmetric system. England was the centre country. It used its monetary policy (bank rate) to maintain gold convertibility. Other countries accepted the dictates of fixed parities and allowed their money supplies to respond passively. His regressions support this view – the French and German central banks adapted their domestic policies to external conditions, whereas the British did not.

The benefits to England as leader of the gold standard – from seigniorage earned on foreign-held sterling balances, from returns to financial institutions generated by its central position in the gold standard and from access to international capital markets in wartime – were substantial enough to make the costs of not following the rule extremely high.

Finally, Eichengreen (1993) argues that episodic central bank cooperation may have also strengthened the credibility of the gold standard. Lines of credit arranged between the Banque de France, other central banks and the Bank of England during incipient financial crises such as 1890 and 1907 may in turn have encouraged private stabilizing capital movements to offset threats to convertibility.

The classical gold standard, the gold exchange standard and Bretton Woods

Eichengreen (1994) posits three prerequisites for a successful international monetary arrangement: the capacity to undertake relative price adjustment; adherence to robust monetary rules; and ability to contain market pressures. According to him, the classical gold standard contingent rule satisfied these criteria for the core countries because the credible commitment to maintain convertibility above all else allowed the escape clause to accommodate major shocks, and because central bank cooperation eased market pressures in the face of speculative attacks. By contrast, in the case of peripheral countries, the credibility of commitment to the gold standard was considerably weaker reflecting strong domestic political pressures to alter exchange rates (Frieden, 1994).

Though gold convertibility was restored by 1926 by most countries, the inter-war gold exchange standard was a much less successful application of the gold standard rule. The escape clause could not be invoked (lest it lead to destabilizing capital outflows) in the absence of a credible commitment to maintain gold parity in the face of a politicized money supply process, and according to Eichengreen (1993), the failure of cooperation.

The Bretton Woods international monetary system can also be viewed within the context of the gold standard rule, although it is a distant variant of the original gold standard. Under the rules of Bretton Woods, only the USA, as central reserve country and provider of the nominal anchor, was required to peg its currency to gold; the other members were required to peg their currencies to the dollar (McKinnon, 1993). They also were encouraged to use domestic stabilization policy to offset temporary disturbances. The Bretton Woods system had an escape clause for its members – a change in parity was allowed in the face of a fundamental disequilibrium, which could encompass the contingencies under the gold standard rule – but it was not the same as under the gold standard because it did not require restoring the original parity.[10] The rule for members (other than the USA) was enforced, as under the gold standard, by access to US capital and to the International Monetary Fund's resources. For the USA, there was no explicit enforcement mechanism other than reputation and the commitment to gold convertibility. Capital controls were viewed as a method to contain market pressures.

The system was successful as long as the USA maintained its commitment to convertibility (i.e. maintained price stability). But the escape clause mechanism quickly proved defective as the fundamental disequilibrium contingency was never spelled out and hence parity changes would be accompanied by speculative attacks which became more serious as capital controls became increasingly ineffective. Ultimately, by following highly expansionary monetary and fiscal policies beginning in the mid-1960s, the USA attached greater importance to domestic concerns than to its role as the centre of the international monetary system and the system collapsed.

Thus, although the Bretton Woods system can be interpreted as one based on rules, the system did not provide a credible commitment mechanism.[11] The USA was unwilling to subsume domestic considerations to the responsibility of maintaining a nominal anchor. At the same time, other G-7 countries became increasingly unwilling to follow the dictates of the USA-imposed world inflation rate.

Finally, we consider a way in which gold could be used as a commitment mechanism in present circumstances in which gold no longer plays a key role in either the domestic or international monetary system. Since freeing the market price of gold in 1968, the price of gold, according to many observers, is a good barometer of underlying inflationary pressures (Moore, 1988; 1990; 1991; Ranson, 1991). Indeed, recently several Federal Reserve officials have suggested its use as a possible policy indicator (Angell, 1987; Johnson, 1988; Greenspan, 1993). This suggests that movements in the price of gold may offer an indirect form of commitment mechanism. Central banks may see rising gold prices as a predictor of future inflation (which may or may not be reflecting their own past actions) and so follow a contractionary policy. In other words, to the extent that gold prices are related to measures of monetary policy, they may in future serve as a possible indicator of commitment to low inflation.

3.3 Historical overview of the gold standard as a rule

Specie and gold standards

In this section we survey the record of adherence to the gold standard rule – commitment to a fixed parity with an escape clause. Table 3.1 gives a snap-shot record of the conformity of twenty-one countries to the rule. The table covers the period from the early nineteenth century until the final breakdown of the gold exchange standard in the 1930s.

Table 3.1 Dates of specie convertibility and suspensions over twenty-one countries in seven groupings

Country	Dates of bimetallic or silver convertibility	Dates of suspensions	Reasons for suspensions	Dates of gold convertibility	Dates of suspensions	Reasons for suspensions	Change in parity
Core countries							
France	1803	1848–50	Government overthrown	1878	1914	War	Yes
Germany	1850	1870–8	War	1928	1936	Depression	Yes
				December 1871	1914	War	Yes
				1924	1931	Depression	Yes
UK	1694	1797–1821	War	1816–21	1847[a]	Panic	No
					1857[a]	Panic	No
					1866[a]	Panic	No
					1914	War	No
				1925	1931	Crisis	Yes
USA	1792	1834[b]		1875–9	1893	Panic[c]	No
	1834	1837[c]	Panic	1893	1907	Panic[c]	No
	1838	1857[c]	Panic	1908	1933	Depression	Yes
	1858	1862	War				
		1873[c]	Panic				
Anglo-Saxon countries of new settlement							
Australia	1829			1852	1915	War	No
				April 1925	December 1929	Crisis	Yes
				March 1930			
Canada	1821	1837	Crisis	1853	1914	War	No
	1839						No
				June 1926	September 1931	Crisis	Yes

Country	Dates of bimetallic or silver convertibility	Dates of suspensions	Reasons for suspensions	Dates of gold convertibility	Dates of suspensions	Reasons for suspensions	Change in parity
Latin America							
Argentina	1822	1825	War	1863	May 1876	Conversion failed	No
				1881		Lax fiscal policy	No
				1883	January 1885	Conversion failed	Yes
				1899	1914	Lax fiscal policy	Yes
				August 1927	1929	War	
						Crisis	
Brazil		1833	Lax fiscal policy	1846	1857	Crisis	
				1888	1889	Government overthrown	Yes
				1906	1914	War	Yes
				1927	1930	Crisis	Yes
Chile	1818	1851		1887		Conversion failed	Yes
	1851	1866		1895	1898	War threat	Yes
	1870	1878	Crisis	1925	1931	Crisis	Yes
Southern Europe							
Greece	February 1833	April 1848	Panic	January 1885	August 1885	Conversion failed	No
	January 1849	December 1868	War	April 1910	December 1914	War	Yes
				May 1928	April 1932	Lax fiscal policy	Yes
Italy	August 1870	May 1877	War	1884	1894	Lax fiscal policy	Yes
	1862	1866	Lax fiscal policy; war				

Portugal	1846			December 1927	October 1936	Depression	Yes
Spain	1868			1854	1891	Crisis	Yes
	1883	Crisis		July 1931	09/1931	Crisis	Yes
Scandinavian countries							
Denmark				December 1872	December 1914	War	No
				January 1927	September 1931	Crisis	Yes
Finland				1877	1914	War	Yes
				January 1926	October 1931	Crisis	Yes
Norway				1875	1914	War	No
				May 1928	September 1931	Crisis	Yes
Sweden	1803	1809	War	1873	1914	War	No
	1834	1873		1922–4	1931–	Crisis	Yes
Western Europe							
Belgium	1832	1848	Crisis	1878	1914	War	Yes
				October 1926	March 1935	Crisis	Yes
The Netherlands	1847			1875	1914	War	No
				April 1925	October 1936		Yes
Switzerland	1850			1878	1914	War	No
				1929	1936	Crisis	Yes
Japan							
Japan	1885	1897		1897	1917	Crisis	No
				Dec–30	Dec–31	Crisis	Yes

Source: Bordo and Schwartz (1993).

Notes
a Suspension of Banking Act of 1844.
b Change in mint ratio.
c Restriction of payments by banks.

The countries are divided into two main groupings: four core countries (the USA, the UK, France and Germany) and seventeen peripheral countries divided into geographical groupings. In the table, the experience of bimetallism or adherence to a silver standard which prevailed in many countries before the last quarter of the nineteenth century is demarcated from the gold standard that followed. For each standard and each country the table shows dates when a commitment was made to convert the national currency into specie, dates of suspension of the commitment and the reasons for suspension. In the case of the gold standard, an additional column indicates whether a change in parity was made on resumption of convertibility after suspension. The column is omitted for bimetallic or silver experience because in these cases we have not established the dates of devaluations or revaluations after resumptions.

Turning first to the four core countries we discuss the record for these countries before the gold standard. For the bimetallic/silver standard period, there are no entries for Germany, as it was not unified until 1871. The individual German states, however, were on a bimetallic standard, as were the other three core countries.

The date of convertibility of the French franc into gold or silver is given as 1803 in the table. A bimetallic system nevertheless predated that entry by centuries, but before 1803 France had endured devaluations, revaluations, John Law's inflationary inconvertible paper money experiment (1716–20) and the revolutionary war assignat hyperinflation (1789–95). So 1803 marks the beginning of a stable system, with only two interruptions until 1878, when France switched to gold. The two interruptions were suspensions in 1848–50, following the overthrow of the July monarchy, and 1870–8, following the Franco-German war. Both of these interruptions qualify as consistent with adherence to specie rules, as the suspensions were valid exercises of the escape clauses.

Although the table shows 1694, the year the Bank of England was founded, as the date for convertibility of the British pound into silver, Britain was on a silver standard as far back as the thirteenth century. De facto the country was on a gold standard from 1717 on, owing to the overvaluation of gold by Sir Isaac Newton, the Master of the Mint; de jure the country adopted the gold standard in 1816, while suspension of convertibility was still in effect. There had been banking crises in 1763, 1772, and 1783, but no suspensions until the war with France ended convertibility from 1797 to 1821. This again we regard not as a breach of the rule but proper invocation of the escape clause not only for the duration of the war but for a period of adjustment thereafter. Resumption at the pre-war parity also respects the rule (Bordo and Kydland, 1992).

The US Coinage Act of 1792 defined the bimetallic standard at a mint ratio of 15:1. In 1834, and again in 1837, the mint ratio was altered, remaining unchanged thereafter at 16 to 1. Banking panics in 1837 and 1857 led to temporary restriction of payments by banks but no suspension of convertibility. The Civil War, however, occasioned suspension from 1862 until 1878. In 1873 there was a banking panic, like the earlier ones, in which the banks restricted payments of high-powered paper money. Despite contentious political opposition to deflation that resumption enforced, on 1 January 1879 resumption was achieved at the pre-war parity, in line with the declaration of the Resumption Act of 1875. Under the classical gold standard, both France and Germany observed specie rules until the outbreak of the First World War. Each then suspended convertibility, and both devalued before resuming in the 1920s. Convertibility by France lasted for 8 years, by Germany for 7 years, and then both devalued after suspending in 1931. Because of war and financial crisis, the public probably regarded suspension per se as permissible under the escape clause. The change in parity, however, diluted the credibility of the countries' attachment to specie rules.

The UK's record before the First World War is the epitome of proper conduct under the gold standard. As the country at the centre of the system, operating with a small gold reserve, it nevertheless managed to serve both its domestic and international interests while maintaining convertibility. Three banking panics in 1847, 1857 and 1866 led to suspension of the Banking Act of 1844, which limited the Bank of England's fiduciary issue but did no damage to the convertibility commitment. Thereafter, the Bank acted to defuse panics before they emerged, as in 1890 and 1907. Convertibility was abandoned by the Bank in the First World War (de facto in 1914 and de jure in 1919), taking advantage of the escape clause, and the return to the gold standard at the pre-war parity was delayed until 1925, also consonant with the provisions of the escape clause. The convertibility commitment, however, lasted only for 6 years, and devaluation followed.

The record of commitment by the core countries to specie rules is unblemished under the pre-First World War gold standard. Neither France nor Germany played by those rules during the inter-war period, having resumed convertibility with devalued gold content of their currencies. The UK reverted to its pre-war parity when it resumed convertibility in 1925, but by 1931 it had devalued and abandoned rules for discretion. The USA followed the UK in devaluing in 1933, and adopted a gold standard in 1934 that diverged in fundamental ways from the pre-First World War standard.

A number of peripheral countries also followed the rule as well as the USA and the UK. These included Canada, Australia, Sweden, the Netherlands, Switzerland and Japan. In marked contrast to this group are the ABC (Argentina, Brazil and Chile) countries of Latin America and the countries of southern Europe. The Latin American countries suspended convertibility in wartime and also in the face of declining economic activity. They usually returned to gold at a depreciated parity. Their experience was characterized by higher money growth rates, higher fiscal deficits and higher inflation rates than the other countries (Bordo and Schwartz, 1994). For them, gold convertibility was the exception rather than the rule. For the southern European countries, adherence to the gold standard was an important objective, but for most of them was difficult to achieve. Their experience of low money growth, low fiscal deficits (with the principal exception of Italy) and exchange rates that never drifted far from parity suggests that following the rule was important (Bordo and Schwartz, 1993).

The inter-war gold exchange standard and Bretton Woods

The inter-war gold exchange standard was an attempt to recreate the classical gold standard with lower gold reserves and greater freedom for domestic financial policy. As an application of the contingent rule it was much less successful. Because monetary policy was highly politicized in many countries, the commitment to credibility was not believed and devaluation would have led to destabilizing capital flows. Unlike the pre-war gold standard, central bank cooperation was ineffective (Eichengreen, 1992a). The system collapsed in 1931 and subsequent years in the face of the shocks of the Great Depression.

Bretton Woods was our last convertible regime. It can be viewed within the context of the gold standard rule, although it is a distant variant of the original gold standard. The architects of Bretton Woods wanted to combine the flexibility and freedom for policy makers of a floating rate system with the nominal stability of the gold standard rule. Under the rules of Bretton Woods, only the USA, as central reserve country and provider of the nominal anchor, was required to peg its currency to gold; the other members were required to peg their currencies to the dollar (Bordo, 1993a).

As is well known, the system got off to a bad start with the UK's unsuccessful attempt to restore dollar convertibility in 1947 and then its devaluation in September 1949, followed by a large number of countries. The speculative attacks accompanying that event seemed to discourage members from using the escape clause of devaluation in the event of fundamental disequilibrium, and encouraged them to utilize capital controls and other means to preserve their parities longer than was consistent with fundamentals. In addition, the contingencies under which changes in parties could occur were not as clear cut as under the classical gold standard. Fundamental disequilibrium was originally intended to mean the types of shocks that occurred beyond the control of the domestic monetary and fiscal activities. As events unfolded, key countries such as France in 1957, 1958 and 1969 and Britain in 1967 may have devalued as a consequence of lax financial policies. As capital controls became less effective and the markets understood that governments were following policies inconsistent with exchange rate stability, speculative attacks became more serious.

Ultimately the system was successful as long as the USA – the nominal anchor to the system – maintained its commitment to convertibility, i.e. maintained price stability. As events turned out, by following highly expansionary monetary and fiscal policies to finance the Vietnam War, beginning in the mid-1960s, the USA attached greater importance to domestic concerns than to its central international monetary role, thus weakening the system.

An additional force in the downfall of Bretton Woods was French gold conversion policy. An implication of the role of the USA as key reserve centre was that US dollars supplied by 'deficits without tears' served as a growing substitute for gold as international reserves. In other words, unlike other deficit countries, as reserve centre the USA did not have to adjust her domestic economy to the external deficits. Cumulative US deficits, reflecting US capital outflows, had their counterpart in cumulative European surpluses accompanied by dollar inflows. The French, and to a lesser extent the other western European powers, resented the dollar's exorbitant privilege and in reaction converted outstanding dollar holdings into gold. Such conversions threatened to deplete the US monetary gold stock. In the end, following a brief hiatus in 1968 with the creation of a two-tier gold market, the USA terminated gold convertibility in August 1971.

The French have been interpreted as torpedoing Bretton Woods for purely nationalistic reasons. In Bordo *et al.* (1994), it is argued that the French, from 1960 to 1968, were following a strategy consistent with their inter-war policies at Genoa in 1922 and the Tripartite Agreement in 1936. They wanted a cooperative gold exchange standard based on several key currencies and gold. De Gaulle viewed France as leading western Europe in a campaign for a more cooperative international monetary system. The threat of gold conversions was used to force the Americans to make concessions in the bargaining over reform of the international monetary system that was then taking place.

Like the gold standard, Bretton Woods was a convertible regime. As with the gold standard, it was associated with a high degree of macroeconomic stability compared with the inter-war period and the subsequent floating exchange rate regime. Like the gold standard, Bretton Woods was based on a contingent rule. But the Bretton Woods system was less durable than the gold standard. This may reflect the fact that the rules were not well designed – the contingency under which the escape clause mechanism would be invoked was not made clear. It may also reflect the lack of a credible commitment by the USA to maintain price stability. Finally, as argued by an earlier generation of scholars, it may reflect the inherent design flaw of a gold exchange standard – which is what Bretton Woods evolved into – that, as dollar reserves of the rest of the world increase relative to the monetary gold holdings of the centre country, the likelihood of a run on the monetary gold stock of the reserve centre increases.

In conclusion, the survey of adherence to rules before and after Bretton Woods reveals a decay of respect for rules over the century covered. Rules were not universally honoured even during the classical gold standard era. A core group of countries was usually faithful to specie rules and, in addition, countries in western Europe, the new Anglo settlement countries, and the Scandinavian countries also conducted their financial affairs so that the fixed price of gold that defined their currencies was unchanged for extended periods. Monetary and fiscal policies in the remaining countries were such that suspensions of the specie rule were not exceptional, and they were followed by changes in the former parity if resumption occurred. Only extraordinary events such as wars occasioned departures from the standard among the core and their cohorts and until the First World War resumption took place at the pre-war parity.

In the inter-war period, a return to the gold standard was sometimes at the earlier parity, but often at a devalued rate. During most of the period floating exchange rates were common. The attempt under the Bretton Woods agreement to impose a rule that the par value of its currency with the dollar that each country member declared would be changed only under extraordinary circumstances as under the classical gold standard failed. Domestic economic objectives proved to be paramount to international obligations.

3.4 Some evidence on the performance of gold as a commitment mechanism

In this section we present some evidence on the gold standard rule's record in achieving nominal stability. Were the commitment to gold convertibility credible, we would expect monetary authorities to follow monetary policies consistent with preserving price stability. We would also expect the performance of nominal variables such as the inflation rate and long-term interest rates to be superior to those under fiat monetary regimes.

To examine these issues, we present evidence for three variables (money growth, inflation and long-term interest rates) over the past 110 years, for the countries identified in Table 3.1. We demarcate the data into four monetary regimes: the classical gold standard (1880–1914); the inter-war period (1919–39); the Bretton Woods international monetary system (1946–70); and the recent managed float (1971–89). The Bretton Woods system, as a variant of the contingent gold standard rule, is directly comparable to the classical gold standard. The recent managed float, a regime not based on the rule, and the inter-war period, which comprises episodes of free floating, adherence to the gold standard, and managed floating, are presented as contrasts to the two rule-based regimes.[12]

Table 3.2 presents descriptive statistics on the rate of monetary growth (M2) for each of the twenty-one countries identified in Table 3.1. These data are plotted in Figure 3.1. For each country, we present two summary statistics: the mean and standard deviation. In addition, for each of the seven country groupings from Table 3.1, and four aggregate groupings [all countries; all except the four core countries; the G-10 countries plus Switzerland, (G-11); and all except the G-11], we show the grand mean.

Money growth was considerably more rapid across all countries after the Second World War than before the war (see Figure 3.1).[13] In the case of the core countries and most of the G-11 countries, there is not much difference between the Bretton Woods system and the subsequent floating regime. Southern Europe, Latin America and Japan exhibited considerably higher money growth under the Bretton Woods system than the others. In the case of the Latin American countries, money growth rates accelerated over the entire postwar period, reaching their highest levels under the float. By contrast with the postwar period, the gold standard exhibited lower money growth in both core and peripheral countries alike, with the principal exception of Japan; however, it was still higher in core than in peripheral countries. The observance of lower money growth in both core and peripheral countries is probably a reflection of the omnipresence of the gold standard rule.

In the core and G-11 countries, money growth was least variable under the gold standard. Under that regime, money growth variability was higher in the periphery than in the core. Across all countries, money growth was least variable in the inter-war period and most variable in the recent float. Under the Bretton Woods system and the recent float, the difference between core and peripheral money growth variability is less obvious, again with the principal exception of Latin America, which exhibits considerably greater money growth variability than all other countries. Among these countries, the increase in money growth variability reflects the breakdown of any linkage to a commitment regime.

In sum, money growth was generally lowest and most stable across all countries under the gold standard, followed by the Bretton Woods system. Core countries within each regime followed more prudent and stable monetary policies than peripheral countries. By contrast, under the float, money growth was considerably higher and less stable across all countries. Lower and more stable money growth in the core countries under the gold standard compared with the periphery may reflect better adherence to the commitment mechanism or, alternatively, that there was less pressure to gear monetary policy to domestic purposes (Eichengreen, 1993). The fact that peripheral countries' money growth was still relatively low and stable compared with later regimes may reflect their intention to adhere to the rule when conditions were favourable. A similar but more muted pattern is observed in comparing the Bretton Woods system with the subsequent float.

Table 3.3 presents evidence for the inflation rate (the GDP deflator) arranged in the same manner as Table 3.2. The data can be seen in Figure 3.2. The classical gold standard had the lowest rate of inflation of any monetary regime for all twenty-one countries, and during the inter-war period mild deflation was experienced by all countries except Latin America (see Figure 3.2). Within the classical gold standard regime, the inflation rate was lowest in countries identified in Table 3.1 as following the convertibility rule: the four core countries, some of the different European groupings and the Anglo countries of new settlement (see Figure 3.2). It was considerably higher in Latin America and Japan. This pattern can also be seen in a comparison of the G-10 plus Switzerland aggregate (an expanded core group) with the other peripheral countries. The former grouping contains nine countries which followed the rules; the latter only three.

Under Bretton Woods, like the gold standard, a distinct difference can be observed between the core countries and a number of other groupings (Anglo-Saxon new settlement, other western Europe, Japan), which had low inflation, and a set of countries with higher inflation (Latin America, to a lesser extent countries in southern Europe and Scandinavia). This observed difference between country groupings is also found under the recent float. The evidence on inflation suggests that, if the gold standard rule or its variant did provide a credible commitment mechanism for low inflation, it was strongest in the gold standard period, followed by Bretton Woods. Within these regimes, observance of the rule clearly demarcates inflation performance between countries.

The gold standard period had the most stable inflation rate of any regime (across all countries), judged by the standard deviation. This was followed by Bretton Woods, the inter-war and then the float. For the G-11 countries, the recent float is the most stable period. Within the gold standard regime, core countries and countries following the gold standard rule exhibited greater price stability than the others. For Bretton Woods, a similar difference between country groupings is observed,

Table 3.2 Money growth (M2) in twenty-one countries 1880–1900. Descriptive statistics annual data: means and standard deviations[a]

	Gold standard (1881–1913)		Inter-war (1919–38)		Bretton Woods (1946–70)		Floating exchange (1974–90)	
Core countries								
USA	0.3	3.1	-1.8	7.6	2.4	2.6	5.6	2.4
UK	0.3	3.1	-1.5	7.8	3.7	2.2	9.4	6.1
Germany	0.6	2.6	-2.1	4.7	2.7	4.0	3.3	1.2
France	0.0	4.9	2.2	9.1	5.6	4.1	8.8	3.2
Mean	0.3	3.4	-0.8	7.3	3.6	3.2	6.8	3.2
Anglo-Saxon countries of new settlement								
Australia	0.5	3.9	0.3	5.7	5.1	4.9	10.0	3.0
Canada	0.4	1.4	-1.9	6.1	2.7	3.0	7.3	2.6
Mean	0.5	2.6	-0.8	5.9	3.9	4.0	8.6	2.8
Latin America								
Argentina	2.6	14.2	-1.7	6.3	22.9	14.7	122.9	77.0
Brazil	4.3	17.5	3.0	6.3	24.3	14.8	94.5	87.0
Chile	5.2	9.1	5.5	7.3	27.7	13.0	30.9	41.2
Mean	4.0	13.6	2.3	6.6	25.0	14.2	82.8	68.4
Southern Europe								
Greece	NA	NA	1.8	5.4	7.8	9.7	15.9	3.2
Italy	0.6	3.2	-1.1	11.7	3.8	11.5	12.9	4.6
Portugal	0.6	3.5	7.9	15.4	2.2	3.2	17.4	3.6
Spain	-0.2	1.2	-0.7	7.3	8.6	5.8	12.6	4.5
Mean	0.3	2.6	2.0	10.0	5.6	7.5	14.7	4.0

Scandinavia								
Denmark	-0.3	3.1	-1.6	7.6	3.5	5.4	7.4	3.1
Finland	0.8	3.4	4.6	10.8	9.1	10.2	9.0	3.8
Norway	0.7	3.1	-3.1	9.7	3.7	3.9	7.6	3.6
Sweden	0.4	3.1	-2.3	6.1	3.9	4.0	8.4	3.0
Mean	0.4	3.2	-0.6	8.5	5.0	5.9	8.1	3.4
Other Western Europe								
Belgium	0.2	4.9	3.8	4.4	2.4	3.2	4.9	2.5
The Netherlands	1.0	2.2	-3.1	5.6	4.1	3.1	3.6	2.9
Switzerland	NA	NA	-2.2	4.3	2.8	1.9	3.5	1.8
Mean	0.6	3.6	-0.5	4.8	3.1	2.7	4.0	2.4
Japan	4.6	5.5	-1.7	7.3	4.5	4.6	2.6	2.4
All countries								
Mean	1.2	4.9	0.2	7.4	7.3	6.2	19.0	12.5
All except four core countries								
Mean	1.4	5.3	0.4	7.5	8.2	6.9	21.9	14.7
G-10 + Switzerland								
Mean	0.8	3.4	-1.1	6.8	3.5	4.0	6.4	3.0
All except G-10 + Switzerland								
Mean	1.6	6.3	1.4	8.2	11.2	8.4	32.6	22.9

Source: Appendix to Bordo and Schwartz (1993).

Notes

a Mean growth rate calculated as the time coefficient from a regression of the natural logarithm of the variable on a constant and a time trend.
NA, not available.

(a) Core countries

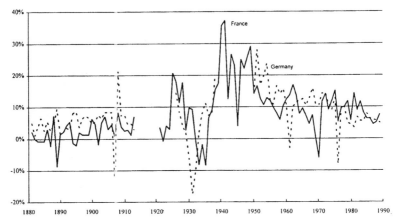

(a) Continued

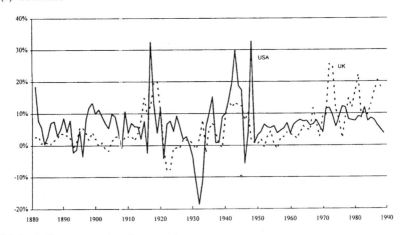

(b) Anglo-Saxon countries of new settlement

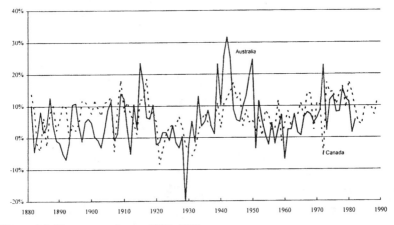

Figure 3.1 Money growth rate, 1881–1990.

(c) Latin America

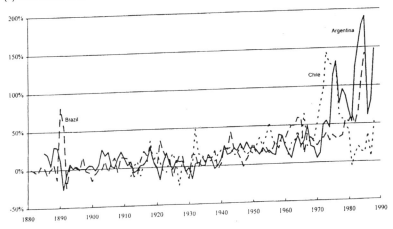

(d) Southern Europe

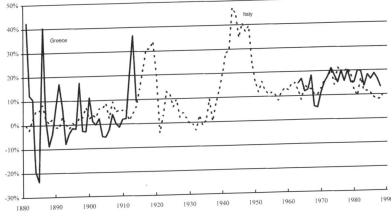

(d) Continued

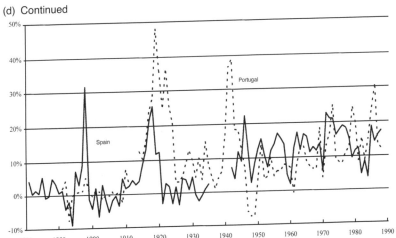

Figure 3.1 Continued.

(e) Scandinavia

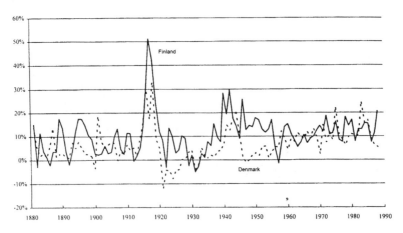

(e) Continued

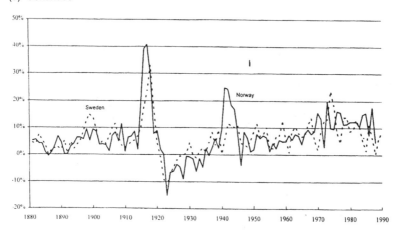

(f) Other Western Europe

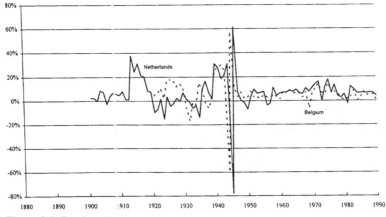

Figure 3.1 Continued.

(f) Continued

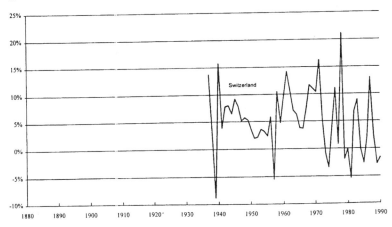

(g) Japan

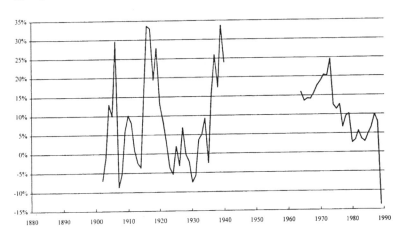

Figure 3.1 Continued.

with Japan joining the stable inflation group, and southern Europe the unstable inflation group. These differences persist into the recent float.

The evidence of a high degree of price stability under the gold standard (and to a lesser extent under Bretton Woods) and of greater price stability during those periods in countries following the rules compared with those that did not is thus consistent with the traditional view that commodity money based regimes provide a stable nominal anchor.

A third variable that would be sensitive to the adherence to the gold convertibility rule is the long-term interest rate. According to McKinnon (1988; 1992) the classical gold standard and Bretton Woods periods were characterized by lower and more stable long-term bond yields than under the managed floating regime. This would

Table 3.3 Inflation (GDP deflator). Twenty-one countries 1880–1900: descriptive statistics annual data: means and standard deviations

	Gold standard (1881–1913)		Inter-war (1919–38)		Bretton Woods (1946–70)		Floating exchange (1974–90)	
Core countries								
USA	0.3	3.1	−1.8	7.6	2.4	2.6	5.6	2.4
UK	0.3	3.1	−1.5	7.8	3.7	2.2	9.4	6.1
Germany	0.6	2.6	−2.1	4.7	2.7	4.0	3.3	1.2
France	0.0	4.9	2.2	9.1	5.6	4.1	8.8	3.2
Mean	0.3	3.4	−0.8	7.3	3.6	3.2	6.8	3.2
Anglo-Saxon countries of new settlement								
Australia	0.5	3.9	0.3	5.7	5.1	4.9	10.0	3.0
Canada	0.4	1.4	−1.9	6.1	2.7	3.0	7.3	2.6
Mean	0.5	2.6	−0.8	5.9	3.9	4.0	8.6	2.8
Latin America								
Argentina	2.6	14.2	−1.7	6.3	22.9	14.7	122.9	77.0
Brazil	4.3	17.5	3.0	6.3	24.3	14.8	94.5	87.0
Chile	5.2	9.1	5.5	7.3	27.7	13.0	30.9	41.2
Mean	4.0	13.6	2.3	6.6	25.0	14.2	82.8	68.4
Southern Europe								
Greece	NA		1.8	5.4	7.8	9.7	15.9	3.2
Italy	0.6	3.2	−1.1	11.7	3.8	11.5	12.9	4.6
Portugal	0.6	3.5	7.9	15.4	2.2	3.2	17.4	3.6
Spain	−0.2	1.2	−0.7	7.3	8.6	5.8	12.6	4.5
Mean	0.3	2.6	2.0	10.0	5.6	7.5	14.7	4.0

Scandinavia								
Denmark	−0.3	3.1	−1.6	7.6	3.5	5.4	7.4	3.1
Finland	0.8	3.4	4.6	10.8	9.1	10.2	9.0	3.8
Norway	0.7	3.1	−3.1	9.7	3.7	3.9	7.6	3.6
Sweden	0.4	3.1	−2.3	6.1	3.9	4.0	8.4	3.0
Mean	0.4	3.2	−0.6	8.5	5.0	5.9	8.1	3.4
Other Western Europe								
Belgium	0.2	4.9	3.8	4.4	2.4	3.2	4.9	2.5
The Netherlands	1.0	2.2	−3.1	5.6	4.1	3.1	3.6	2.9
Switzerland	NA	NA	−2.2	4.3	2.8	1.9	3.5	1.8
Mean	0.6	3.6	−0.5	4.8	3.1	2.7	4.0	2.4
Japan	4.6	5.5	−1.7	7.3	4.5	4.6	2.6	2.4
All countries								
Mean	1.2	4.9	0.2	7.4	7.3	6.2	19.0	12.5
All except four core countries								
Mean	1.4	5.3	0.4	7.5	8.2	6.9	21.9	14.7
G-10 + Switzerland								
mean	0.8	3.4	−1.1	6.8	3.5	4	6.4	3
All except G-10 + Switzerland								
Mean	1.6	6.3	1.4	8.2	11.2	8.4	32.6	22.9

Source: Appendix to Bordo and Schwartz (1994).

Notes

a Mean growth rate calculated as the time coefficient from a regression of the natural logarithm of the variable on a constant and a time trend.
NA, not available.

(a) Core countries

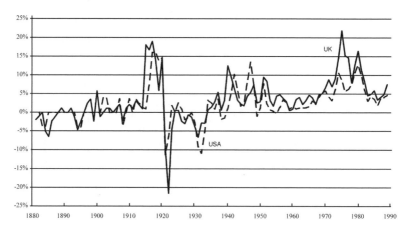

(a) Continued

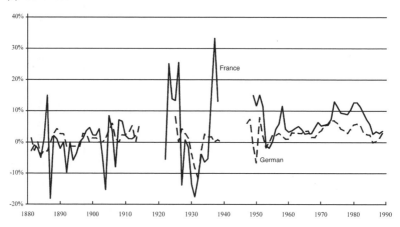

(b) Anglo-Saxon countries of new settlement

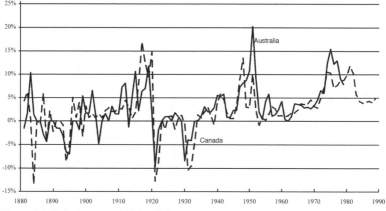

Figure 3.2 Inflation rate, 1881–1990.

(c) Latin America

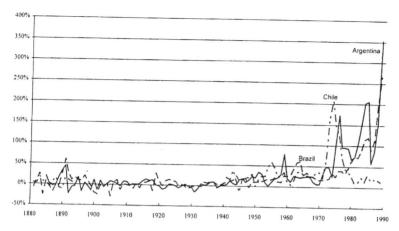

(d) Southern Europe

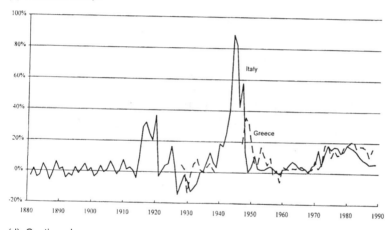

(d) Continued

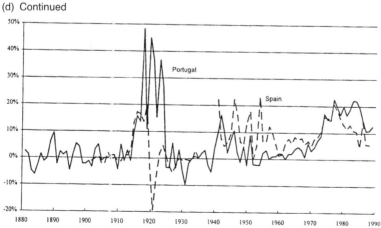

Figure 3.2 Continued.

(e) Scandinavia

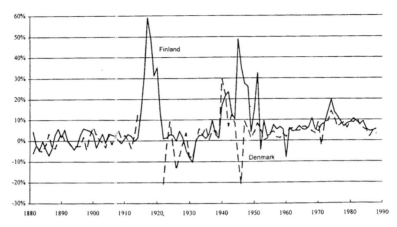

(f) Other Western Europe

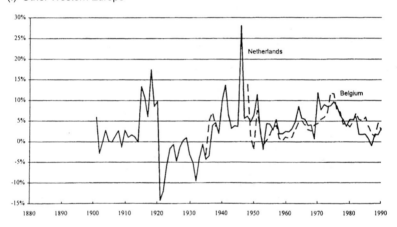

(f) Continued

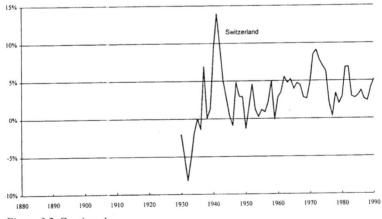

Figure 3.2 Continued.

(g) Japan

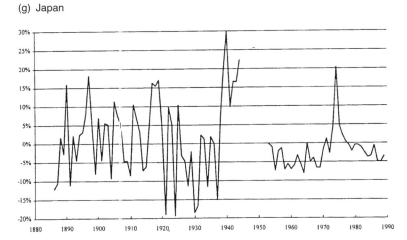

Figure 3.2 Continued.

reflect more sanguine inflationary expectations and a belief in long-term monetary stability. Table 3.4 shows the same descriptive statistics as Tables 3.2 and 3.3 for a smaller set of countries – for which comparable data is available – the G-10 plus Switzerland. The underlying data can be seen in Figure 3.3.

As with inflation rates, long-term interest rates for the G-10 plus Switzerland are lowest under the gold standard, followed by the inter-war and Bretton Woods. They also are more stable under the gold standard and Bretton Woods. The contrast is most marked between the gold standard and the recent float. These findings corroborate McKinnon's results and suggest that adherence to the gold convertibility rule was associated with a climate favourable to long-term investment.

Thus, the behaviour of three nominal variables suggests that adherence to the gold convertibility rule, whether in its pure form under the classical gold standard or the indirect form under the Bretton Woods system, was important. Under these regimes, all three variables had lower growth rates and were more stable. This result holds for both core and peripheral countries treated as groups. However, a significant difference between the performance of the two groups persists across regimes - nominal performance is superior in the core. These results are consistent with the chronology of adherence to convertibility in Table 3.1. They suggest that adherence to the gold convertibility rule made a difference, although the presence of the rule in the core countries may also have constrained the monetary authorities of peripheral countries to follow more stable policies than would otherwise be the case.[14]

A final piece of evidence on regime performance is the persistence of inflation. Evidence of persistence in the inflation rate suggests that market agents expect the monetary authorities to continually follow an inflationary policy; its absence would be consistent with the belief that the authorities are following a stable monetary rule such as the gold standard's convertibility rule.

Barsky (1987) presented evidence for the UK and USA, based on both

Table 3.4 Long-term interest rates in eleven countries, 1880–1900 annual data: means and standard deviations

	Gold standard (1881–1913)		Inter-war (1919–38)		Bretton Woods (1946–70)		Floating exchange (1974–90)	
USA	3.8	0.3	4.2	0.6	3.9	1.3	10.4	2.1
UK	2.9	0.2	4.1	0.7	5.2	1.8	12.1	2.8
Germany	3.7	0.2	6.8	1.6	6.3	0.7	7.8	1.5
France	3.2	0.3	4.6	0.8	5.7	0.8	10.9	2.4
Japan	NA	NA		7.0	0.1		7.1	1.8
Canada	3.5	0.4	4.7	0.8	4.5	1.5	11.0	2.0
Italy	4.2	0.5	5.9	0.6	6.0	0.7	13.7	3.3
Belgium	3.2	0.3	4.7	0.8	5.2	1.1	9.9	2.0
The Netherlands	3.3	0.3	4.1	0.7	4.3	1.3	8.4	1.5
Sweden	3.8	0.3	4.5	0.4	4.3	1.6	11.1	1.7
Switzerland	3.8	0.2	4.7	0.9	3.5	0.8	4.9	1.1
Mean	3.5	0.3	4.8	0.8	5.1	1.1	9.8	2.0

Source: Data Appendix to Bordo (1993b).

Note
NA, not available.

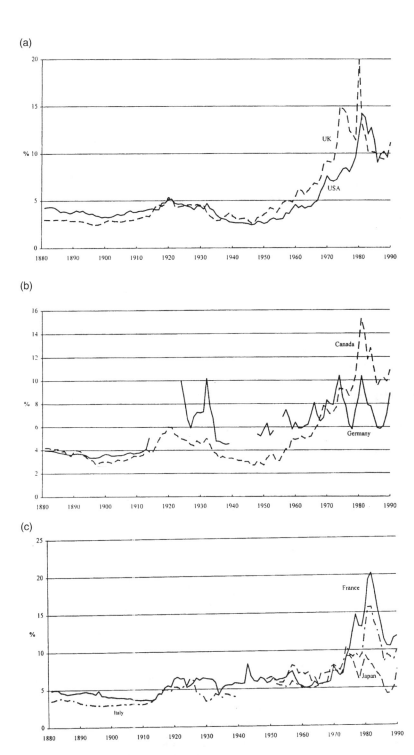

Figure 3.3 Long-term interest rate, 1881–1990.

(d)

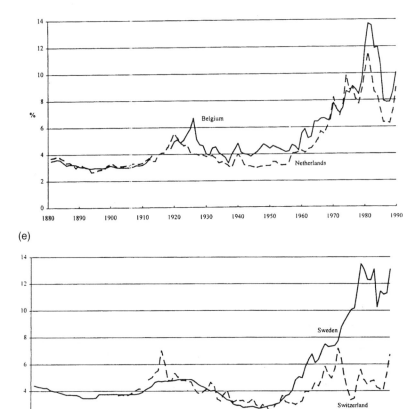

(e)

Figure 3.3 Continued.

autocorrelations and time series models, that inflation under the gold standard was very nearly a white noise process, whereas in the period after the Second World War the inflation rate exhibited considerable persistence. Alogoskoufis and Smith (1991) also showed, based on AR(1) regressions of the inflation rate, that inflation persistence in the two countries increased between the classical gold standard period and the inter-war period and between the inter-war period and the post-Second World War period.[15]

Table 3.5 presents the inflation rate coefficient [from the type of AR(1) regressions on Consumer Price Index (CPI) inflation] estimated by Alogoskoufis and Smith (1991), for all of the twenty-one countries over successive regimes since 1880,[16] as well as the standard errors and the Dickey–Fuller tests for a unit root.[17] The results, as in Alogoskoufis and Smith, show an increase in inflation persistence for most G-11 countries between the classical gold standard and the inter-war period. In a number of countries, most notably the USA and France, it rises under the Bretton Woods regime compared with the inter-war period, while in twelve others, most notably the UK, Germany and Japan, it declines. In virtually all countries, inflation persistence increases between Bretton Woods and the float. No significant differences can be detected between the performance of core and peripheral countries.

In sum, the general pattern observed of rising inflation persistence as the century progressed (with the principal exception in twelve countries of a decline during the Bretton Woods regime) is consistent with the general pattern observed in Table 3.1, of a gradual evolution away from convertible monetary regimes.

In conclusion, this section has presented evidence that adherence to the gold convertibility is associated with superior performance of inflation and other nominal variables. The pattern of performance differs between strong adherents (core countries) and others as theory predicts.

3.5 The price of gold as an indirect commitment mechanism

Since the closing by Richard Nixon of the gold window on 15 August 1971, the role of gold in the US domestic monetary system and the international monetary system has been greatly reduced (*US Gold Commission* Report, 1982: vol. 1) Gold is no longer used to settle international balance of payments or as legal backing for the domestic money supplies of any country. Thus, gold can no longer be viewed as a commitment mechanism to ensure stable money and low inflation in the sense developed in this chapter.

Nevertheless, gold may play an important role in guiding monetary policy actions under the fiat money regime which prevails today to produce stable money and low inflation. It may do this if authorities use the price of gold as an indicator for monetary policy actions, as has been recently suggested by a number of former Federal Reserve officials (Angell, 1987; 1994; Johnson, 1998).

Because monetary policy actions affect the price level with long and variable lags, policy makers need to rely on some indicator of the future consequences of their actions. The case for using a commodity price index or particular commodities such as gold as a guide for discretionary monetary policy is based mainly on empirical evidence that commodity prices, especially that of gold, are a leading indicator of inflation (Moore, 1988). In addition, commodity price indices provide information on future movements of the price level which is additional to that provided by monetary aggregates and other factors thought to be important determinants of inflation (Horrigan, 1986).

Commodity prices, including gold price, may be leading indicators of inflationary pressure for a number of reasons. First, the initial consequence of expansionary monetary policy is that it encourages the purchase of financial assets and real commodities which are traded in impersonal 'auction' markets characterized by highly flexible prices (Bordo, 1980). The increase in demand raises their prices. Second, supply shocks, such as the oil price shocks of the 1970s (believed by many to be a cause of inflation), affect commodity prices directly.[18] Third, many commodities,

Table 3.5 Persistence of CPI inflation, twenty-one countries 1880–1900 annual data: coefficient of AR1 regression (standard error), t-statistic for unit root test

(a) Core countries

	USA			UK			Germany			France		
Gold standard	0.27	(0.18)	4.05	0.30	(0.18)	4.03	0.51	(0.16)	3.06	−0.22	(0.18)	6.78
Inter-war	0.45	(0.17)	3.18	0.35	(0.20)	3.37	0.51	(0.21)	2.33	0.42	(0.24)	2.42
Bretton Woods	0.49	(0.19)	2.68	0.33	(0.19)	3.38	−0.03	(0.21)	4.90	0.56	(0.16)	2.75
Floating exchange	0.68	(0.18)	1.76	0.69	(0.17)	1.67	0.83	(0.14)	1.21	0.85	(0.16)	0.94

(b) Anglo-Saxon countries of new settlement

	Australia			Canada		
Gold standard	0.39	(0.19)	3.19	0.08	(0.18)	5.11
Inter-war	0.23	(0.19)	4.13	0.35	(0.20)	3.25
Bretton Woods	0.60	(0.19)	2.09	0.39	(0.19)	3.21
Floating exchange	0.60	(0.18)	2.27	0.75	(0.17)	1.47

(c) Latin America

	Argentina			Brazil			Chile		
Gold standard	0.59	(0.30)	2.37	0.47	(0.17)	3.11	0.23	(0.31)	2.48
Inter-war	−0.17	(0.19)	6.14	0.53	(0.19)	2.53	0.16	(0.23)	3.68
Bretton Woods	0.27	(0.20)	3.61	0.81	(0.12)	1.58	0.56	(0.16)	2.66
Floating exchange	0.74	(0.22)	1.18	1.29	(0.08)	−9.62	0.85	(0.14)	1.11

(d) Southern Europe

	Greece		Italy		Portugal		Spain	
Gold standard	NA		0.28 (0.14)	5.14	0.14 (0.19)	4.54	−0.22 (0.11)	10.6
Inter-war	0.18 (0.24)	3.37	0.28 (0.18)	4.00	0.63 (0.36)	1.02	0.14 (0.24)	3.63
Bretton Woods	0.72 (0.26)	1.08	0.21 (0.12)	6.58	−0.13 (0.17)	6.77	0.13 (0.23)	3.75
Floating exchange	0.30 (0.18)	3.89	0.75 (0.17)	1.47	0.63 (0.18)	2.03	0.61 (0.20)	1.92

(e) Scandinavia

	Denmark		Finland		Norway		Sweden	
Gold standard	0.27 (0.17)	4.21	0.46 (0.17)	3.08	0.44 (0.17)	5.14	0.42 (0.17)	3.53
Inter-war	0.24 (0.25)	3.04	0.64 (0.25)	1.45	0.31 (0.31)	4.14	0.50 (0.11)	4.44
Bretton Woods	−0.12 (0.16)	7.20	0.30 (0.30)	2.37	0.10 (0.20)	4.58	0.13 (0.21)	4.26
Floating exchange	0.16 (0.14)	2.73	0.57 (0.12)	3.51	0.45 (0.19)	1.05	0.53 (0.21)	2.25

(f) Other Western Europe

	Belgium		The Netherlands		Switzerland	
Gold standard	0.11 (0.18)	4.83	−0.36 (0.26)	5.14	NA	
Inter-war	0.49 (0.20)	2.57	0.34 (0.16)	4.14	0.16 (0.15)	5.77
Bretton Woods	−0.09 (0.22)	5.07	0.31 (0.15)	4.58	0.24 (0.20)	3.75
Floating exchange	0.78 (0.16)	1.40	0.88 (0.11)	1.05	0.69 (0.18)	1.80

(g) Japan

	Japan	
Gold standard	0.22 (0.18)	4.33
Inter-war	0.70 (0.25)	1.20
Bretton Woods	0.52 (0.18)	2.67
Floating exchange	0.70 (0.19)	1.58

Source: Data Appendix to Bordo and Schwartz (1993).

Note
Per cent significance level for unit root test with twenty-five observations is 3.00.

and especially gold, are held as a hedge against inflation. Hence, the bid-up of their prices reflects investors' fears of future inflation.[19]

In this section we treat the price of gold as a leading indicator of Federal Reserve policy actions on the assumption that Federal Reserve officials act as if they view it as an indicator (along with other forward-looking variables) of inflation. We test to see if past movements in the price of gold Granger cause (temporally precede) movements in three key monetary policy instruments (the Federal Funds rate, non-borrowed reserves and the monetary base) using monthly data from 1971 to 1991.[20]

Admittedly, such an exercise should be treated with a large grain of salt. As has been pointed out by McCallum (1990), and others, such an approach, based on a reduced-form equation between a policy indicator and an instrument, will be biased. This is because the underlying structural model that links policy instruments to policy targets to the real economy and hence to inflation needs to be fully specified (an undertaking beyond the scope of this chapter). Nevertheless, we present some evidence based on simple bivariate regressions as a rough measure of gold's indirect commitment power and as a guide to future research.

Table 3.6 displays the results of bivariate Granger causality tests on changes in the logs of the CPI inflation rate, the price of gold and three well-known instruments of Federal Reserve policy – the Federal Funds rate, non-borrowed reserves; and the monetary base – using monthly data from 1971 to 1991. Granger causality represents a measure of temporal precedence. If, for example, it is found that changes in the price of gold Granger cause CPI inflation, this means that past values of the price of gold have a statistically significant influence on future inflation, once account has been taken of past changes in inflation.

Table 3.6 presents the $\bar{R}^2$ and F-statistics for eight experiments, treating each of the four variables as dependent variables. We experimented with successive blocks of lags ranging from 3 months to 12 months. The best fit of twelve lags, displayed in the table, is based on the F-statistic, which indicates the contribution of all of the lagged coefficients to the regression equation. Significant F-statistics (P-values less than 5 per cent) suggests that regressors being tested help to explain the behaviour of the dependent variable.

Equations (1) and (2) test for the influence of the price of gold on inflation and vice versa. As found in earlier studies, changes in the price of gold (with up to twelve lags) have explanatory power over the inflation rate. This relationship, however, is significant in the reverse direction as well. The results suggest that the price of gold is a leading indicator of inflation, but the presence of reverse causality dictates that policy makers should exhibit caution in basing policy conclusions upon the relationship – without the aid of a structural model linking monetary policy to inflation and the price of gold.

For equations (3) and (4), the greater significance of the F-statistic on the change in the price of gold (1.5 per cent) when inflation is treated as dependent variable than of the F-statistic on inflation when the price of gold is treated as dependent variable suggests that the price of gold is a good leading indicator of this tool of Federal Reserve policy-making. Indeed, these results are consistent with the view

Table 3.6 Tests of Granger causality of changes in the price of gold inflation, the Federal Funds rate, non-borrowed reserves and the monetary base: US monthly data 1971–91

Equation no.	Regression		$\bar{R}^2$	F-tests	
	Dependent variable	*Regressors (no. of lags)*		*Excluded variable*	*F-statistic (P-value)*
1	Δp	c, Δpg (12)	0.522	Δpg (12)	1.88*
		Δp (12)			(0.038)
2	Δpg	c, Δpg (12)	0.126	Δp (12)	1.99*
		Δp (12)			(0.026)
3	Δff	c, Δpg (12)	0.287	Δpg (12)	2.15*
		Δff (12)			(0.015)
4	Δpg	c, Δpg (12)	0.119	Δff (12)	1.83*
		Δff (12)			(0.045)
5	Δnbs	c, Δpg (12)	0.115	Δpg (12)	1.35
		Δnbs (12)			(0.172)
6	Δpg	c, Δpg (12)	0.078	Δnbs (12)	1.00
		Δnbs (12)			(0.463)
7	Δmb	c, Δpg (12)	0.093	Δpg (12)	1.13
		Δmbs (12)			(0.339)
8	Δpg	c, Δpg (12)	0.094	Δmb (12)	1.25
		Δmbs (12)			(0.251)

Sources: Price of gold, *Quarterly Bulletin,* Bank of England, 1971 Q1 to 1991 Q4; CPI, Federal Funds rate, non-borrowed reserves and the monetary base, *Federal Reserve Bulletin*, various issues.

Notes
Δp　Change in the log of the CPI; *significant at the 5 per cent level.
Δpg　Change in the log of the price of gold.
Δff　Change in the log of the Federal Funds rate.
Δnbs　Change in the log of non-borrowed.
Δmb　Change in the log of the monetary base.

that gold may be an indirect commitment mechanism for policy-making. Equations (5) and (6) suggest that changes in the price of gold have only limited influence on non-borrowed reserves and equations (7) and (8) suggest almost no effects on the monetary base.

Given the overall results of Table 3.6, we next ascertain more precisely in Table 3.7 the impact of changes in the price of gold on future movements of inflation and the three policy indicators by showing the significance added by successive blocks of three lags of the price of gold to the best fit univariate regression of the dependent variable. Of special interest are equation (1c), which shows that changes in the price of gold today help to explain the behaviour of inflation 7–9 months later, equation (2a), which indicates that it helps explain the federal funds rate 1–3 months later, and equation (3a), which indicates that it helps explain (although less strongly) the behaviour of non-borrowed reserves 1–3 months later.

In sum, the results from both tables that the price of gold is a significant leading

Table 3.7 Tests of the influence of lagged changes in the price of gold on inflation, the Federal Funds rate, non-borrowed reserves and the monetary base: US monthly data 1971–91

Equation no.	Regression		$\bar{R}^2$	F-tests	
	Dependent variable	Regressors (no. of lags)		Excluded variable	F-statistic (P-value)
1a	Δp	c, Δp(2) Δpg(1–3)	0.462	Δpg(1–3)	0.29 (0.835)
1b	Δp	c, Δp(2) Δpg(4–6)	0.469	Δpg(4–6)	1.45 (0.230)
1c	Δp	c, Δp(2) Δpg(7–9)	0.495	Δpg(7–9)	5.67* (0.001)
1d	Δp	c, Δp(2) Δpg(10–12)	0.464	Δpg(10–12)	0.72 (0.549)
2a	Δff	c, Δff(2) Δpg(1–3)	0.284	Δpg(1–3)	6.85* (0.000)
2b	Δff	c, Δff(2) Δpg(4–6)	0.229	Δpg(4–6)	0.58 (0.628)
2c	Δff	c, Δff(2) Δpg(7–9)	0.237	Δpg(7–9)	1.41 (0.240)
2d	Δff	c, Δff(2) Δpg(10–12)	0.241	Δpg(10–12)	1.91 (0.128)
3a	Δnbs	c, Δnbs(1) Δpg(1–3)	0.140	Δpg(1–3)	3.08* (0.028)
3b	Δnbs	c, Δnbs(1) Δpg(4–6)	0.113	Δpg(4–6)	0.53 (0.661)
3c	Δnbs	c, Δnb(1) Δpg(7–9)	0.112	Δpg(7–9)	0.42 (0.741)
3d	Δnbs	c, Δnb(1) Δpg(10–12)	0.118	Δpg(10–12)	0.94 (0.423)
4a	Δmb	c, Δmb(1) Δpg(1–3)	0.013	Δpg(1–3)	1.96 (0.121)
4b	Δmb	c, Δmb(1) Δpg(4–6)	0.110	Δpg(4–6)	1.40 (0.243)
4c	Δmb	c, Δmb(1) Δpg(7–9)	0.104	Δpg(7–9)	0.81 (0.492)
4d	Δmb	c, Δmb(1) Δpg(10–12)	0.105	Δpg(10–12)	0.93 (0.426)

Sources: Price of gold, *Quarterly Bulletin,* Bank of England, 1971 Q1 to 1991 Q4; CPI, Federal Funds rate, non-borrowed reserves and the monetary base, *Federal Reserve Bulletin,* various issues.

Notes
Δp   Change in the log of the CPI; *significant at the 5 per cent level.
Δpg   Change in the log of the price of gold.
Δff   Change in the log of the Federal Funds rate.
Δnbs   Change in the log of non-borrowed.
Δmb   Change in the log of the monetary base.

indicator of both inflation and the Federal Funds rate suggests to us that gold may have value as an indirect commitment mechanism for achieving a low-inflation monetary policy.

3.6 Conclusion and implications for gold's future role

Gold played a major role as a commitment mechanism for close to a century, ensuring that monetary authorities of different countries refrained from inflationary activity. In this chapter we document gold's role as a commitment mechanism through the gold standard rule of convertibility. The rule which prevailed before 1914 for many countries, was a contingent one, or a rule with an escape clause – to be abandoned temporarily in the face of a well-understood emergency such as a war. Before 1914 even peripheral countries, which had considerable difficulty in adhering to convertibility, were relatively restrained in pursuing inflationary policies compared with later in the twentieth century.

Although the link to gold was stretched and weakened under the inter-war gold exchange standard and the postwar Bretton Woods systems, the importance of convertibility was recognized until the early 1970s. Since then, its appeal has lessened, as the world has turned to a fiat regime with generalized floating exchange rates and higher and more variable inflation than under convertibility.

Without the ethos of convertibility, does gold still have a role as a credible (anti-inflation) mechanism? In the previous section, it is argued that it may serve as an indirect credibility mechanism – as a way of keeping policy makers honest. To the extent that the price of gold, determined in free, world auction markets, is a good harbinger of inflationary trends, gearing policy on the basis of its movements may succeed in achieving low inflation.

Moreover, gold may have other uses as a commitment device. Recently, a number of scholars have expressed interest in reducing exchange rate volatility through increased policy coordination within well-specified target zones (Williamson and Miller, 1987; Bergsten, 1993). Such schemes may be enhanced by using gold as a possible nominal anchor (Mundell, 1994).

Second, major central banks of the Organization for Economic Cooperation and Development (OECD) have expressed continued reluctance to sell off their gold stocks. This may reflect a collective central bank folk memory of gold as a former successful anti-inflation commitment mechanism or, alternatively, reflect fears that markets would interpret such actions as indicating that central banks have lost such memories. Regardless of the motivation, their inertia suggests that for them retaining their gold reserves is treated with some importance.

Third, several newly emerging former communist bloc countries (NECs) have been using or considering using gold as an earnest to facilitate access to international capital markets. In a sense, they treat gold as a form of commodity reserve (Bordo and Schwartz, 1993).

Fourth, although evidence is scanty, gold appears to have been in demand by the central banks and other official agencies of a number of developing countries. This may reflect its role as a second line of defence (secondary international reserve) in the face of shocks to the balance of payments (Bordo and Klug, 1994).

Finally, gold may be desired by the NEC and less developed country (LDC) countries because of its past successful history as a credible commitment mechanism, i.e. because of its good brand name. Though no longer used for such purposes by the OECD countries, the fact that it was associated for so many years with low inflation may give it value to countries trying to emulate the OECD's earlier successful record.

Notes

1   The Currency school in England in the early nineteenth century made the case for the Bank of England's fiduciary note issue to vary automatically with the level of the Bank's gold reserve ('the currency principle'). Following such a rule was viewed as preferable (for providing price-level stability) to allowing the note issue to be altered at the discretion of the well-meaning and possibly now well-informed directors of the Bank (the position taken by the opposing Banking School). For a discussion of the Currency Banking School debate, see Viner (1937), Fetter (1965) and Schwartz (1987).

2   Viewed, however, as a rule in the traditional sense – as an automatic mechanism to ensure price stability – bimetallism may have had greater scope for automaticity than the gold standard because of the possibility of a switch from one metal to the other. See Friedman (1990).

3   The description is consistent with a result from a model of Lucas and Stokey (1983), in which financing of wars is a contingency rule that is optimal. In their example, in which the occurrence and duration of the war are uncertain, the optimal plan for the debt is not to service it during the war. Under this policy, people realize when they purchase the debt that it will be defaulted on in the event the war continues.

4   A case study comparing British and French finances during the Napoleonic Wars shows that Britain was able to finance its wartime expenditures by combination of taxes, debt and paper money issue – to smooth revenue – whereas France had to reply primarily on taxation. France had to rely on a less efficient mix of finance than Britain because she had used up her credibility by defaulting on outstanding debt at the end of the American Revolutionary War and by hyper-inflating during the Revolution. Napoleon ultimately returned France to the bimetallic standard in 1803 as part of a policy to restore fiscal probity, but because of the previous loss of reputation France was unable to take advantage of the contingent aspect of bimetallic standard rule. See Bordo and White (1991).

5   The behaviour of asset prices (exchange rates and interest rates) during suspension periods suggests that market agents viewed the commitment to gold as credible. For the USA see Roll (1972) and Calomiris (1988), who present evidence of expected appreciation of the greenback during the American Civil War based on negative interest differential between bonds that were paid in greenbacks and those paid in gold. Also, see Smith and Smith (1993), who demonstrate that movements in the premium on gold from Resumption Act of 1875 until resumption was established in 1879 were driven by a credible belief that resumption would occur. For the case of Britain's return to gold in 1925, see Smith and Smith (1990) and Miller and Sutherland (1992; 1994). An application of the stochastic process-switching literature suggests that the increasing likelihood that resumption would occur at the original parity gradually altered the path of dollar pound exchange towards the new ceiling, several months in advance.

6   For suggestive evidence, see Bordo and Kydland (1992).

7   Also see Officer (1993). His calculations of speculative bands (bands within which

uncovered interest arbitrage prevails consistent with gold point arbitrage efficiency) for the inter-war dollar sterling exchange rate show serious violations only in 1931, at the very end of the gold exchange standard.

8 A case study of Canada during the Great Depression provides evidence for the importance of the credible commitment mechanism of adherence of gold. Canada suspended the gold standard in 1929 but did not allow the Canadian dollar to depreciate or the price level to rise for 2 years. Canada did not take advantage of the suspension to emerge from the depression because of concern for its credibility with foreign lenders. See Bordo and Redish (1990).

9 Eschweiler and Bordo (1993) provide evidence for this interpretation for Germany over the period 1883–1913 based on an estimation of the Reichsbank's reaction function. They find that the central bank's pursuit of an interest rate smoothing policy (an obvious violation of the 'rule of the game') was subordinate to its commitment to keep the exchange rate within the gold points.

10 The USA could change the dollar price of gold if a majority of members (and every member 10 per cent or more of the total quotas) agreed.

11 Indeed, Giovannini's (1993) calculations show that during the Bretton Woods regime convertible bounds on interest rates for the major currencies, in contrast to the classical gold standard, were frequently violated.

12 For earlier applications of similar regime comparisons in a different context see Bordo (1993a,b), Bordo and Jonung (1994) and Bordo and Schwartz (1994).

13 The data sources for Figure 3.1 and all subsequent figures are listed in the Data Appendices in Bordo (1993b), Bordo and Jonung (1994) and Bordo and Schwartz (1993).

14 A comparison of means and standard deviations of the growth rates of real output for the twenty-one countries in Bordo and Schwartz (1993) reveals the Bretton Woods regime as the most rapidly growing and stable regime, with the classical gold standard ranked behind the recent float. The remarkable performance of Bretton Woods may reflect adherence to the convertibility rule but it may reflect also the absence of significant supply shocks compared with the other regimes, as well as other favourable circumstances (see Bordo, 1993b). It is more difficult to relate real than nominal economic performance to the type of monetary regime followed.

15 Also see Alogoskoufis (1992), who attributes the increase in persistence to the accommodation by the monetary authorities of shocks. This evidence is also consistent with the results of Klein (1975).

16 The regression run was $\Delta \log P_t = B_0 + \Delta B_1 \log P_{t-1} + e_t$. We ran the same regression for the GNP deflators, with similar results.

17 Eichengreeen (1992b) also presents these statistics for four of the countries.

18 In fact, however, inflation results only if monetary expansion ensues to offset the contractionary effects of the supply shock on sectors of the economy in which prices are sticky.

19 Use of commodity prices such as gold as an indicator of inflation has been criticized on a number of grounds. First, a commodity index, or a commodity such as gold, is not a terribly reliable indicator of inflation. Commodity prices may be capturing the non-monetary effects of changes in relative prices, in turn reflecting supply shocks such as bad harvests, geological discoveries, technical change and the formation or dissolution of cartels – rather than the inflationary consequences of expansionary monetary policy. These phenomena may be temporary or permanent. The index, or commodity price, cannot distinguish between the different sources of change or their duration. Second, a commodity price index or a particular commodity may incorporate what the market expects policy makers to do in the future. The market may react to speeches by policy makers or other actions interpreted as harbingers of future policy. Consequently, guiding actual policy decisions by such an indicator may be highly misleading if the market perceptions are incorrect. Third, because gold has so many uses in industry, in the arts, as jewellery, as international reserves in some

countries and as a speculative asset, movements in its price are sensitive to both real and monetary disturbance. As a speculative asset, movements in its prices are highly sensitive not only to inflationary expectations but also to political uncertainty and other information which may subject to high-volatility swings.

20 See Ranson (1991) for an earlier econometric examination of the link between the price of gold and Federal Reserve policy indicators and Barsky *et al.* (1992) for the application of Granger causality tests to various leading indicators of inflation.

References

Alogoskoufis, G.S. (1992) 'Monetary accomodation, exchange rate regimes and inflation persistence', *Economic Journal*, 2(5): 461–80.

—— and Smith, R. (1991) 'The Phillips curve, the persistence of inflation and the Lucas critique: evidence from exchange-rate regimes', *American Economic Review*, 8(2): 1254–73.

Angell, W. (1987) *A Commodity Price Guide to Monetary Targeting*, New York: Lehrman Institute.

——(1993) 'Commodity prices and other novel indicators in a policy aimed at general price stability: a synthesis and evaluation', mimeo, University of Michigan.

——(1994) 'Virtue and inflation', *Wall Street Journal*, June 24.

Barro, R.J. (1979) 'Money and the price level under the gold standard', *Economic Journal*, 89(353): 13–33.

Barro, R.J. and Gordon, D.B. (1983) 'Rules, discretion and reputation in a model of monetary policy', *Journal of Monetary Economics*, 12: 101–21.

Barsky, R.B. (1987) 'The Fisher hypothesis and the forecastability and persistence of inflation', *Journal of Monetary Economics*, 19(1): 3–24.

Barsky, R., *et al.* (1992). 'The Worldwide Change in the Behavior of Interest Rates and Prices in 1914 by Monetary Regime Transformations.' *International Library of Macroeconomic and financial History,* 3, pp. 91–122, Aldershot, UK: Elgar Reference Collection series.

Bergsten, C.F. (1993) 'The collapse of Bretton Woods: implications for international monetary reform', in M.D. Bordo and B. Eichengreen (eds) *A Retrospective on the Bretton Woods System*, Chicago: University of Chicago Press.

Bloomfield, A. (1959) *Monetary Policy under the International Gold Standard, 1800–1914*, New York: Federal Reserve Bank of New York.

Bordo, M.D. (1980) 'The effect of monetary change on relative commodity prices and the role of long term contracts', *Journal of Political Economy*, 88(6).

——(1984) *The Gold Standard: The Traditional Approach; A Retrospective on the Classical Gold Standard*, 1821–1931, pp. 23–113, National Bureau of Economic Research Conference Report series, Chicago: University of Chicago Press

——(1993a) 'The Bretton Woods international monetary system: a historical overview', in M.D. Bordo and B. Eichengreen (eds) *A Retrospective on the Bretton Woods System: Lessons for International Monetary Reform*, Chicago: University of Chicago Press.

——(1993b) 'The gold standard, Bretton Woods and other monetary regimes: a historical appraisal', *Federal Reserve Bank of St. Louis Review*, 75(2): 123–91.

——(1994) 'The specie standard as a contingent rule: some evidence for core and peripheral countries, 1880–1990', mimeo, Rutgers University.

—— and Jonung, L. (1994) 'Monetary regimes, inflation and monetary reform: an essay in honour of Axel Leijonhufvud', mimeo, Rutgers University.

—— and Klug, A. (1994) 'Optimal gold reserves', mimeo, World Gold Council.

—— and Kydland, F.E. (1992) 'The gold standard as a rule', Federal Reserve Bank of Cleveland Working Paper No. 9205.

—— and Redish, A. (1990) 'Credible commitment and exchange rate stability: Canada's interwar experience', *Canadian Journal of Economics*, XXIII(2): 357–80.

—— and Schwartz, A.J. (1993) 'The changing relationship between gold and the money supply', *Research Study No. 4*, World Gold Council.

—— and White, E. (1991) 'A tale of two currencies: British and French finance during the Napoleonic War', *Journal of Economic History*, 51(2): 303–16.

——Simard, D. and White, E. (1994) *An Overplayed Hand: France and the Bretton Woods International Monetary System, 1960–8*, International Monetary Fund Working Paper.

Calomiris, C.W. (1988) 'Price and exchange rate determination during the greenback suspension', *Oxford Economic Papers*, December.

Canzoneri, M. (1985) 'Monetary policy games and the role of private information', *American Economic Review*, 75: 1056–70.

——and Henderson, D.W. (1991) *Monetary Policy in Interdependent Economies*, Cambridge, MA: Massachusetts Institute of Technology Press.

Dekock, G. and Grilli, V. (1989) 'Endogenous exchange rate regime switches', NBER Working Paper No. 3066.

Eichengreen, B. (1985) 'Editor's introduction', in B. Eichengreen (ed.) *The Gold Standard in Theory and History*, London: Methuen.

—— (1987) 'Conducting the international orchestra: Bank of England leadership under the classical gold standard', *Journal of International Money and Finance*, 6: 5–29.

—— (1989) 'Hegemonic stability theories of the international monetary system' in N. Cooper, B. Eichengreen, R. Putnam, G. Holtham, C. and Henning (eds). *Can Nations Agree? Issues in International Economic Cooperation*, pp. 255–98, Studies in International Economics Series, Washington, DC: Brookings Institution.

—— (1992a) 'The gold standard since Alee Ford', in S.N. Broadberry and N.F.R. Crafts (eds) *Britain in the International Economy: 1870–1939*, Cambridge: Cambridge University Press.

—— (1992b) *Golden Fetters: The Gold Standard and the Great Depression, 1919–39*, Oxford: Oxford University.

—— (1993) 'Three perspectives on the Bretton Woods system', in M.D. Bordo and B. Eichengreen (eds), *A Retrospective on the Bretton Woods System*, Chicago: University of Chicago Press.

—— (1994) *History and Reform of the International Monetary System*. Center for International and Development Economics Research Working Paper: C94-041, pp. 30, Berkeley, CA: University of California.

Eschweiler, B. and Bordo, M.D. (1993) *Rules, Discretion and Centra; Banfe Independence: The German experience 1880–1989*, NBER Working Paper No. 4547.

Fetter, F. (1965) *Development of British Monetary Orthodoxy, 1797–875*, Cambridge, MA: Harvard University Press.

Fishlow, A. (1987) 'Market force, or group interest inconvertible currency in pre-1914 Latin America', mimeo, University of California at Berkeley.

Fishlow, A. (1989) 'Conditionality and willingness to pay: some parallel from the 1890s', in B. Eichengreen and P. Lindert (eds) *The International Debt Crisis in Historical Perspective*, Cambridge, MA: Massachusetts Institute of Technology Press.

Flood, R.P. and Isard, P. (1989) *Simple Rules, Discretion and Monetary Policy*, NBER Working Paper No. 2934.

Frieden, J.A. (1994) 'The dynamics of international monetary systems: international and domestic factors in the rise, reign, and demise of the classical gold standard', in J. Snyder and R. Jervis (eds) *Coping with Complexivity in the International System*, Boulder, CO: Westview Press.

Friedman, M. (1990) Bimetallism revisited', *Journal of Economic Perspectives*, 4(4): 85–104.

Gallarotti, G.M. (1993) 'The scrambler for gold: monetary regime transformation in the 1870s', in M.D. Bordo and F. Capie (eds) *Monetary Regimes in Transition*, Cambridge: Cambridge University Press.

Giovannini, A. (1989), 'How do fixed exchange-rate regimes work?: the evidence from the gold standard, and Bretton Woods and the EMS', in M.D. Bordo and B. Eichengreen (eds) *A Retrospective on the Bretton Woods Systems,* Chicago: University of Chicago Press.

—— (1993) 'Bretton Woods and its precursors: rules versus discretion in the history of international monetary regimes', in M.D. Bordo and B. Eichengreen (eds) *A Retrospective on the Bretton Woods Systems*, Chicago: University of Chicago Press.

Greenspan, A. (1993). 'Changing capital markets: implications for monetary policy: opening remarks.' *Changing Capital Markets: Implications for Monetary Policy,* A symposium sponsored by the Federal Reserve Bank of Kansas City, Jackson Hole, Wyoming, August 19-21, 1993, Kansas City, WY.

Grossman, H. J. and Van Huyck, J.B. (1988), 'Sovereign debt as a contingent claim: excusable default, repudiation, and reputation', *American Economic Review*, 78: 1088–97.

Hayashi, F. (1989) *Japan's Saving Rate: new Data and Reflections,* NBER Working Paper No. 3205.

Horrigan, B. (1986) *Monetary Indicators, Commodity Prices, and Inflation*, Federal Reserve Bank of Philadelphia Working Paper No. 86.7.

Johnson, M. (1988) 'Current perspectives on monetary policy', *Cato Journal*, 8(2): 253–60.

Jonung, L. (1984) 'Swedish experience under the classical gold standard, 1873–1914', in M.D. Bordo and A.J. Schwartz (eds) *A Retrospective on the Classical Gold Standard, 1821–1931*, Chicago: University of Chicago Press.

Klein, B. (1975) 'Our new monetary standard: measurement and effect of price and uncertainty, 1880–1973', *Economic Inquiry*, 13: 461–84.

Krugman, P. (1991) 'Target zones and exchange rate dynamics', *Quarterly Journal of Economics*, 56: 669–82.

Kydland, F.E. and Prescott, E. (1977) 'Rules rather than discretion: the inconsistency of optimal plans', *Journal of Political Econo*my, 85: 473–91.

Linder, P. (1969), 'Key currencies and gold, 1900–13', *Princeton Studies in International Finance* No. 24, Princeton, NJ: Princeton University Press.

Lucas, R.E. Jr and Stokey, N.J. (1983) 'Optimal fiscal and monetary policy in an economy without capital', *Journal of Monetary Economics*, 12: 55–93.

McCallum, B. (1990) 'Targets and indicators and instruments of monetary policy', in W.S. Haraf and P. Cagan (eds) *Monetary Policy for a Changing Financial Environment*, Washington, DC: American Enterprise Institute

McKinnon, R.I. (1988) 'An international gold standard without gold', *Cato Journal*, 8: 351–73.

—— (1992) 'Exchange risk and interest rate volatility in historical perspective', *Greek Economic Review,* 14(1): 37–52.

—— (1993) *Bretton Woods, the Marshall Plan, and the Postwar Dollar Standard. A retrospective on the Bretton Woods system: Lessons for international monetary reform.* pp. 598–604. National Bureau of Economic Research Project Report, Chicago: University of Chicago Press,

Mankiw, G. (1987) 'The optimal collection of seigniorage – theory and evidence', *Journal of Monetary Economics*, 20: 327–41.

—— (1993) 'International money in historical perspective', *Journal of Economic Literature*, xxxi(1): 1–44.

Miller, M. and Sutherland, A. (1992) 'Britain's return to gold and entry into the ERM', in P. Krugman and M. Miller (eds) *Exchange Rate Targets and Currency Banks*, Cambridge: Cambridge University Press.

—— (1994) 'Speculative anticipations of stering's return to gold: Was Keynes wrong?', *Economic Journal*, July.

Moore, G. (1988) 'Inflation cycles and metals prices', *Mineral Processing and Extractive Metallurgy Review*, 3: 95–104.

—— (1990) 'Gold prices and a leading index of inflation', *Challenge*, July–August: 52–6.

—— (1991) 'Gold and inflation', *Gold Review*, Jan–Feb, New York: World Gold Council.

Mundell, R.A. (1994) *Prospects for the International Monetary System*, World Gold Council Research Report.

Obstfeld, M. (1991) *Destabilizing Effects of Exchange Rate Escape Clauses*, NBER Working Paper No 3606.

Officer, L. (1986) 'The efficiency of the dollar-sterling gold standard, 1880–1908', *Journal of Political Economy*, 94: 1038–73.

—— (1993) 'Gold-point arbitrage and uncovered interest arbitrage under the 1925–31 dollar–sterling gold standard', *Explorations in Economic History*, 30(1): 98–127.

Ranson, D. (1991) 'Gold; a leading indicator of financial market conditions', in the *Gold of the Institutional Portfolio*, New York: World Gold Council.

Roll, R. (1972) 'Interest rates and price expectations during the civil war', *Journal of Economic History*, XXXII.

Schwartz, A.J. (1984) 'Introduction', in M.D. Bordo and A.J. Schwartz (eds) *A Retrospective on the Classical Gold Standard, 1821–1931*, Chicago: University of Chicago Press.

—— (1987) 'Banking school, currency school, free banking school', in *New Palgrave Dictionary of Economics*, London: Macmillan.

Simon, H.C. (1951) 'Rules versus authorities in monetary policy', in A.E.A. *Readings in Monetary Theory*, Homewood, IL: Richard D. Irwin.

Smith, G. and Smith, T (1993) 'Wesley Mitchell and Irving Fisher and the greenback gold returns 1865–79', mimeo, Queens University.

Smith, W. S. and Smith, R.T. (1990) 'Stochastic process switching and the return to gold', *Economic Journal*, 100: 1641–75.

Svennson, L. (1994) 'Why exchange rate bands? Monetary independence in spite of fixed exchange rates', *Journal of Monetary Economics*, 33(1): 157–99.

US Gold Commission (1982) *The Role of Gold in the Domestic and International Monetary System*, Washington, DC: US Gold Commission.

Viner, J. (1937) *Studies in the Theory of International Trade*, Chicago: University of Chicago Press.

Williamson, J. and Miller, M. (1987) *Targets and Indicators: a Blueprint for the International Coordination of Economic Policy*, Washington, DC: Institute for International Economics.

Yeager, L. (1984) 'The image of the gold standard', in M.D. Bordo and A.J. Schwartz (eds) *A Retrospective on the Classical Gold Standard, 1821–1931*, Chicago: University of Chicago Press.

4 The misuse of central bank gold holdings

Ernst Juerg Weber

Introduction

Although the gold standard era has long passed, central banks continue to hold large quantities of gold. At the end of the 1990s, central banks owned about one billion troy ounces of gold, with a market value of US$270 billion.[1] Using an interest rate of 4 per cent, the cost of financing these gold holdings was US$10.8 billion. Why do central banks invest in gold at great economic cost? A popular view holds that official gold reserves make a currency more secure. The idea is that central banks are unable to inflate a currency that is covered by gold because, unlike paper money, gold is a physical commodity for which the supply is not contolled by monetary authorities. In this chapter it is demonstrated that this argument goes astray by applying principles that were true under the gold standard to the modern monetary system. Section 4.1 reviews the monetary role of gold during the gold standard. Section 4.2 ascertains that central bank gold holdings do not provide effective protection against inflation in the modern paper standard. In section 4.3, the analysis is extended to other physical assets. In section 4.4, it is found that central bank gold holdings, far from being an innocuous relic, do indeed compromise financial markets and monetary policy. Consequently, central banks should dispose of their gold reserves because they are costly, they are an ineffective cover of the currency, they interfere with the operation of financial markets, and they are detrimental to the conduct of monetary policy.

4.1 The gold standard

The gold standard ties the purchasing power of money to gold by defining the monetary unit as a fixed quantity of gold. The inverse of the gold weight of the monetary unit is the official gold price. The market price of gold moves between narrow limits, the so-called gold points, whose spread is determined by the cost of striking gold coins and melting them down. Gold coins are struck when the gold price falls below the lower gold point, and coins are hoarded or melted down when the gold price rises above the upper gold point. In the past, the operation of the gold standard required a profit-seeking agent who struck coins when the gold price was low. This agent could be the government or the public, as the right of free coinage was common already during the Middle Ages. With free coinage, the public handed in gold bullion for coinage at the mint, which charged a fee for minting costs (brassage) and often a seigniorage tax.

In practice, idiosyncratic measuring units, whose origins are lost in history, complicated monetary calculations considerably. For example, Great Britain maintained three pound systems during the nineteenth century. As a monetary unit of account, one pound equalled 20 shillings and one shilling was 12 pence. In commerce, the so-called avoirdupois pound was used to weigh all goods except precious metals and stones, and medicines. The avoirdupois pound was divided into the ounce (1/16 of a pound) and dram (1/16 of an ounce). Gold and silver weights were measured in troy pound, a somewhat lighter pound weight that was equal to 0.823 avoirdupois pounds. The subdivisions included the troy ounce (1/12 troy pound), pennyweight (1/20 troy ounce) and grain (1/24 pennyweights). After the Napoleonic Wars, Great Britain returned to the gold standard, restoring the historic sovereign coin. The gold weight of the sovereign determined the gold weight of the pound because one sovereign was tariffed at one pound. The new sovereign weighed 123.3 grains and its fineness was 11/12, yielding 113 grains of pure gold. As one sovereign was equal to one pound, the gold weight of the pound was 113 grains. The inverse of this was the official gold price, 2.1 pence per grain of pure gold.[2]

In the gold standard the purchasing power of money equalled the gold weight of the monetary unit times the purchasing power of gold.

Purchasing power of money (C/M) = Gold weight of monetary unit
(G/M) × Purchasing power of gold (C/G)   (4.1)

The purchasing power of money shows how many commodity units one monetary unit buys (C/M), where the commodity units constitute a basket that is representative of household consumption expenditures. The gold weight of the monetary unit is measured as gold units per monetary unit (G/M), and the purchasing power of gold is commodity units per gold unit (C/G). The gold standard did not give rise to a monolithic monetary unit whose purchasing power never changed. Equation (4.1), the arbitrage condition, shows that changes in the purchasing power of money arose from two sources. First, the government could change the official gold weight of the monetary unit, the first item on the right-hand side. Second, the purchasing power of gold, the second item on the right-hand side, was a relative price that depended on market conditions.

Contrary to popular opinion, metallic monetary standards never provided a safeguard against deliberate inflation through willful adulteration of coins and changes in their valuations.[3] Equation (4.1) shows that the purchasing power of money changed one-to-one with a change in the gold weight of the monetary unit. Institutional factors determined the mechanics of a change in the gold weight of the monetary unit. The government could modify the weight of gold coins and their fineness. In countries with multiple weight systems, a common occurrence, the ratio of monetary weights relative to commercial weights could be manipulated. As seen, the weight of the monetary troy pound had fallen to 82.3 per cent of the avoirdupois pound in Great Britain by the nineteenth century. Finally, pre-industrial coins lacked value marks, giving the government the power to change the value of the monetary unit by adjusting the official valuation of coins by 'crying' them up or down in terms of money of account.[4]

The second determinant of the purchasing power of money was the purchasing power of gold, which was a relative price that was subjected to market forces. In equation (4.1), an autonomous change in the purchasing power of gold will produce a one-to-one change in the purchasing power of money. The purchasing power of gold fell when there were gold discoveries or advances in mining technology. During much of the history of the gold standard, war booty was considered a legitimate source of gold, putting downward pressure on the purchasing power of gold in the victorious country and raising it in the vanquished one.[5] In the last quarter of the nineteenth century, economic growth increased the demand for gold for monetary and industrial needs, raising the purchasing power of gold. In this situation, monetary authorities could have reduced the gold weight of the monetary unit in order to avoid deflation. However, monetary authorities put up with deflation because they did not yet distinguish between money and gold. Drawing upon Roman law, a reduction in the gold weight of the monetary unit was condemned as being a fraudulent diminution of the currency.[6]

Paper money, which has a much longer history in China, became common in the West only during the eighteenth and nineteenth centuries. First private banks and then central banks issued bank notes that were backed by precious metals. The gold standard worked differently with free banking as opposed to central banking. Private bank notes, which were legally related to bills of exchange, embodied an unconditional promise by the issuer to convert notes into gold on demand. Free banking disciplined banks because any suspension of gold convertibility by a private bank led to immediate bankruptcy. In the nineteenth century, the move to central banking watered down the principle of gold convertibility because governments do not allow central banks to fail. This made the legal connection between bank notes and bills of exchange meaningless.[7]

An important consequence of central banking is that the gold standard can be suspended by giving paper money legal tender status. The leading industrial nations – Great Britain, Germany, France and the USA – suspended gold convertibility only during major wars, but other countries exercised less restraint. Bordo and Kydland (1996) view the gold standard as a contingent rule allowing for the suspension of gold convertibility during wars and other national emergencies, on the understanding that convertibility would eventually be restored at the old gold price. The commitment to return to the old gold parity facilitated access to credit markets during the emergency. Bordo and Eichengreen (1999) also find that the commitment encouraged stabilizing capital flows during currency crises. On the downside, the return to the old gold price required a deflationary process after the emergency. This had no adverse effect on economic activity only if the promise to return to the old gold price had remained credible during the emergency, with the public expecting that inflation would be followed by deflation.

A contentious issue in the literature on the gold standard concerns the effect of central banks on the purchasing power of money when convertibility is maintained.[8] A central bank that overissued bank notes experienced a loss of gold through the balance of payments. The price–specie–flow mechanism of David Hume (1711–76) posits that an excess supply of money raises domestic prices relative to foreign prices, making domestic goods uncompetitive in world markets. Accordingly, the central bank had the power to influence the purchasing power of money for a limited time, although sustained inflation was incompatible with the gold standard. In the nineteenth century, improvements in transportation (railway and steamboat) and communication (telegraph) accounted for a massive reduction in transaction costs in international trade. Central banks were unable to influence domestic prices if they were linked to foreign prices through international commodity arbitrage. As a consequence, monetary policy ceased to have an effect on the price level, making the price–specie–flow mechanism obsolete.[9] The monetary approach to the balance of payments abandons the notion that changes in relative price levels were the main force behind the balance of payments in fixed exchange rate regimes, including the gold standard. Instead, it is maintained that monetary policy affected the balance of payments directly, through aggregate spending.[10]

To sum up, the gold standard tied the purchasing power of money more or less securely to gold. The government could change the gold weight of the monetary unit by adjusting the weight and fineness of coins and, in pre-industrial times, by manipulating monetary weights and changing the official valuation of unmarked coins. The introduction of bank notes did not change the nature of the gold standard as long as bank notes were supplied competitively. The emergence of central banks undermined the principle of convertibility because central banks are exempt from bankruptcy laws. Although central banks were constrained by international gold flows, they had the power to influence the economy in the short run. As a consequence, the gold standard had lost its main operational advantage, the ability to work automatically without government interference, well before its demise in the twentieth century.

4.2 Inconvertible paper money

The gold standard ended during the Great Depression in the 1930s, although gold continued to play a residual role until the demise of the Bretton Woods international monetary system in 1971. The adoption of flexible exchange rates produced a monetary system in which central banks can print paper money at will. A modern central bank can inflate or deflate the monetary unit without limit because it is not obliged to defend a fixed gold price or exchange rate. The public no longer has the right to exchange bank notes for gold at a fixed price. Therefore, an excessive amount of paper money increases all prices, including the gold price. The shift to inconvertible paper money changed the way in which central banks conduct monetary policy. Modern central banks target the inflation rate because the economy lacks a nominal anchor in the form of an official gold price or a fixed exchange rate against a gold currency.

The move to inconvertible paper money makes central bank gold reserves obsolete. The following analysis shows that gold reserves fail to constrain the issuing power of the central bank if the gold price is market determined. For simplicity, it is assumed that the central bank is the only bank in the economy, and central bank transactions accounts are counted as paper money. The starting point is a central bank with 100 per cent gold reserves and no capital. Both the gold reserves and the circulation of paper money amount to US$100.

Assets		(CB 1)	Liabilities
Gold	100	Notes	100
		Capital	–

At first sight, this currency looks rock solid because all bank notes are backed by gold. But look what happens if the central bank prints more paper money, doubling the amount of circulating notes. The perfect gold cover is maintained if the central bank puts the extra notes in circulation by buying more gold.

Assets		(CB 2)	Liabilities
Gold	200	Notes	200
		Capital	–

This is not yet the final state of the central bank balance sheet because the increase in the money stock produces inflation. Ignoring all real effects of inflation and of the purchase of gold, the doubling of the money stock will lead to a doubling of the price level. As inflation involves a uniform increase in the prices of all commodities, the gold price also doubles. After the inflationary process has run its course, the balance sheet is:

Assets		(CB 3)	Liabilities
Gold	400	Notes	200
		Capital	–

Thus, the central bank makes a profit on its gold reserves of US$200. The reason for this is that physical gold holdings are valued at the market-determined price of gold, which has doubled. The profit is added to the capital account.

This argument shows that gold reserves do not limit central bank discretion in the modern paper standard. Gold reserves do not prevent the central bank from starting an inflationary process by printing paper money and buying gold, printing more paper money and buying more gold, and so on. Central banks are free to choose the money growth rate because inflation increases the nominal value of their gold reserves. Even if the central bank just printed paper money without buying extra gold, the gold backing of the currency would be maintained. Clearly, it is futile to tie a nominal quantity, the price level, to another nominal quantity, the value of gold reserves.

Errata

<u>Page 68:</u>

Assets		(CB 3)	Liabilities
Gold	400	Notes	200
		Capital	200

<u>Page 69:</u>

Assets		(P 1)	Liabilities
Notes	100	Wealth	600
Gold	500		
CB Capital	-		

The gold purchase by the central bank leads to a change in asset holdings of the public, reducing gold by US$ 100 and increasing bank notes by US$ 100. . . . . . .

Assets		(P 2)	Liabilities
Notes	200	Wealth	1200
Gold	800		
CB Capital	200		

Central bank gold holdings are problematic because they create an incentive to inflate. The balance sheet (CB 3) shows that the central bank makes a profit of US$200 on its gold holdings by doubling the price level. In fact, central banks made huge profits when the gold price was freed in response to inflationary pressures in 1971. Central banks held about 1 billion troy ounces of gold, which, at US$35 per ounce, was worth US$35 billion. Using a price of US$400 per ounce, the value of central bank gold holdings reached US$400 billion in the 1980s. Hence, central banks made a staggering profit of US$365 billion simply by inflating.[11]

Yet, inflation does not create wealth; there is no free lunch. The following two balance sheets show that the central banks' profit was funded by the public. The public holds paper money, gold and the shares of the central bank. There are not many countries where the public actually holds central bank shares, a notable exception being Switzerland. Still, the capital of the central bank is included among the assets of the public because, in a democratic society, government agencies are answerable to the public. Initially, the capital of the central bank is nil and the shares are valueless. The public wealth (US$600) equals the gold stock in the economy, which is split between the public (US$500) and the central bank (US$100).

Assets	(P 1)		Liabilities
Notes	100	Wealth	600
Gold	200	Notes	200
CB Capital	–		–

The gold purchase by the central bank leads to a change in asset holdings of the public, reducing gold by 100 per cent and increasing bank notes by 100 per cent. The next balance sheet directly shows the situation after the doubling of the price level in response to the doubling of the money stock. Public wealth increases because gold holdings double in value from US$400 to US$800 and the value of central bank capital, which is assigned to the public, increases from zero to US$200.

Assets	(P 2)		Liabilities
Notes	200	Wealth	600
Gold	800	Notes	200
CB Capital	200		–

Although wealth nominally increases from US$600 to US$1200, the public is no better off in real terms because the price level has also doubled. Not surprisingly, inflation that is fuelled by paper money creation does not create wealth. However, public wealth is only unaffected if the central bank's profit of US$200 is really transferred to the public via the capital item. The increase in the value of central bank shares compensates the public for the reduction in the purchasing power of money. The public is worse off if it does not receive the central bank profit. Thus, the crucial question is: what happened to the US$365 billion that central banks earned in the 1970s?

Basically, central banks may have used the profit in three ways: transferred it to the Treasury, used it to cover losses in their foreign exchange dealings and other speculative activities, or hidden it by undervaluing their gold holdings. Consider the welfare implications of each of these actions.

1   The Treasury can pass on the profit to the public by reducing taxes. If the windfall is used to finance extra government expenditures, the effect on public welfare depends on the nature of these government expenditures.
2   Using the profit to cover losses in the foreign exchange market amounts to a subsidy to banks and foreign exchange dealers, which is hard to justify.
3   Hiding the profit by undervaluing gold is unproblematic only if the central bank capital is represented by shares that can be traded. These shares would reflect the true value of central bank gold holdings and people could sell the shares. But the hands of the public are tied because most central banks do not issue shares. Even the shares of the Swiss National Bank do not reflect the true value of gold holdings because dividend payments are strictly regulated. In effect, central banks that kept their gold after the increase in the gold price made a risky investment on behalf of the public.

4.3 Other monetary fallacies

The idea that physical assets are suitable to back up bank notes has a long tradition in commercial banking. In the eighteenth and nineteenth centuries, the emergence of bank notes raised concerns that banks may overexpand the currency. In particular, it was feared that banks might fuel a speculative boom in real estate or shares by discounting financial bills. It was considered a sound banking principle that banks discounted only bills of exchange that had been created in commercial transactions involving the purchase and sale of commodities. Prudent banks avoided so-called financial bills that arose from the extension of credit without an underlying commercial transaction. This is the real bills doctrine, which was embraced by the banking school in the nineteenth century.[12] In practice, it was difficult to distinguish between commercial bills and financial bills because a bill may have passed through several hands before it was discounted by a bank. There is no doubt that banks often invested in financial bills despite the prominence of the real bills doctrine. In fact, financial bills provided a convenient vehicle for unsecured loans because the rigorous bankruptcy rules for bills of exchange made them tradable in secondary markets.

The real bills doctrine accounted for much mischief in early central banking (Friedman and Schwartz, 1963: 191–3, 373). Central bankers believed that the discount of commercial bills would produce an elastic currency whose circulation harmonized with the business cycle. Commercial bills were thought to be more closely linked to economic activity than financial bills, which might be used for speculative activities. During the Great Depression in the 1930s, central bankers, whose monetary policy conception was still rooted in the nineteenth century, adopted a hands-off policy, claiming that it was futile to force money into circulation beyond business needs. Curiously, the central element of the real bills doctrine, the belief that business needs determined the nominal money stock, re-emerged in Japan during the recession in the 1990s. The Bank of Japan steadfastly refused to implement a monetary expansion that would have halted deflation. It could easily have reflated the economy by buying government securities, monetizing the huge government budget deficit that arose from ineffectual fiscal policy.[13]

The central concern of the banking school, that it was possible to overissue bank notes, has to be taken seriously because a central bank was unlikely to experience a loss of gold as long as an asset price boom was in the making. However, the proposed cure, the real bills doctrine, was ineffective. The main flaw of the real bills doctrine is that it ties the nominal money stock to another nominal quantity, the value of commercial bills on the balance sheet of the central bank. Suppose that the central bank reduces the discount rate below the level that is compatible with price stability. The amount of discount loans would increase, expanding the money stock and fuelling inflation. A central bank that accommodates business needs would replace expiring commercial bills with nominally inflated new ones in order to keep real central bank credit constant. This would further increase the money supply, fuelling more inflation. As in the case of gold, the discount of commercial bills does not provide a nominal anchor because the face value of commercial bills rises one-to-one with the price level.

The spectacular collapse of John Law's financial empire exposed the same fallacy.[14] John Law (1671–1729), the son of a Scottish banker, proposed that inconvertible paper money would be perfectly safe if it was backed up by land, a physical asset that, like gold, had the advantage that it was available in all countries. His breakthrough came when he became a confidant of the French regent in 1715. The concept of paper money must have appeared to the regent, who ruled on behalf of the infant king, like manna from heaven, as the royal house was broke. Law rapidly established the Banque Général (later Banque Royale) and the Compagnie de Commerce d'Occident (Compagnie des Indes), which eventually monopolized the entire colonial trade of France. In 1720, shortly before his downfall, Law reached the pinnacle of his career, achieving the position of minister of finance.

Law monetized the French public debt through a two-tier process. The Compagnie d'Occident raised capital by issuing shares; the unusual aspect was that the public could pay for the shares with government securities. This was popular because the Compagnie d'Occident accepted government securities at face value, even though they had fallen below par. In turn, the Banque Royale issued bank notes by extending credit, accepting the shares of the Compagnie de Commerce d'Occident as collateral for margin loans. This two-tiered procedure effectively monetized the French public debt. As a consequence of the monetary expansion, the shares of the Compagnie de Commerce d'Occident rose fiftyfold and the general price level doubled. In 1720, the scheme collapsed and the bank notes became worthless. Law fled to Venice, where he died an impoverished gambler.

Economists owe to John Law the practical proof that real asset holdings do not limit a central bank's ability to issue inconvertible paper money because inflation increases the price of these assets. In fact, the value of the shares that the Banque Royale held as collateral for margin loans rose even faster than the price level during the inflationary process. Law's experiment demonstrated early on that a central bank had the power to influence the price level by issuing paper money. However, central bankers did not draw the right lesson from Law's misadventure, instead adhering to the real bills doctrine, which suffers from the same flaw as Law's scheme, until the twentieth century.

4.4 Moral hazard

As gold no longer serves a monetary purpose, central banks are rightfully reducing their gold holdings. In September 1999, fifteen European central banks, including the European Central Bank, signed an agreement in Washington that limited gold sales to 400 tonnes per year for the next 5 years. This equals about one-sixth of the annual gold production in the world. The purpose of the Washington Agreement is to prevent a fire sale of official gold that would lead to a collapse of the gold price. The Washington Agreement is reproduced below.

Washington Agreement, 26 September 1999

1   Gold will remain an important element of global monetary reserves.
2   The above institutions will not enter the market as sellers, with the exception of already decided sales.
3   The gold sales already decided will be achieved through a concerted program of sales over the next 5 years. Annual sales will not exceed approximately 400 tonnes and total sales over this period will not exceed 2,000 tonnes.
4   The signatories to this agreement have agreed not to expand their gold leasings and the use of gold futures and options over this period.
5   This agreement will be reviewed after 5 years.

The signatories are Oesterreichische Nationalbank, Banque Nationale de Belgique, Suomen Pankki, Banca d'Italia, Banque centrale du Luxembourg, De Nederlandsche Bank, Banque de France, Deutsche Bundesbank, Central Bank of Ireland, Banco do Portugal, Banco de España, Sveriges Riksbank, Schweizerische Nationalbank, Bank of England, and European Central Bank.

The first clause of the agreement, which states that gold will remain an important element of global monetary reserves, is opaque. It may either be an empty declaration that aims at calming down the gold market or it may be an indication that, even three centuries after John Law, central banks still do not fully understand the operation of an inconvertible paper currency. Clauses 2 and 3 determine gold sales for the next 5 years. During the first year, the signatories strictly abided by the agreement, selling about 400 tonnes of gold. Three countries – the Netherlands, Switzerland and the UK – accounted for more than 90 per cent of official gold sales (World Gold Council, 2000). Clause 4, which refers to gold loans and gold derivatives, is designed to curb short-selling of gold by private institutions. Short-selling operations that use central bank gold put downward pressure on the gold price to the detriment of central banks that wish to sell gold.

The Washington Agreement triggered a panic in the gold market, which had become used to the easy availability of central bank gold. The gold price, which had been hovering just above US$250 during the summer, shot above US$300 in response to the limitation on official gold sales. Short-sellers were struggling to cover their positions either by buying gold outright or by borrowing it. The freezing of gold loans by central banks led to a tightening of the credit market for gold, raising the interest rate on gold loans, which are payable in gold, to 10 per cent in the first few days after the agreement. By the end of the year, the gold price was still about 10 per cent higher than before the agreement, while the gold interest rate had fallen to 1–2 per cent, the rate which 'the market is historically used to' (The Washington Central Banks Agreement on Gold, World Gold Council, October 1999).

Central bank gold holdings may interfere in three ways with the primary goal of modern monetary policy, price stability. First, the central bank may not be impervious to profits and losses on its gold holdings; nor should it be, because these profits and losses are ultimately carried by the public. Second, the application of principles of modern asset management to official gold holdings, in particular the use of gold loans and derivatives, may expose the central bank to risk in a way that the preservation of central bank investments becomes a concern in the conduct of monetary policy. Finally, the central bank's gold holdings may become embroiled in political controversy. The following paragraphs show how central bank gold holdings threaten monetary policy independence in the modern paper standard.

Central bank gold holdings create a moral hazard because the central bank can earn a profit by inflating the currency. The increase in the gold price produced enormous accounting profits in the 1970s. It is irrelevant whether central banks really succumbed to the temptation to enrich themselves by inflating during the 1970s. Monetary regulations belong to the basic constitutional framework of a country, which is designed to last for generations. An important objective of constitutional constraints is to limit moral hazard by officials and government bodies. Monetary regulations should avoid the moral hazard inherent in central bank gold holdings when paper money is inconvertible. Any regulatory framework must address the issue of moral hazard – there is nothing special about monetary regulations in this regard.

In practice, central bankers are not impervious to the profit motive. Many central banks actively manage their gold holdings in order to make a profit. The asset managers of central banks have found a way to put gold to productive use by making gold loans and dealing in gold derivatives. Clause 4 in the Washington Agreement mentions gold loans (leasings), gold futures and options. The size of these operations is substantial, although information is hard to come by as they often involve off-balance-sheet items. A report commissioned by the World Gold Council estimates that:

... the amount of gold in the lending and swaps market (total liquidity) at end-1999 was 5,230 tons, with 90 per cent of it – 4,710 tons – supplied by central banks and other formal official holders (BIS, ECB, etc.) . . . Analyzing the position of 118 countries (those with traceable reserves), the [report] found that 29 didn't lend at all or lent no more than 10 per cent of their gold reserves, 4 lent 10–25 per cent, 48 lent 25–50 per cent, while 37 lent more than 50 per cent. When all known official reserves are taken into account (including those of the BIS, ECB, etc.), average lending was found to be 14 per cent – or 25 per cent if the USA, Japan, the IMF and non-lending European countries are excluded.

World Gold Council (2000)

Central banks in the Middle East, Latin America and Africa are particularly active in the gold market, although their gold holdings are small (World Gold Council, 2000).

Private parties borrow gold from central banks in order to sell it in the spot market. The motives for these short-selling operations include hedging and specula-tion, with the hedging being done mostly by gold mining companies. It is common practice to finance a new gold mine by borrowing gold from a central bank and selling it in the spot market. The short-selling operation locks in the gold price and, at the same time, it generates immediate cash that can be used to finance the development of the mine. Central bank gold loans are immensely popular among gold miners because they make it possible to finance a mining project at a very low interest rate, about 1–2 per cent. The mining company carries no gold price risk because the gold loan, principal plus interest, can be paid back with newly produced gold when the mine becomes operational. The World Gold Council, which is not a disinterested party, estimates that hedging by mining companies 'accounted for three-fifths – 3,021 ton – of total use [of gold loans] at the end of 1999. In contrast, the financing of consignment and other inventory stocks accounted for only 1,465 tons, net speculative short positions for some 394 tons, and other uses some 350 tons' (World Gold Council, 2000).[15]

The central banks' dealings with gold miners are questionable. Although the lure of gold remains strong, there is really nothing special about gold that would justify preferential treatment of the gold industry. As with other primary commodities, the production of gold can be hedged by selling it forward, and capital costs of gold mines can be financed through bank loans and share market floats. Central bank gold loans, which effectively subsidize the production of gold, contributed to the expansion of gold mining in the 1990s. World gold production increased from an average output of about 2,250 tonnes per year in the first half of the decade to about 2,500 tonnes per year from 1996 to 1999 (World Gold Council, 2000). Central banks have finally become aware of the connection between gold loans and gold production. Clause 4 in the Washington Agreement freezes gold loans because the expansion of gold mining is depressing the gold price at a time when central banks want to sell gold.

Besides the gold mining industry, the beneficiaries of central bank gold loans include speculators who sell gold short. The World Gold Council's estimate of net speculative short positions are 647 tonnes and 394 tonnes at the end of June and December 1999 respectively. Central banks face a dilemma when speculators to whom they have lent gold run into trouble. Similarly, gold futures and options involve contingent liabilities that entangle the central banks' interests with those of private parties. This may compromise monetary policy during a financial crisis, just when the central bank needs a free hand. A central bank that is entangled with the private sector may bail out a financial institution to protect its own direct and indirect exposure. The central banks' involvement in financial markets – not only gold – gives rise to moral hazard in monetary policy. What were the motives of the US Federal Reserve when it hastily brokered a rescue, albeit without using its own funds, for Long-Term Capital Management (LTCM), a hedge fund, in September 1998?[16] The rescue package involved a cost in terms of loss of monetary policy independence. The easing of money market conditions in the fourth quarter of 1998, which cannot be explained by macroeconomic conditions, was a pay-off to the financial institutions that participated in the rescue package for LTCM.

A bail-out of speculators is detrimental to the efficient allocation of capital because it undermines accountability, giving rise to moral hazard in financial markets. The rescue of LTCM rewarded excessive risk taking by the wealthiest investors in the world. Asset prices impart a realistic appraisal of investment opportunities only if risk is valued correctly. A culture of bail-outs leads to the undervaluation of risk, distorting the risk–return trade-off. As a consequence, capital flows to industries where risk is subsidized, here the gold industry. Why do central banks assume the price risk of gold producers by lending them gold? It is doubtful that central banks can carry this risk at a lower cost than gold producers who have first hand knowledge of the gold industry. Central banks make these gold loans simply because they are stuck with a large quantity of gold that would otherwise remain idle.

Official gold sales will not stop when the Washington agreement is reviewed after 5 years (clause 5). The sale of 2,000 tonnes of gold makes barely a dent in central bank gold holdings, which will fall by only 6.4 per cent. After the sales, central banks will still hold more than ten times the annual world production of gold. The sale of gold by central banks will depress the gold market for many years to come. At the going rate of 400 tonnes per year, it will take almost 80 years until all central bank gold is sold. Not surprisingly, the central banks' gold policy has become the focus of public contention. Gold producers oppose the inevitable disposal of official gold with the same vehemence as silver producers resisted the demonetization of silver at the end of the nineteenth century (Friedman and Schwartz, 1963: section 3.2). In 1997, the sale of a small quantity of gold by the Reserve Bank of Australia caused a stir among Australian gold producers. The World Gold Council, the premier lobbyist of the gold industry, spends a fortune on propaganda material praising the monetary role of gold.[17] The Council poured scorn on the Washington Agreement, being particularly incensed by the freezing of central bank gold loans. In Switzerland, a citizens-initiated referendum is pending on the distribution of gold holdings of the Swiss National Bank. The referendum, which is opposed by the government, asks for the transfer of 'excess' gold to the Swiss old age pension fund. A highly politicized debate of central bank gold is detrimental to the conduct of independent monetary policy. As the central bank does not operate in a political vacuum, it may find it necessary to compromise on monetary policy in order to accommodate public opinion on an issue that is peripheral to monetary policy.

4.5 Conclusion

The gold standard tied the purchasing power of money to gold by defining the monetary unit as a fixed quantity of gold. The official gold price served as a nominal anchor for the price system as long as the government did not set sail for another anchorage. Although abuse did happen, the gold standard provided a high degree of monetary stability for long stretches of time. It took central banks about two decades, from the onset of inflation in the 1960s to the 1980s, to achieve the same degree of price stability that was common under the gold standard. Have central banks finally learnt the right lesson from John Law's misadventure that it is possible to overissue paper money? The price stability that has been achieved in major industrial countries warrants some optimism, but the jury on the central banks' ability to manage the paper standard that emerged in 1971 is still out. A poor understanding of the operation of the modern paper standard explains the Bank of Japan's failure to prevent deflation in the 1990s.

In the gold standard era, gold reserves were crucial for the defence of the official gold price. A central bank that overexpanded the currency was penalized by a loss of gold through the balance of payments. A monetary authority that was seriously committed to a fixed gold price had to use the discount rate in a way to reinforce the effect of international gold flows on the money stock. In the modern paper standard, central banks are free to choose the inflation rate by setting the money growth rate. Exchange rate changes account for international adjustment instead of international gold flows. Central banks have kept their gold reserves without having any real use for them. Despite the high cost of official gold holdings, central banks have so far escaped public censure. The popular attachment to gold arises from a vague notion that central bank gold holdings somehow make the currency more secure. This argument falsely applies principles that were true under the gold standard to the modern paper standard. Central bank gold holdings no longer provide a safeguard against deliberate inflation because their value increases with a general increase in prices. The same is true for other real assets, including commercial bills (real bills doctrine), land (proposed by John Law) and shares (used by John Law). In fact, asset prices often race ahead during an inflationary spell.

Central bank gold holdings are a risky investment in the name of a disenfranchised public. Given the high volatility of the gold price, central banks grossly underprice gold loans. The meagre return, about 1–2 per cent, does not provide adequate compensation for the risk on gold holdings, which is similar to that on shares. The underpricing of risk distorts the allocation of capital in financial markets.

The implied subsidy to gold producers contributed to the recent expansion of gold mining and the falling gold price. Inflationary accounting profits on gold constitute a moral hazard in monetary policy. The central banks' entanglement with speculators through gold loans and derivatives threatens monetary policy independence. Central bank gold holdings are not an innocuous relic from the gold standard era. They should be disposed of because they are costly, they are an ineffective cover of inconvertible paper money, they undermine the efficient operation of financial markets, they give rise to moral hazard in monetary policy, and they may become the focus of political attention. As an immediate measure, central bank gold holdings should be transferred into a special fund that is given the task to dispose of it without disrupting the gold market.

Another view holds that central bank gold holdings provide emergency cash for the government. But what kind of emergency should this be, realistically? Certainly, it must be a global crisis because it is easy to set aside funds for a national disaster, for example an earthquake, by accumulating international assets that yield more than gold. A country may also borrow internationally, as Italy did after the severe earthquake on 23 November 1980 (Neely, 1999). Yet a return to the gold standard would not be an option during a global economic crisis of the type of the Great Depression in the 1930s. The gold standard was a contributing factor to the Great Depression because the fixed gold price precluded a monetary easing after the stock market crash in 1929. In any case, gold cannot protect against a global catastrophe because, like any other good, gold has value only as long as it can be exchanged into another commodity, somewhere. On this account, gold would be downright useless after a full-blown world war. The only eventuality in which gold may again become useful as an international means of payment is a rise of rogue states and an emergence of global thuggery that would end international borrowing and lending. The Great Depression and the Second World War provide a historical precedent of a collapse of international financial relations along these lines. However, it is not really worthwhile to prepare for this dire eventuality because it presupposes a social and economic retrogression in which monetary issues would be a mere bagatelle.

Notes

1 IMF, International Financial Statistics.
2 Applying metric measuring units, one avoirdupois pound equals 453.6 grams and one troy pound is 373.2 grams. Although the avoirdupois pound is heavier than the troy pound, the avoirdupois ounce is lighter than the troy ounce because the two pound units are divided into 16 ounces and 12 ounces respectively. One avoirdupois ounce equals 28.35 grams and one troy ounce is 31.1 grams.
3 Spufford (1988) discusses monetary debasements during the Middle Ages. Weber (1996) analyses the inflationary process in Basle from 1365 to 1429.
4 Weber (2001) deals with the significance of the introduction of value marks in coinage during the Industrial Revolution.
5 In the nineteenth century, the incipient international law distinguished between private gold holdings, which were protected, and official gold holdings, which remained fair game.

 6 Sargent and Velde (2002: Chapters 5 and 6) discuss the evolution of the concept of money in jurisprudence.
 7 Selgin (1999) argues that 'a completely free banking system, where no bank enjoys special government privileges or immunities, would be most likely to stick to its commitments'. Dowd (1992) includes a collection of essays on the experience of free banking.
 8 Frenkel and Johnson (1976) and Bordo (1984) review the historic literature on the gold standard. Modern research on the gold standard can be found in the volumes edited by Bordo and Schwartz (1984), Eichengreen (1985), Bayoumi *et al.* (1996), and the collected essays of Bordo (1999). Sargent and Velde (2002) consider the effect of token coinage on the price level during the Middle Ages.
 9 An increase in the money stock had a small effect on domestic prices by raising world prices. The strength of this effect depended on the country's share in the world money supply.
10 McCloskey and Zecher (1976) apply the monetary approach to the balance of payments to the gold standard.
11 An appreciation of the home currency relative to the US dollar reduced the central bank's profit on its gold holdings in terms of home currency.
12 The real bills doctrine preceded the controversy between the currency school and the banking school by several decades. Viner (1937), Mints (1945) and Fetter (1965) review the development of monetary theory in the eighteenth and nineteenth centuries.
13 The Japanese gross public debt as a share of GDP increased from 57.9 per cent in 1990 to 105.4 per cent in 1999 (OECD *Economic Outlook*, December 2000: 242). The inaction of the Bank of Japan has been criticized by many economists, including Ito and Itoh (1998), Itoh (1998), Krugman (1998a,b) and Meltzer (1999a,b). McKinnon and Ohno (2000) argue that exchange rate expectations make Japanese monetary policy ineffective. Okina (1999) defends the monetary policy of the Bank of Japan.
14 Garber (2000: 91–107), Niehans (1990: 48–51) and Pohl (1993: 139–49) discuss John Law's monetary system.
15 The report also includes figures for June 1999.
16 The Federal Reserve does not deal in gold loans and gold derivatives, but it manages a portfolio of foreign exchange and government securities. The Federal Reserve may also have acted on behalf of other central banks.
17 This material is available on the Internet at www.gold.org.

References

Bayoumi, T., Eichengreen, B. and Taylor, M.P. (eds) (1996) *Modern Perspectives of the Gold Standard*, Cambridge: Cambridge University Press.
Bordo, M.D. (1984) 'The gold standard: the traditional approach', in M.D. Bordo and A.J. Schwartz (eds) *A Retrospective of the Classical Gold Standard, 1821–1931*, Chicago: University of Chicago Press.
—— (1999) *The Gold Standard and Related Regimes*, Cambridge: Cambridge University Press.
—— and Eichengreen, B. (1999) 'Is our current international economic environment unusually crisis prone?', in D. Gruen and L. Gower (eds) *Capital Flows and the International Financial System*, conference proceedings, Reserve Bank of Australia.
—— and Kydland, F.E. (1996) 'The gold standard as a commitment mechanism', in T. Bayoumi, B. Eichengreen and M.P. Taylor (eds) *Economic Perspectives of the Classical Gold Standard*, Cambridge: Cambridge University Press.

—— and Schwartz, A.J. (eds) (1984) *A Retrospective of the Classical Gold Standard, 1821–1931*, Chicago: University of Chicago Press.

Dowd, K. (ed.) (1992) *The Experience of Free Banking*, London: Routledge.

Eichengreen, B. (ed.) (1985) *The Gold Standard in Theory and History*, New York: Methuen.

Fetter, F.W. (1965) *The Development of British Monetary Orthodoxy, 1717–1875*, Cambridge, MA: Harvard University Press.

Frenkel, J.A. and Johnson, H.G. (1976) 'A monetary approach to the balance of payments: essential concepts and historical origins', in J.A. Frenkel and H.G. Johnson (eds) *The Monetary Approach to the Balance of Payments*, Toronto: University of Toronto Press.

Friedman, M. and Schwartz, A.J. (1963) *A Monetary History of the United States, 1867–1960*, Princeton, NJ: Princeton University Press.

Garber, P.M (2000) *Famous First Bubbles*, Cambridge, MA: MIT Press.

Ito, T. and Itoh, M. (1998) 'Can target 3–4 per cent inflation be achieved by quantitative easing?', *Ronso*, Toyo Keizai (September).

Itoh, M. (1998) 'Inflation policy is also an option', *Nihon Kezai Shimbunn* (25 June).

Krugman, P. (1998a) 'Japan's trap'. Available online at http://web.mit.edu/krugman/www/japtrap.html (accessed 8 January 2002).

—— (1998b) 'Japan's slump and the return of the liquidity trap', *Brookings Economic Papers*, 2: 137–206.

McCloskey, D.N. and Zecher, J.R. (1976) 'How the gold standard worked', in J.A. Frenkel and H.G. Johnson (eds) *The Monetary Approach to the Balance of Payments*, Toronto: University of Toronto Press.

McKinnon, R. and Ohno, K. (2000) 'The foreign exchange origins of Japan's economic slump and low interest liquidity trap'. Available online at http://www-econ.stanford.edu/faculty/workp/swp00010.html (accessed 8 January 2002).

Meltzer, A.H. (1999a) 'Comment: What more can the Bank of Japan do?', *Monetary and Economic Studies*, Bank of Japan (December), 189–91.

—— (1999b) 'Liquidity claptrap', *International Economy*, 13 (November/December): 18–23.

Mints, L. (1945) *A History of Banking Theory in Great Britain and the United States*, Chicago: University of Chicago Press.

Neely, C.J. (1999) 'An introduction to capital controls', *Federal Reserve Bank of St. Louis Review* (November/December): 13–30.

Niehans, J. (1990) *A History of Economic Theory*, Baltimore: Johns Hopkins University Press.

Okina, K. (1999) 'Monetary policy under zero inflation: a response to criticisms and questions regarding monetary policy', *Monetary and Economic Studies*, Bank of Japan, December: 157–88.

Pohl, H. (ed.) (1993) *Europäische Bankengeschichte*, Frankfurt am Main: Fritz Knapp Verlag.

Sargent, T. and Velde, F. (2002) *The Big Problem of Small Change*, Princeton: Princeton University Press.

Selgin, G. (1999) 'Ludwig von Mises and the case for gold', *Cato Journal* 15(Fall): 259–77.

Spufford, P. (1988) *Money and Its Use in Medieval Europe*, Cambridge: Cambridge University Press.

Viner, J. (1937) *Studies in the Theory of International Trade*, New York: Harper and Brothers.

Weber, E.J. (1996) ' "Imaginary" or "real" moneys of account in medieval Europe? An econometric analysis of the Basle pound, 1365–1429', *Explorations in Economic History*, 33: 479–95.

—— (2001) *A history of bimetallism: Greece – Rome – Middle Ages – modern times*, University of Western Australia Working Paper (December).

World Gold Council (1999) *The Washington Central Banks Agreement on Gold*, London: World Gold Council.

World Gold Council (2000) *Gold in the Official Sector*, London: World Gold Council.

5 International barriers to gold trade

Chris Allen, Taron Brearley, Antony Clarke, Julie Harman and Peter Berry

Despite gold being one of the most actively and widely traded commodities in the world, there are a number of restrictions on gold and jewellery trade in various countries. Reduction of these barriers to gold trade would be of benefit from a global industry perspective.

Better market access would benefit Australian gold producers because it would tend to increase demand for gold bullion exports, Australian gold jewellery and other manufactured gold products.

Why gold trade barriers exist

Governments erect barriers to trade for many reasons; however, historical motivations for restricting gold trade can be classified into two broad categories.

First, some gold trade regulations are linked with gold's now dominant and growing role as a commodity used in jewellery, electronics, dentistry and other specialist industrial applications. These restrictions largely take the form of barriers (typically tariffs, but quotas in some instances) to imports of gold jewellery or other semimanufactured gold products; they generally serve to protect domestic manufacturing industries from world competition. Such restrictions often function as de facto 'luxury' taxes on expensive gold jewellery imports. Substantial barriers to such imports remain in a number of important markets.

Second, some gold trade regulations (generally applied to gold bullion or coin) are linked with gold's historical role as a medium of exchange. After the collapse of the Bretton Woods gold–dollar exchange system in 1973, many economies in the world adopted some form of floating exchange rate system and liberalized (but to differing degrees) their foreign exchange and capital markets, including liberalizing restrictions on international gold bullion trade. Significant barriers to gold bullion trade only remain in countries where domestic currency and capital markets are relatively highly regulated. Flows of gold to these countries are restricted as a form of government control over the domestic money supply and exchange rates.

Trade barriers and recent reforms

Tariffs on imports of gold bullion, jewellery and other semimanufactured gold products account for the majority of barriers to gold trade in the world, and there appear to be few cases where quotas are used to regulate trade in these products. There are also other (generally minor) import tariffs on other gold products: South Korea, for example, levies an 8 per cent import tariff on gold used for manufacturing semiconductors.

Compared with the numerous and widespread tariffs on gold imports, non-tariff barriers to gold trade are less common and are concentrated in a few countries. India has banned imports of gem-set gold jewellery, but not imports of plain gold jewellery and gems (separately subject to various import tariffs). Vietnam and China impose various non-tariff barriers on gold imports, reflecting the highly regulated foreign exchange and capital markets in these countries. All gold imported to China must be authorized by the People's Bank of China, and similarly all gold imports to Vietnam require approval of the State Bank of Vietnam (which set a 34-tonne quota on allowable gold imports in 1996) (World Gold Council, 1997).

The People's Bank of China also heavily regulates gold production and distribution within its country. Gold producers in China are required to sell their output to the bank at the official Chinese price, which in the past year or so has been slightly higher than world prices. The People's Bank of China is the only legitimate source of bullion for gold manufacturers, and it has previously sold bullion at a premium of around 10 per cent above the official price (Bannock *et al.*, 1997). Foreign manufacturers (through a Chinese partner) are allowed to operate in China (mainly for exporting), but foreign-owned gold retailers face an effective ban in China (Bannock *et al.*, 1997).

The People's Bank of China recently adjusted the country's official bullion selling price (the price at which the bank sells gold to fabricators) closer to the world gold price, to discourage smuggling and to increase revenues from authorized gold imports.

Patterns in gold trade liberalization

Import tariffs on gold jewellery are more widespread and larger (in nominal terms) than import tariffs on gold bullion (Table 5.1). To indicate the significance of these tariffs to the market, the Australian Bureau of Agricultural and Resource Economics (ABARE) calculated weighted-average jewellery and bullion import tariff rates. Jewellery tariffs have been weighted by each country's share of world gold in jewellery consumption, and bullion import tariffs have been similarly weighted by an estimate of each country's share of gold bullion imports.

Like the size and frequency of tariffs on gold and jewellery, the weighted-average tariff rates indicate the relative importance of these restrictions. The world weighted-average import tariff on gold in jewellery (10.5 per cent) is around four times larger than the world weighted-average import tariff on gold bullion (2.2 per cent). The fact that import tariffs on gold jewellery are generally larger and more

Table 5.1 Major international gold import tariffs[a]

	Gold import tariff		
	Jewellery (%)	*Bullion (%)*	*Market share[b] (%)*
Australia	5	0	1
Brazil	21	5	2
China	40	8	6
Dubai	4	0	2
European Union	4	1	9
India[c]	15	6	22
Indonesia[d]	25	0	1
Malaysia	100	3	
Philippines	20	3	0
Saudi Arabia	12	0	6
South Korea	30	3	3
Thailand	22	0	1
Turkey[e]	2	0	6
United States	6	0	11
Vietnam[f]	40	5	1
Other	0	0	25
Total (weighted average)[g]	10.5	2.2	100

Notes
a   There are tariffs on various other gold products, but jewellery and bullion represent the most widespread tariffs here. Tariff rates are approximate and may include numerous subcategory tariffs. Jewellery includes Australian Harmonised Export Commodity Classification Codes (AHICC) 7113–5; bullion includes AHICC 7108.
b   Market share is based on a country's share of world gold fabrication in1997 (Gold Fields Minerals Services, 1998).
c   Applies to plain gold jewellery items only. Gem-set jewellery to India is banned. Tariff is calculated on the basis of a 6 per cent import duty and a 4.5 per cent premium for purchasing a Special Import Licence through an Indian resident partner.
d   A 40 per cent rate applies to ASEAN countries.
e   Applies to non-EU countries only; 60 per cent applies elsewhere.
f   Bullion imports to Vietnam are subject to authorization of the State Bank of Vietnam, which set a quota of 34 tonnes on imports in1996 (World Gold Council, 1997).
g   Averages weighted by market shares.

widespread than those on gold bullion reflects the different economic policy and industry protection objectives of these tariffs.

Gold bullion

Since the breakdown of the Bretton Woods system in 1973, rapid financial liberalization in many economies has been accompanied by liberalization of the gold bullion trade (see Box 5.1 for an overview). The latter has tended to follow broader financial and economic liberalization because a government that opens up its foreign exchange and capital markets to global trade no longer has an incentive

Box 5.1   Financial liberalization and gold bullion

The modern world gold 'market' only came into existence following the abolition of the Bretton Woods gold–US dollar exchange system in 1973. Given the US government's concern over controlling the value of gold under the Bretton Woods system, private US citizens were not allowed to buy or sell bullion. After the collapse of the Bretton Woods system in 1973 and a move to a managed floating exchange regime, this concern for controlling private gold holdings disappeared. The restrictions were formally removed in 1975. Similar restrictions were removed in other countries such as Japan (1973) and the UK (1979), following the deregulation of 'Bretton Woods era' foreign exchange trading regulations (Warwick-Ching,1993).

Following these reforms in developed countries during the 1970s, similar liberalization of gold bullion trade has proceeded in developing countries during the 1980s and 1990s. The liberalization of Turkey's gold trade in the 1980s resulted from broader financial and economic liberalization of the Turkish economy during that time (Ertuna, 1994). Prior to these reforms, gold imports into Turkey were banned, although annual (illegal) imports of around 80 tonnes were smuggled into the country. Following Turkey's liberalization of gold trade, domestic gold price premiums rose by around 85 per cent, contributing to significant growth in Turkey's gold jewellery export industry (Ertuna, 1994).

Similar gold trade liberalization measures have recently been undertaken in India (as part of broader economic liberalization since 1991) after the economy suffered a major balance of payments crisis. Prior to1991 private gold bullion ownership and imports were banned in India, leading to significant domestic price premiums over world prices (reflecting the additional costs of smuggling gold into India). After removing the Gold Control Act in 1991, India progressively liberalized importation controls on gold. Over the period 1992–94, schemes were enacted to allow non-resident Indians to import up to 10 kilograms a year, and similar Special Import Licence schemes were set up for gold jewellery and other products exporters. Unofficial (smuggled) imports have since fallen dramatically (Table 5.2), as have local price premiums (down from US$200 an ounce in 1990 to less than US$20 an ounce in 1998) (Figure 5.1).

In 1997, a group of experts brought together by the Ministry of Finance and the Reserve Bank of India outlined plans for full capital account convertibility of the rupee (Baru,1997). Following this, the Open General Licence importing scheme was introduced in October 1997, whereby eight banks and three authorized importing agencies are allowed to freely import gold bullion subject to the current rate of 250R/10 g imports, equivalent to a 6 per cent import tariff at current rates. The tariff rate was originally set at 225R/10 g in 1997, then raised in May 1998 (following depreciation of the rupee and the threat of economic sanctions following India's nuclear detonations) as a means of increasing foreign exchange revenues. The tariff was again raised in January 1999 to 400R/10 g (equivalent to a 10 per cent import tariff).

to control bullion trade (that is, allowing a country's citizens to buy and sell foreign exchange freely is analogous to allowing them to buy and sell gold bullion freely) (Frankel, 1994).

Gold bullion trade was liberalized in most developed countries during the 1970s. Important reforms occurred in Turkey during the 1980s and in India during the 1990s. Policy on gold bullion trade in India changed from an outright ban on imports in 1990 to a modest 6 per cent import tariff. As a result, domestic gold premiums (the difference between the domestic gold price and the world gold price expressed in domestic currency terms at official exchange rates) have fallen dramatically in that country, smuggling has declined, and domestic prices have approached equivalent world prices as legal import volumes have increased (Figure 5.1).

The extent of these recent reforms to gold bullion trade in India, Turkey and other important gold-consuming economies has significantly reduced barriers to world gold bullion trade, with modest imports tariffs remaining in India, China, Vietnam and Brazil (Table 5.1). (As discussed earlier, China and Vietnam also impose non-tariff barriers on gold bullion imports, but the equivalent tariff of these restrictions has not been determined.) These historical trends in financial and gold bullion trade liberalization, and the prospect of progressive foreign exchange and capital market deregulation in China, Vietnam and other developing countries in the next decade, suggest that gold bullion trade liberalization is likely to continue over the medium to longer term.

Jewellery and other semi-manufactured gold products

Despite the progress made on the liberalization of gold bullion trade, restrictions on trade in gold jewellery and other gold products remain widespread. This reflects the domestic industry interests and other socioeconomic factors that influence trade policies for such manufactured products.

It is apparent that significant jewellery import tariffs occur in some countries with substantial local jewellery manufacturing industries, such as India, Thailand, Saudi Arabia, the United Arab Emirates and the USA. Protection appears to be

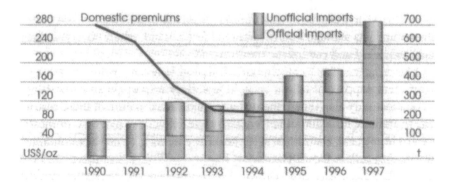

Figure 5.1 Indian gold imports and price premiums.

concentrated in markets where gold manufacturing (such as jewellery making) is particularly labour intensive. This association suggests that gold-using manufacturing industries that sustain high levels of regional employment may exert considerable influence over levels of protection from competitive gold imports.

A good example of this is the ban of gem-set jewellery imports to India (where the manufacture of gem-set items is fairly labour intensive). Companies wanting to import plain gold jewellery into India must find a resident partner to obtain a special import licence (which sells at a premium of over 4 per cent). The importer then has to pay an import duty of around 6 per cent, leading to an equivalent import tariff (ignoring the transaction costs of obtaining the licence) of around 11 per cent.

Gem-set imports are also highly restricted in Thailand, where such jewellery is both exported and part of the tourism trade.

Government support of tariffs on gold jewellery imports in some developing countries may also reflect the de facto 'luxury tax' nature of these restrictions. In India, China and other 'Eastern'-style jewellery markets, domestic prices of high-carat, traditional-style jewellery items may not be maintained at levels that reflect the full extent of import tariffs because there are high levels of domestic price competition. On the other hand, domestic prices at the 'higher end' of the jewellery market in these countries (which typically includes 'Western'-style jewellery items that have a higher fabrication value-added component and per unit cost) are likely to be increased by the full extent of import tariffs.

Thus, import tariffs may effectively discriminate against the high-value end of jewellery markets, and thereby serve as a form of 'luxury taxation' on expensive 'Western'-style jewellery imports. From an economic perspective, a single tax on expensive gold jewellery items – rather than an import tariff that affects both consumption and domestic production decisions and distorts jewellery trade – could achieve this objective more effectively.

Benefits of world gold trade liberalization

Trade protection-related restrictions

Gold is traded competitively in an extensive network of global spot and forward markets (O'Callaghan, 1993), which have been found to be efficient (that is, when the gold price fully reflects market information) using standard tests (see Sjaastad and Scacciavillani, 1996). The evident ability of competitive world markets to efficiently provide gold and jewellery commodities and products means, from a global perspective, that social welfare would be maximized by liberalizing remaining barriers to gold and jewellery trade and enabling open and competitive markets for that trade. [This assumes that the hoarding of gold by central banks does not create (removable) distortions in world gold trade.]

Removal of trade barriers would mean that consumers in previously restricted markets would benefit by being able to purchase additional gold and jewellery at lower domestic prices. Social gains would also be realized when resources previously used in protected gold mining and manufacturing industries were redirected to other more socially valued uses. Producers of jewellery and gold in the rest of the world would benefit from being able to provide additional output to these markets. These effects would be of net benefit to society over the longer term, although the recipients of protection would face adjustment costs in the short term.

Monetary policy and exchange control-related restrictions

A few countries retain restrictions on gold trade for monetary reasons, and there may be some justification for continuing these restrictions until wider economic reforms proceed. These restrictions may be valid if it is likely that private gold bullion ownership and trade (without subsequent removal of restrictions on foreign exchange transactions) could destabilize the domestic currency (and lead to associated economic losses) through citizens preferring to use gold. The magnitude of these costs would clearly depend on a number of factors, including the stocks of gold in relation to domestic money supply, citizens' preferences for holding wealth in gold and the transactions costs involved.

In principle, the optimum order of liberalization is to remove all trade, foreign exchange and capital distortions immediately (Caves *et al.*, 1993). However, where all barriers cannot be removed at once, research has found that international capital market liberalization should follow domestic trade and capital market liberalization (McKinnon, 1992).

It is beyond the scope of this chapter to ascertain whether the few remaining barriers to gold bullion trade may be justifiable under these conditions. However, the issue of gold bullion trade liberalization is of secondary importance to liberalization of world gold jewellery trade for two reasons. First, tariffs on gold bullion are not large or widespread compared with tariffs on gold jewellery (Table 5.1). Second, it is apparent that tariffs on world gold bullion trade are progressively being eliminated as broader economic and financial liberalization proceeds in developing countries.

Smuggling and domestic competition issues

The existence of smuggling can reduce the economic efficiency losses from trade restrictions, and subsequently reduce the potential net benefits of liberalization (Pitt, 1981). Given gold's high unit value, it is easily smuggled: black markets for gold have operated widely in the past, and continue in countries that impose substantial trade restrictions.

Prior to India's removal of the Gold Control Act in 1990, ownership and trade of gold bullion was prohibited. However, the unofficial gold flow into India was 222 tonnes in 1989 – equivalent to 9 per cent of world fabrication demand in that year (Figure 5.1). Similarly, domestic gold consumption in Vietnam was estimated at around 20 tonnes in 1997, yet no gold was imported through the official State Bank of Vietnam quota scheme (Gold Fields Minerals Services, 1998: 16). Market analysts also suggest, despite the restrictions on gold jewellery and bullion imports to China, that significant volumes of gold jewellery are smuggled into China from Hong Kong and Singapore (Gold Fields Minerals Services, 1998: 49).

Another factor that may reduce the effect on domestic gold prices of gold trade import restrictions is the extent to which domestic competition in protected gold manufacturing industries undermines any price advantages derived from such restrictions. The average making charge on plain gold jewellery in India, for example, is around US$4 an item (Naqvi, 1998). Moreover, domestic competition (among over 250,000 jewellery stores within India) keep these costs low. Thus, it is unlikely that tariffs on plain gold jewellery in India significantly affect the domestic prices of items with low fabrication content.

However, the removal of existing barriers to jewellery imports would be expected to benefit importers at the 'higher-value end' of the jewellery market – that is, importers of lower-carat 'Western'-style jewellery (which generally has a higher value-added component and per unit cost). For jewellery that has a higher value-added component, and which is diverse and differentiated from local products by virtue of its origin (for example, Italian designer jewellery), local prices tend to fully reflect the costs of import tariffs and other trade restrictions.

While the existence of black markets for gold and domestic competition for some jewellery products may reduce the effect on domestic prices of gold jewellery trade restrictions, this does not mean that trade liberalization will not be beneficial. Given that black markets and smuggling reduce the effectiveness of barriers to trade, they undermine the value of setting high barriers, and thus add to the argument for liberalization.

Other distortions in the world gold market

Despite barriers to international gold trade being the most important form of distortion in the world gold market, Bannock *et al.* (1997) found numerous other regulatory policies that affect gold ownership and production in various countries. Some of these policies are generally considered beneficial to the efficiency of the world gold market. Standards on gold and jewellery hallmarking, for example, ensure that all market participants have equal information about the quality of products – a condition required for markets to work efficiently.

Other gold regulations found by Bannock *et al.* (1997) that are likely to be distortionary (that is, they lower economic efficiency) are restrictions on ownership and production in China and Italy. In addition to the barriers to gold trade in China, all gold producers in China are required to sell their output to the People's Bank of China at the official price (which has been above the international market price); this amounts to a domestic production subsidy and leads to higher levels of gold production in China than would occur at world prices. However, deregulation of these policies affecting gold production, ownership and trade in China is likely to proceed as wider economic and financial liberalization progresses.

Similarly, Italy has recently revoked laws restricting private investment purchases of gold bullion, and there is an amendment before the Italian parliament to enable private investors to sell bullion.

Gold taxation

Bannock *et al.* (1997) cited various domestic taxes on gold consumption as possibly being discriminatory. However, the optimal (or efficient) level of taxation on consumption of gold will tend to vary from country to country. It is difficult to identify aspects of gold taxation policies (for consumers) in different countries that may be economically inefficient. Moreover, the different consumption taxation arrangements in various countries would make it difficult to consider taxation reform issues as part of international negotiations.

One possible exception relates to the differential treatment of taxation on financial transactions and gold sales for 'commercial' purposes. The European Union Commission released a directive in July 1998 to harmonize all existing value-added gold taxes in EU member states and to set the tax at zero on gold used for purely 'financial' transactions. It has not been ascertained whether this differentiation occurs in other economies, but it would appear to be appropriate (from an economic perspective) to tax purely 'financial' transactions in gold in the same manner as similar transactions using other forms of exchange.

Australia's perspective

In Australia, two major groups are likely to benefit from further liberalization of international barriers to gold trade. First, Australian gold jewellery manufacturers are likely to gain through increased access to overseas export markets, and through higher prices (than otherwise may occur) for existing exports as world gold and jewellery consumption rises. Australian gold producers also stand to gain from higher world gold prices, other things being equal, given that they are 'price takers' in the world gold market.

The nature of gold jewellery markets with trade restrictions suggests that Australian jewellery manufacturers are unlikely to gain significantly from additional access to plain-gold, high-carat jewellery markets in parts of Asia, the Middle East and India, because domestic jewellery prices are unlikely to fully reflect jewellery import tariffs. However, Australian jewellery manufacturers would be expected to benefit from such tariff reductions through greater access to the 'higher end' of these markets (such as 14- and 16-carat jewellery items with a significant fabrication component), particularly where specific 'Australian origin' jewellery has a premium.

The benefits to Australian jewellery manufacturers from increased access to the restricted jewellery markets (Table 5.1) could be expected to increase over time as incomes in these regions increase. Benefits are especially likely to increase if jewellery tastes shift towards more 'Western'-style products. Recent analysis has found rising consumption of gem-set jewellery in China and growing levels of 14-carat jewellery manufacture in Turkey – two markets that have traditionally sold 22-carat, plain-gold items (Gold Fields Minerals Services, 1998).

Currently, the Australian government is pursuing the issues of gold jewellery trade liberalization through the Asia Pacific Economic Cooperation (APEC) forum's Early Voluntary Sectoral Liberalization Process, and through various other multilateral and bilateral negotiations through APEC. Future negotiations through the World Trade Organization may also provide a forum for pursuing these trade liberalization issues.

Unlike Australian jewellery manufacturers, which face differentiated potential markets, Australian gold producers essentially operate in a global, homogeneous product market – that is, world gold demand for bullion. Australian gold producers may benefit from further gold trade liberalization when such reforms result in lower domestic jewellery prices in restricted markets, leading to higher gold jewellery consumption in these markets and therefore higher world gold consumption and prices than would otherwise occur.

Import tariffs on gold jewellery represent the most widespread and significant barrier to world gold trade. A simple model of the world gold and jewellery markets (see below) has been used by ABARE to estimate changes in world gold prices that would result from the simultaneous removal of all of the gold jewellery tariffs shown in Table 5.1. The results of this analysis are presented in Table 5.2.

The impact on the world gold price of removing existing import tariffs on gold jewellery is sensitive to the price responsiveness of gold supply from both mine production and above-ground stock sales. The more responsive these sources of supply, the smaller the increase in the world gold price when tariffs on gold jewellery imports are removed.

Given considerable uncertainty about investor and central bank market behaviour over the medium term, ABARE used a wide range of price elasticities for sales of above-ground stocks. Values from zero to ten were tested to illustrate a feasible range of potential (long-term) price increases (Table 5.2).

A price elasticity of zero for sales of above-ground stocks (which produces the largest increase in the equilibrium price of gold – 5.4 per cent) represents a scenario in which sales of such stocks do not change when world gold prices increase. A price elasticity of ten represents a scenario in which annual sales of above-ground stocks increase by 26 per cent (or around 510 tonnes) when world gold prices increase by 2.6 per cent following liberalization. Despite using this range in potential supply responses from above-ground stocks, the range of resulting world gold price increases flowing from the removal of tariffs is reasonably limited, ranging from 1.7 to 5.4 per cent (Table 5.2).

The long-term price elasticity of gold production in Australia was found to be 2.15. Thus, given the future removal of current tariffs on gold jewellery imports shown in Table 5.1, Australian gold production could increase by an estimated 4–12 per cent.

The modelling approach used to derive these estimates is necessarily simplified. Issues with these simplifications and their effect on the overall analysis are discussed in the the next section. Nevertheless, the results show a range of price increases that suggests that gold jewellery trade liberalization is a worthwhile policy objective not only for exporters of Australian jewellery, but also for Australian gold producers (via the indirect price and volume benefits).

Table 5.2   Estimated changes in the world gold price from the removal of world gold
jewellery import tariffs[a]

	Elasticity of above-ground stock sales		
	Zero *(0.0)*	*Mid* *(5.0)*	*High* *(10.0)*
Change in world gold price on tariff removal (%)[b]	5.40	2.60	1.70
Other assumptions			
Price elasticity of world gold production	2.15	2.15	2.15
Price elasticity of gold jewellery demand[c]	–0.85	–0.85	–0.85

Notes
a   See appendix for Chapter 5 for a detailed explanation of the method and assumptions underpinning
these results.
b   This is a long term equilibrium price increase, and prices may increase by more or less than this
amount initially.
c   Elasticity of gold in jewellery demand with respect to the gold price.

Illustrative model – effect on the world gold price of removing tariffs on gold jewellery imports

A simple model has been developed by ABARE to examine the effect on the world
gold price of removing all the import tariffs on gold jewellery (which are presented
in Table 5.1). The results of this analysis are shown in Table 5.2.

Key assumptions and model structure

In principle, the effect of removing all import tariffs on gold jewellery would be
a lower domestic price of gold jewellery in restricted markets, leading to higher
gold jewellery consumption in these markets and therefore a higher world gold
price. The illustrative model developed here estimates the magnitude of the
potential world gold price increase and examines the sensitivity of this result to
key assumptions.

World jewellery market

For the purposes of the illustrative model, gold jewellery was treated as a globally
homogeneous product, using estimated world averages for the proportion of gold
in jewellery (caratage) and jewellery manufacturing costs. Annual gold jewellery
consumption in a country was assumed to depend on gold jewellery prices in
that country. For simplicity, price elasticities of gold jewellery consumption were
assumed to be the same in all markets. [Note that Batchelor and Gulley (1995)
found that price elasticities of gold jewellery consumption in the USA, Germany,
France, Italy, Japan and the UK were not significantly different.]

Further, it was assumed that the technology in jewellery manufacture uses inputs (including gold) in fixed proportions to output, and that prices of these inputs are given and independent of volumes used. Domestic jewellery prices were assumed to fully reflect the effect of any import tariffs on gold jewellery.

World gold market

Gold jewellery accounted for around 80 per cent of world gold consumption in 1997, with industrial uses and (to a lesser extent) purchases of gold bars and coins accounting for the remainder. This volume of non-jewellery gold consumption in 1997 was assumed to remain constant on removal of import tariffs on gold jewellery. Thus, the only variable influence on gold consumption in the model is through gold jewellery consumption.

There are two distinct sources of world gold supply: production from gold mines and sales of above-ground gold stocks. Since 1988, annual world gold consumption has been greater than world gold mine production, with sales of above-ground stocks making up the difference (42 per cent of supply in 1997). Annual world gold supply from both sources was assumed to positively depend on the world gold price.

Equations

Specific gold jewellery consumption, world gold mine production and above-ground stock holding equations were not estimated because the exercise is illustrative only. (Given that these equations are written in general form, there will be a linearization error in the empirical exercise presented later, which could be removed if the functional forms for these expressions were known and used.) In the following equations, variables denoted by lower-case letters indicate relative (percentage) changes, whereas upper-case letters indicate levels.

World price of jewellery

$$P^j_w = \alpha P^g_w + \beta \tag{5.1}$$

Domestic price of jewellery in country i

$$P^j_i = P^j_w(1 + T_i) \tag{5.2}$$

Consumption of jewellery in country i

$$C^j_i = f(P^j_i) \tag{5.3}$$

World gold mine production

$$X^g = f(P^g_w) \tag{5.4}$$

Gross sales of above-ground gold stocks

$$S = f(P_w^g)$$ (5.5)

Consumption of gold in jewellery

$$C_i^{gj} = C_i^j \alpha$$ (5.6)

World gold market clearing condition

$$\sum_{i=1}^{n} C_i^{gj} + C_0^g = X_w^g + S$$ (5.7)

If equations (5.1) to (5.7) are converted to linear equations in variables expressed in terms of percentage changes from base year levels, then the following equation can be obtained for the percentage change in the world gold price, P_w^g on percentage changes in gold jewellery import tariffs, t_i for each country i (equation 5.8).

$$P_w^g = \frac{\displaystyle\sum_{i=1}^{n} C_i^{gi}(0)t_i \frac{T_i(0)}{1+T_i(0)}}{\dfrac{\varepsilon X_w^g(0) + \sigma S(0)}{\eta^j} - \alpha \dfrac{P_w^g(0)}{P_w^j(0)} \displaystyle\sum_{i=1}^{n} C_i^{gi}(0)}$$ (5.8)

where $X(0)$ indicates the base level of variable X.

Endogenous variables

P_w^j = world jewellery price
P_w^g = world gold price
P_i^j = price of jewellery in country i
C_i^j = annual consumption of jewellery in country i
C_i^{gj} = annual consumption of gold in jewellery in country i
X_i^g = annual world production of gold
S = annual (gross) sales of above-ground gold stocks

Exogenous variables and parameters

α = proportion of gold in jewellery
note: α = caratage $\times$ 100/24
C_0^g = annual rate of non-jewellery gold consumption
β = manufacturing cost per ounce of jewellery
η^j = price elasticity of world jewellery consumption

ε = price elasticity of world gold mine production
σ = price elasticity of above-ground gold stock sales
T_i = *ad valorem* import tariff rate (expressed as a fraction) on gold jewellery in country i

Model estimation and results

Equation (5.8) was used to calculate the effect on the world gold price of removing all gold jewellery import tariffs shown in Table 5.1. Key values for the initial market conditions and parameters are shown in Tables 5.3 and 5.4. The result of this analysis for the world gold price was shown in Table 5.2, and the effects on jewellery prices and consumption in individual countries are shown in Table 5.5.

Estimates of the price elasticity of gold jewellery consumption were taken from a recent study by Batchelor and Gulley (1995), who applied a seemingly unrelated regression model to data on gold in retail jewellery purchases across a range of developed countries. Batchelor and Gulley (1995) found direct long-term price elasticities of gold in jewellery (as a function of the gold price) in the range of –0.25 (France) to –1.1 (Japan). The weighted (by gold in jewellery consumption) average of the elasticities reported by Batchelor and Gulley for developed countries is –0.85.

Given that the price elasticity estimated by Batchelor and Gulley (1995) is the elasticity of consumption of gold in jewellery with respect to the world gold

Table 5.3 Model's parameter estimates

Parameter	Description	Value
	Initial world price	US$300/oz
α	Proportion of gold in gold jewellery (by weight)	82% (Table 5.5)
β	World cost of gold jewellery manufacture per ounce of jewellery	US$200/oz
	Initial world gold price of gold jewellery	US$346/oz
	Initial annual consumption of gold in jewellery in country i	See Table 5.5
	Initial annual world consumption of gold in jewellery	3,328 tonnes
	Annual rate of non-jewellery gold consumption	926 tonnes
$S(0)$	Initial annual sales of above-ground stocks	1,790 tonnes
	Initial world gold mine production	2,464 tonnes
η^i	Price elasticity of gold jewellery consumption	–1.5
ε	Price elasticity of world gold mine production	2.15
σ	Price elasticity of above-ground stock sales	0–10
$T_i(0)$	Gold jewellery import tariff in country i	See Table 5.5
$t_i(0)$	Percentage change in the import tariff in country i	–100% for all countries

Table 5.4 Model's initial market conditions

	C_i^g (t)	T^i (%)[a]	α (%)[b]
Australia	5	0	1
Brazil	21	5	2
China	40	8	6
Dubai	4	0	2
European Union	4	1	9
India[c]	15	6	22
Indonesia	25	0	1
Malaysia	10	0	3
Philippines	20	3	0
Saudi Arabia	12	0	6
South Korea	30	3	3
Thailand	22	0	1
Turkey	2	0	6
USA	6	0	11
Vietnam	40	5	1
Other	0	0	25
Total (weighted average)	10	2	100

Notes
a   See footnote to Table 5.1 for detail.
b α is assumed to be equal across markets because gold is treated as a homogeneous product, but this column shows how the average value of α was determined. Estimate of caratage is derived from Warwick-Ching (1993, p. 205).
c   Weighted by share of jewellery consumption.

price, it is necessary to convert this to the elasticity of jewellery consumption with respect to the jewellery price (η^j), which is used in equation 5.16. The relationship between these two elasticities (derived using equations 5.9, 5.10 and 5.14) is shown in equation 5.17. The price elasticity of gold jewellery consumption of -1.5 was therefore derived from the weighted-average elasticity from Batchelor and Gulley (1995), and from estimates of the average mark-up of the jewellery price over gold content (300 per cent) and the average gold in jewellery content (70 per cent) for the countries studied by Batchelor and Gulley (after Warwick-Ching, 1993).

$$\eta^j = \eta^j_{p_w^g} \frac{P_w^j C^j}{P_w^g C^g} = \eta^j_{p_w^g} \frac{P_w^j}{\alpha P_w^g} \tag{5.9}$$

where $\eta^j_{p_w^g}$ = elasticity of consumption of gold in jewellery with respect to the world gold price.

Other key parameters used include the proportion of gold in gold jewellery (α in equation 5.1), which is related to plain gold jewellery caratage. An estimate of the weighted world average (by jewellery consumption) gold content in jewellery of 82 per cent was used (Table 5.5). This is close to 18-carat jewellery (24-carat

Table 5.5 Change in domestic jewellery consumption and prices following tariff removal[a]

	Jewellery consumption[b]			Jewellery price
	1997 t	Tariff reduction t	Increase (%)	Increase (%)
Australia	17	18	5.13	−3.33
Brazil	58	72	24.54	−15.92
China	214	304	41.82	−27.14
Dubai	72	75	3.72	−2.41
European Union	292	301	3.00	−1.95
India	734	865	17.89	−11.61
Indonesia	30	39	28.61	−18.57
Malaysia	114	127	11.80	−7.66
Philippines	3	4	23.48	−15.23
Saudi Arabia	199	227	14.30	−9.28
South Korea	114	152	33.36	−21.64
Thailand	31	39	25.58	−16.60
Turkey	202	204	0.81	−0.53
USA	362	386	6.52	−4.23
Vietnam	45	64	41.82	−27.14
Other	841	822	−2.21	1.43
Total (weighted average)	3328	3698	(11.12)	

Notes
a   These results correspond to the world gold supply elasticity of 5 in Table 5.2.
b   Gold in gold jewellery. See footnote to Table 5.1 for detail.

gold jewellery has 100 per cent gold content, 18-carat has 75 per cent gold content, and so on), which has long been the standard in a number of leading jewellery manufacturing countries (Warwick-Ching, 1993). The average fabrication cost per ounce of gold jewellery was assumed to be US$200.

These assumptions imply an average 81 per cent mark-up of the jewellery price over the value of the gold content per unit of jewellery. This value was chosen as the weighted average of the mark-ups that Warwick-Ching (1993) suggests are typical in Eastern jewellery markets (10–20 per cent) and Europe or North America (200–400 per cent).

The impact on the gold price of removing existing import tariffs on gold jewellery is sensitive to the assumed value of the price elasticity of gold supply from both mine production and above-ground stock sales. The more price elastic these sources of supply, the smaller the increase in the world gold price following the removal of tariffs on gold jewellery imports. However, mine production takes time to respond to significant price changes, given the decision timing and development delays affecting gold producers. Thus, the price elasticity of world mine production would increase over time, to approach a long-term value. In Appendix A of *Australia in the World Gold Market* (1999), the long-term price elasticity of gold production in Australia was found to be 2.15, and this value was used to proxy for the price elasticity of world gold mine production (Table 5.3).

Compared with the price responsiveness of mine supply (which would increase over time), the price responsiveness of above-ground stocks is likely to decline over time (assuming that above-ground holdings are gradually reduced to desirable levels). These contrasting supply responses, and the apparent willingness of the official sector and private investors to significantly reduce their large gold holdings (as outlined in Chapter 2 of *Australia in the World Gold Market*), suggest that the price elasticity of above-ground stocks would be greater than the price elasticity of world gold mine production over the short term, but that this difference would decline and possibly reverse over the longer term. It is not clear to what extent these countervailing influences will affect the aggregate gold supply elasticity over time, and therefore whether the price increasing effect of liberalization increases or decreases over time.

Given the uncertainty surrounding the responsiveness of above-ground stock sales to higher prices, a range of price elasticities for above-ground stocks was used (from zero to ten) to illustrate a feasible range of potential (long-term) price increases (Table 5.2). A price elasticity of zero for sales of above-ground stocks (which produces the largest increase in the equilibrium price of gold – 5.5 per cent) represents the case in which sales of above-ground stocks do not change following an increase in world gold prices. Similarly, the highest price elasticity of ten represents the case in which annual sales of above-ground stocks increase by 17 per cent (or around 300 tonnes) following an increase of 1.7 per cent in world gold price after liberalization.

Despite this range in potential supply responses from above-ground stocks, the range of resulting world gold price increases is reasonably limited – from 5.4 to 1.7 per cent (Table 5.5).

Conclusions

The results presented in Table 5.5 suggest that removing all import tariffs on gold jewellery would lead the world gold price to increase by 1.7–5.4 per cent. Under the midpoint elasticity scenario (price elasticity of above-ground stocks equal to five), the world gold price would increase by 2.6 per cent. The change in domestic gold jewellery prices and jewellery consumption for the various countries that impose gold import tariffs and all other countries using this midpoint elasticity are shown in Table 5.5. Total world gold in jewellery consumption would increase by 11.2 per cent (373 tonnes), but consumption in currently unrestricted markets (and also in some countries with quite low jewellery tariffs) would fall – a result of the world gold price increasing the cost of gold jewellery by more than the price-reducing effect of removing any gold jewellery tariff.

However, given the simplifications of the analysis, the results generated are illustrative only. Perhaps most importantly, the effects of smuggling and domestic competition in jewellery manufacture – which imply lower effective import tariffs – were not considered here, but would lower the resulting price increase.

References

Bannock, G., Doran, A. and Turnbull, D. (1997) *An Overview of Regulatory Barriers to the World Gold Trade*, World Gold Council Research Study no. 17, London: World Gold Council.

Batchelor, R. and Gulley, D. (1995) 'Jewellery demand and the price of gold', *Resources Policy*, 21(1): 37–42.

Caves, R.E., Frankel, J.A. and Jones, R.W. (1993) *World Trade and Payments*, 6th edn, New York: HarperCollins.

Ertuna, O. (1994) *The Liberalization of Turkey's Gold Market*. Research Study No. 7, London: World Gold Council.

Frankel, J.A. (1994) 'Advantages of liberalizing a nation's gold market', *World Gold Council Research Study No. 6*, Geneva.

Gold Fields Minerals Services (1998) *Gold Update*, London, 1 September.

McKinnon, R.I. (1991) *The Order of Economic Liberalization: Financial Control in the Transition to a Market Economy* pp. xii, 200, Johns Hopkins Studies in Development, Baltimore: Johns Hopkins University Press.

—— (1992) 'Taxation, Money, and Credit, in a Liberalizing Socialist Economy', *Economics of Planning* 25(1): 97–112.

Naqvi, K. (1998) 'Gold and silver: India – wedded to gold', Macquarie Equities Research Paper, London.

O'Callaghan, G. (1993) *The Structure and Operation of the World Gold Market*, Occasional Paper No. 105, Washington DC.

Pitt, M.M. (1981) 'Smuggling and price disparity', *Journal of International Economics*, 11(4): 447–58.

Sjaastad, L.A. and Scacciavillani, F. (1996) 'The price of gold and the exchange rate', *Journal of International Finance and Money*, 15(6): 879–98.

Warwick-Ching, T. (1993) *The International Gold Trade*, Cambridge: Woodhead Publishing.

World Gold Council (1997) *Annual Report 1996*, Geneva.

6 The price of gold and the exchange rate

Larry A. Sjaastad and Fabio Scacciavillani

The main objective of this chapter is to identify the effect of major currency exchange rates on the prices of internationally traded commodities. For commodities that are traded continuously in organized markets such as the Chicago Board of Trade, a change in any exchange rate will result in an immediate adjustment in the prices of those commodities *in at least one currency* involved in the trade and perhaps in both currencies if both countries are 'large'. For example, when the dollar depreciates against the Deutschemark, dollar prices of commodities tend to rise (and DM prices fall) even though the fundamentals of the markets – all relevant factors other than exchange rates and price levels – remain unchanged. The power of this effect is suggested by the events surrounding the intense appreciation of the dollar from early 1980 until early 1985, during which time the US price level *rose* by 30 per cent but the International Monetary Fund (IMF) dollar-based commodity price index *fell* by 30 per cent, and dollar-based unit-value indices for both imports and exports of commodity-exporting countries as a group *declined* by 14 per cent. The explanation for this anomaly may lie in the exchange rate: with respect to the DM, for example, the dollar appreciated by more than 90 per cent in nominal terms, and by 45 per cent in real terms.

The potential importance of this phenomenon is not limited to the major currency countries. With more than two-thirds of the minor currencies of the world being directly or indirectly tied to one of the three major currencies (the dollar, the Deutschemark, and the yen) or to a currency basket, shocks to the major currency exchange rates may be felt not only by producers and consumers of internationally traded commodities in the major currency countries but also by many of the smaller, commodity-exporting countries in the form of inflationary (or deflationary) shocks transmitted by fluctuations in the international prices of commodities.[1]

In the first of the five sections to follow, an international pricing model is developed, which predicts that changes in major currency exchange rates will impact on the prices of many commodities in all currencies – major and minor alike. Section 6.2 is concerned with preliminary test of the data and section 6.3 – the core of the chapter – reports the findings of a pilot study of the international market for gold. In section 6.4, we quantify the contribution of floating exchange rates to the coefficient of variation of the international price of gold since the dissolution of the Bretton Woods system in 1973. A short summary section concludes the chapter.

Gold is a prime candidate for a pilot study of the effects on commodity prices of fluctuations in major currency exchange rates. A highly homogeneous commodity, gold is traded almost continuously in well-organized spot and future markets. Moreover, as annual production (and consumption) of gold is minuscule compared with the global stock, the gold-producing countries, whose currencies typically are not traded in organized markets, are unlikely to dominate the world gold market.

6.1 Exchange rates and commodity prices: the model

The model developed in this section focuses on the effect of movements in exchange rates on the international price of a homogeneous commodity that is traded in an organized market; it is not the usual asset-pricing model as it is not concerned with the rate of return on the holding commodity in question.[2] The model has two basic elements: the law of one price and global market clearing in a world of M countries or currency blocs. Ignoring all barriers to trade, and with all variables expressed in natural logarithms, the law of one price for an internationally traded commodity is simply:

$$P_1 = P_j + E_{1j}, j = 1, \ldots, M \tag{6.1}$$

where P_j is the commodity price in currency j and E_{1j} is price of currency j in terms of the reference currency 1. Feedback from the commodity market to exchange rates is assumed to be negligible.

The *excess* demand (i.e. net imports), Q_j, for that commodity in currency bloc j is a function of its *real* price, $P_j^R = P_j - P_j^*$ where P_j^* is the price *level* in that bloc, and a $1 \times N$ vector $X_j = (X_{j1}, X_{j2}, \ldots, X_{jN})$ of (yet to be specified) market 'fundamentals' specific to the commodity in question and currency bloc j:

$$Q_j = Q_j(P_j^R, X_j), \partial Q_j / \partial P_j^R \le 0, j = 1, \ldots, M$$

Global market clearing requires:

$$\sum_{j=1}^{M} Q_j(P_j^R, X_j) = 0$$

and hence a local log-linear approximation can be written as:

$$\sum_{j=1}^{M} (\partial Q_j / \partial P_j^R) \cdot (P_j^R - \bar{P}_j^R) + \sum_{j=1}^{M} \left(\sum_{i=1}^{N} (\partial Q_j / \partial X_{ji}) \cdot (X_{ji} - \bar{X}_{ji}) = 0 \right) \tag{6.2}$$

where $\bar{P}_j^R$ and $\bar{X}_{ji}$ are means of the distributions of P_j^R and X_{ji} respectively.

From equation (6.1), $P_j^R = P_1 - E_1^j - P_j^*$ so equation (6.2) can be rearranged into a fairly simple expression for P_1:

$$P_1 = \text{constant} + \sum_{j=1}^{M} \theta_j \cdot \left(E_{1j} + P_j^* \right) + K(X) \qquad (6.3)$$

where

$$\theta_j = \left(\partial Q_j / \partial P_j^R \right) \Big/ \sum_j^M \left(\partial Q_j / \partial P_j^R \right)$$

while Q_j may be positive or negative, $\partial Q_j / \partial P_j^R$ is non-positive so the θ_j are non-negative fractions that sum to unity. The *global* fundamentals are captured by

$$K(X) = -\sum_j^M \sum_i^N \left[\left(\partial Q_j / \partial X_{ji} \right) \cdot X_{ji} \right] \Big/ \sum_j^M \left(\partial Q_j / \partial P_j^R \right)$$

i.e. X is a vector containing all elements of the country-specific X_j vectors.[3] Since $P_k = P_1 - E_{1k}$ and $E_{kj} = E_{1j} - E_{1k}$, equation (6.3) can be specified in any currency k:

$$P_k = \text{constant} + \sum_{j=1}^{M} \theta_j \cdot \left(E_{kj} + P_j^* \right) + K(X)$$

Changes in the global fundamentals have identical effects on the price of the commodity in question regardless of the currency of denomination.

By subtracting P_1^* from both sides of equation (6.3) we obtain:

$$P_1^R = \sum_{j=1}^{M} \theta_j \cdot E_{1j}^R + K(X) \qquad (6.3R)$$

where $E_{1j}^R \equiv E_{1j} + P_j^* - P_1^*$ is the common purchasing power parity (PPP) *real* exchange rate between currency blocs 1 and j. For the commodity in question, then, θ_j is simultaneously the elasticity of its *nominal* price in currency bloc 1 with respect to the *nominal* exchange rate (or price level) of bloc j, and the elasticity of its real price in currency bloc 1 with respect to the PPP *real* exchange rate between blocs 1 and j, holding all other variables constant in both cases. While θ_j can be estimated with either nominal or real variables, the actual estimation will use forecast errors.

6.1.1   An interpretation of the 'thetas'

The 'thetas' in equation (6.3) are key to the analysis as they measure the relative market power possessed by each participant in the world market for the commodity in question. Consider a small depreciation of currency 1 against all other currencies (holding all P_j^* constant); the effect of that depreciation on P_1 is $\sum_{j=2}^{M} \theta_j = 1 - \theta_1$. If currency bloc 1 is a price-*taker* in, for instance, the world gold market, that depreciation will have no effect on the price of gold in other currencies, so the entire impact falls on the price of gold in currency 1 and hence $\theta_1 = 0$. In other words, currency bloc 1 is the classic 'small' economy in the world gold market.

On the other hand, if bloc 1 is an absolute price-*maker*, that depreciation will have no effect the price of gold in currency 1 as that bloc totally dominates the world gold market, so $\theta_1 = 1$; all of the effect of the depreciation will appear in the price of gold in other currencies.

To dominate the world market for any commodity, a country must have an extremely elastic excess demand for that commodity. When stocks are small compared with annual production and consumption (as in the case of wheat or copper), a country must be a major producer and/or consumer in order to dominate the price of a commodity. Precious metals are unusual in that *stocks* are very large compared with annual production or consumption and hence a country with a high propensity to hoard gold might dominate the world gold market without being a major producer.

Given the high variability of major currency exchange rates since 1973, the term $\Sigma^M_{j=1}\theta_j(E_{ij} + P_j^*)$ of equation (6.3) is a potentially important source of shocks to the price of a commodity such as gold, and hence estimates of the θ_j can be useful.[4] That information can help identify the sources (exchange rates vs. the fundamentals) of the price shocks experienced by consumers and producers of gold, and, to the extent that exchange rates can be predicted, one can forecast the effects of movements in those rates on the price of gold. Finally, information about the θ_j can be exploited for portfolio management; by denominating their assets and liabilities in foreign currency in accordance with the θ_j, firms involved with gold can reduce the financial impact of exchange rate shocks.

6.1.2   The forecast error approach

With appropriate time-series data, the θ_j coefficients in equation (6.3) can be estimated, but that procedure confronts long-standing issues such as the stationarity of exchange rates. However, when the currencies and commodities are traded in both spot and forward markets, those issues can be finessed by using forecast errors, which involves writing equation (6.3) in terms of those errors extracted from spot and forward price and exchange rate data, rather than with actual prices and exchange rates. As forecast error data are usually stationary and, if the relevant markets are 'efficient', as well as serially uncorrelated, the econometric analysis is considerably simplified.

To develop this approach, we begin with spot and forward versions of equation (6.3); apart from notation, the former is identical with equation (6.3):

$$P^S_{1,t} = \text{constant} \sum_{j=1}^{M} \theta_j \cdot \left(E^S_{1j,t} + P^*_{j,t}\right) + K^S\left(X_t\right) \tag{6.3S}$$

and the forward version is written as:

$$P^F_{1,t,n} = \text{constant} + \sum_{j=1}^{M} \theta_j \cdot \left(E^F_{1j,t,n} + P^*_{j,t,n}\right) + K^F\left(X_t\right) \tag{6.3F}$$

where the S and F superscript denote spot and forward, P_j^{*F} and $K^F(X)$ are unobserved market forecasts of P_j^* and $K^S(X)$, and n is the length of the forward contract. The θ_j are set equal in equations (6.3S) and (6.3F) as there is no reason to expect them to differ for short-term (e.g. 90-day) contracts.

The forecast error for the price of the commodity in question, $Z_{1,t,n}$, is the difference between realized and forward prices:

$$Z_{1,t,n} \equiv P_{1,t}^S - P_{1,t-n,n}^F$$

and for exchange rates, the forecast error is:

$$Z_{E1,j,t,n} \equiv E_{1jt}^S - E_{1j,t-n,n}^F$$

Neglecting the constant term, the forecast error version of equation (6.3) is just the difference between equations (6.3F) and (6.3S), with an n-period lag:

$$Z_{1,t,n} = \sum_{j=1}^{M} \theta_j \cdot \left(Z_{E_{1j},t,n} + \left[P_{j,t}^* - P_{j,t-n,n}^{*F} \right] \right) + \left[K^S(X_t) - K^F(X_{t-n}) \right]$$

$$= \sum_{j-1}^{M} \theta_j \cdot Z_{E_{1j},t,n} + \left[P_{W,t}^* - P_{W,t-n}^{*F} \right] + \left[K^S(X_t) - K^F(X_{t-n}) \right]$$

where $P_{W,t}^* = \Sigma_{j=1}^M \theta_j \cdot P_{j,t}^*$ is the 'world' price level and, as $P_{W,t-n}^{*F}$ is the forecast of $P_{W,t}^*$, the terms $P_{W,t}^* - P_{W,t-n}^{*F} \equiv Z_{P,t,n}$ and $K^S(X_t) - K^F(X_{t-n}) \equiv Z_{K,t,n}$ also are forecast errors. Since neither $Z_{P,t,n}$ nor $Z_{K,t,n}$ is observable, the forecast error version of equation (6.3) is written as:

$$Z_{1t,n} = \text{constant} + \sum_{j=1}^{M} \theta_j \cdot Z_{E_{1j},t,n} + \upsilon_{1t} \tag{6.4}$$

where $\upsilon_{1t} \equiv Z_{P,t,n} + Z_{K,t,n}$ is also a forecast error.

If markets are weakly efficient, $K^F(X_{t-n}) = E[K^S(X_t)|I_{t-n}]$ and $P_{W,t}^{*F} - n = E(P_{W,t}^* | I_{t-n})$, where $E(\cdot)$ is the conditional expectation operator and I_{t-n} the information set at time $t-n$, and hence $Z_{P,t,n}, Z_{K,t,n}$, and υ_{1t} are serially uncorrelated. Weak market efficiency implies, then, that all variables in equation (6.4) are serially uncorrelated.[5] Given the potentially superior characteristics of forecast error data, equation (6.4) will be the centrepiece for the empirical implementation of the pricing model.

6.2 Preliminary tests on the data

The spot gold price data consist of daily observations from January 1982 until December 1990 and the forward price data refer to 108 90-day contracts let at the beginning of each month during the same period, both in US dollars. The daily spot gold prices are from the London Gold Market (Reuters), and forward gold prices were computed using closing quotations on 3-month COMEX contracts. Spot and 90-day forward exchange rates between the US dollar and the Deutschemark, the UK pound sterling and the Japanese yen were obtained from the International Monetary Fund Data Bank and cover the same period. Because the forecast errors require a 3-month lag on the forward series, the useful data set is reduced to 105 overlapping (and hence serially correlated) observations. Alternatively, the data can be divided into three subsets of thirty-five non-overlapping observations for the same period. Finally, preliminary tests indicated that the UK 'theta' is approximately zero, so the pound sterling was designated currency 1 and the price of gold and all exchange rates were denominated in pounds.

As the empirical analysis focuses on the relation between exchange rates and the price of gold, and because the fundamentals are difficult to specify in advance (apart from world inflation, which may influence the appeal of gold as a store of value), we made no attempt to do so; accordingly, in estimating equation (6.4), we assume that the exchange rate forecast errors, $Z_{E1j,t,n}$, and those concerning gold market fundamentals, υ_{1t}, are orthogonal. The period of analysis, Federal Funds990, however, was deliberately chosen to exclude the price explosion of 1979–80, which was a result of international political instability; moreover, as the IMF *International Financial Statistics* indicate that central bank gold reserves remained quite constant at just under one billion fine troy ounces throughout the 1982–90 period, the world gold market was not influenced by large net sales of gold on the part of central banks during that period.

6.2.1   Stationarity tests

Two distinct stationarity tests based on all 108 overlapping observations on spot and forward gold prices, and the original US dollar exchange rate data, indicate that all spot and forward series are non-stationary; these results are reported in the Appendix. This finding suggests that those variables may be cointegrated, and hence the relationship described by equation (6.3) might be represented by the Engle–Granger (1987) error correction mechanism. Tests of the no-cointegration null hypothesis were based on a technique proposed by Hamilton (1994, Chapter 19), which consists of estimating the cointegration vector via a regression in which the regressors are exchange rates and the dependent variable is the price of gold, and then testing the residuals for unit roots using the augmented Dickey–Fuller (ADF) (1981) test. The results of the unit-root tests on both spot and forward data are reported in Table 6.1; as the no-cointegration null hypothesis is not rejected in either case, the error correction approach is not appropriate.[6]

As estimation of equation (6.4) requires stationarity of forecast errors rather than prices and exchange rates, the non-overlapping forecast error data were tested for stationarity by ADF unit-root tests with up to five lags. The usual procedure involves testing the ADF statistic corresponding to highest lag with a significant *t*-lag statistic but, as is indicated in Table 6.1, none of the *t*-lag statistics were significant at even

Table 6.1 Augmented Dickey–Fuller unit roots tests on residuals of co-integration
equations: gold prices and exchange rates, July 1982 to December 1990.
Critical values for *t*-ADF statistic: 5% = –3.66, 1% = –4.65[a]

LAG	Spot			Forward		
	t-ADF stat	t-Lag statistic		t-ADF stat	t-Lag statistic	
		Value	P-value		Value	P-value
1	–2.7826	–0.7844	0.4346	–2.7203	–2.1173	0.0369
2	–2.5501	–0.5546	0.5804	–2.1900	–1.7289	0.0872
3	–2.4526	–0.2514	0.8021	–2.0284	–0.3696	0.7125
4	–2.7099	–1.4279	0.1565	–1.5853	–1.4108	0.1617
5	–2.5899	–0.0312	0.9751	–1.5125	–0.0346	0.9725

Note
a   Critical values are for non-zero drift in the explanatory variables.

the 10 per cent level.[7] Although this inconclusive result may be due to sample size,
augmented Dickey–Fuller tests often fail to provide solid evidence.

More conclusive stationarity tests were obtained by using the fractional differencing approach, which involves a non-integer 'order of differentiation', d. For
any time series X_t the Wald representation is:

$$(1-L)^d X_t = A(L)\varepsilon_t$$

where ε_t is white noise, L is the usual lag operator, and stationarity is determined
by the value of d (see the Appendix for further details). We used the Sowell (1991)
maximum likelihood estimate, which gives more reliable results, particularly with
small samples. The parameter d was estimated for each of the three subsets of
thirty-five forecast error observations (based on the original data set), and the results
appear in Table 6.2(a).[8] As none of the estimates of d is significantly different from
zero, the forecast errors for all four series appear to be stationary.[9]

6.2.2   Market efficiency tests

As was argued earlier, if the gold and foreign exchange markets are efficient,
estimation of equation (6.4) is simplified as both the forecast errors and the residuals
of equation (6.4) will be serially uncorrelated. Tests of both weak and semi-strong
market efficiency were conducted.

6.2.2.1   Weak market efficiency

The classic test for weak market efficiency is based on estimating the equation
$P^s_{i,t} = \alpha + \beta \cdot P^F_{i,t-3,3}$ and testing the joint restriction $\alpha = 0$ and $\beta = 1$. But as market
efficiency also requires serially uncorrelated forecast errors, the test for market
efficiency was based on equation (6.5):

Table 6.2 Stationarity and market efficiency tests on forecast error data, February 1982 to April 1990

(a) Stationarity tests on forecast error data

Subset	Maximum likelihood estimates of d (with t-statistics)			
	Gold	DM	Yen	Pound
First	−0.07	0.19	0.03	0.10
	(−0.32)	(0.93)	(0.22)	(1.12)
Second	−0.15	0.15	0.11	0.05
	(−0.30)	(0.88)	(1.53)	(0.18)
Third	−0.08	0.20	0.03	0.18
	(−0.47)	(1.07)	(0.70)	(1.44)

(b) Market efficiency tests

Statistic	Weak (Equation 6.5) Forecast error for:				Semi-strong (Equation 6.6) Forecast error for:			
	Gold	DM	Dollar	Yen	Gold	DM	Dollar	Yen
$\chi^2(1)$[a]	0.03	0.00	1.13	1.05	2.58	17.22	15.02	10.46
P-value	0.87	1.00	0.29	0.31	0.63	0.00	0.00	0.03
$F(1,100)$[b]	0.06	0.00	1.50	1.06	0.48	15.25	4.41	8.74
P-value	0.81	1.00	0.22	0.30	0.75	0.00	0.00	0.00

Notes
a   OLS estimates using White's (1980) robust error routine with two lags.
b   Standard errors estimated by the Hansen–Hodrick (1980) method.

$$Z_{.,t,3} = \gamma + \delta \cdot Z_{.,t-3,3} \tag{6.5}$$

in which estimates of δ should not differ significantly from zero. Four χ^2 statistics on the restriction $\delta = 0$ based on OLS (ordinary least squares) estimates of equation (6.5) for the 105 overlapping observations using White's (1980) robust standard error routine appear in Table 6.2(b); the restriction is not rejected.[10] The standard errors were re-estimated by the Hansen–Hodrick (H–H) (1980) method and since the significance of F-statistics on the $\delta = 0$ restriction, also reported in Panel B of Table 6.2(b), are similar to the χ^2 statistics, weak market efficiency cannot be rejected.

6.2.2.2   Semi-strong market efficiency

In the context of the model developed in section 6.1, semi-strong market efficiency requires past gold price *and* exchange rate forecast errors to be orthogonal with both the current gold price *and* exchange rate forecast errors. The test for the gold market involves estimating the following equation:

$$Z_{1t,+3,3} = \mu + \vartheta_1 \cdot Z_{1,t,3} + \sum_{i=2}^{4} \vartheta_i \cdot Z_{E_{1i},t,3} \tag{6.6}$$

and, for the jth exchange rate, Z_1 is replaced with Z_{E1j}. Semi-strong market efficiency is tested by the joint restriction that estimates of all four θ_i are zero. Table 6.2(b) presents the four χ^2 statistics on that joint restriction, based on OLS robust-error estimates of equation (6.6) using the 105 overlapping observations, and the four F-statistics based on H–H estimates of standard errors; semi-strong market efficiency is not rejected for gold, but is decisively rejected for all exchange rates. In summary, all forecast error series are stationary and hence no filtering is required; in addition, weak market efficiency cannot be rejected for any case, but semi-strong efficiency can be rejected for all exchange rates.

6.3 Estimates of the 'thetas' for the world gold market

As the pound sterling was designated currency 1 (the reference currency) and the price of gold and all exchange rates were denominated in that currency, there are but three parameters to estimate: θ_{DM}, $\theta_{US\$}$ and θ_{yen}. Equation (6.4) was estimated using all 105 overlapping observations with the standard errors estimated by the H–H method.[11] As a t-test on the estimates of the θ_j parameters, reported in Table 6.3(a), indicates that the unit-sum restriction cannot be rejected, that restriction was imposed and the results (again with standard errors estimated by the H–H method) are summarized in Table 6.3(b). As that restriction was not binding, the restricted and unrestricted regressions are nearly identical – apart from an increase in the t-statistics. Apparently, the major gold producers, which include Australia, South Africa and the former USSR, have little power in the world gold market. Rather, that market is dominated by the ECU and dollar blocs (with the ECU having by far the larger weight), and, to a lesser extent, by the yen bloc. Note further that, although the estimates of θ_{DM} and $\theta_{US\$}$ are significant at the 0.001 per cent level, that of θ_{yen} is not significant at the 5 per cent level.[12]

To test whether the θ estimates vary over time, equation (6.4) was re-estimated using two subsamples of equal length, which resulted in the following estimates:

Table 6.3 OLS estimate of equation (6.4): gold, January 1983 to December 1990 (Hansen–Hodrick standard errors)

(a) Unrestricted

Sum of θ_j coefficients	0.9756
Standard error of sum	0.0852
t-Statistic (against unity)	–0.2862
P-value	0.7754

(b) Restricted

Parameter	Estimate	t-Statistic	P-value
θ_{DM}	0.5339	4.0913	0.0001
$\theta_{US\$}$	0.2759	3.4978	0.0007
θ_{Yen}	0.1902	1.8940	0.0614

Note
$\bar{R}^2 = 0.3904$; SEE $= 0.0596$; D–W $= 1.1824$ Q(24) $= 41.7801$, P-value $= 0.0137$.

0.5455 and 0.4995 for θ_{DM}, 0.2472 and 0.3045 for $\theta_{US\$}$, and 0.2073 and 0.1960 for θ_{yen} for, respectively, the subperiods January 1983 to December 1986 and January 1987 to December 1990. While the importance of the dollar bloc may have increased over time (and that of Europe declined), in no case did the difference between the two estimates exceed the smaller of the two standard errors.

6.3.1   World inflation and the price of gold

The estimate of equation (6.4) reported in Table 6.3 does not include any variables for the fundamentals, which are captured in equations (6.3S) and (6.3F) by $K^S(X_t)$ and $K^F(X_{t-3})$. A likely candidate is world inflation, changes in which may affect the price of gold (but not exchange rates). The 'world' price level, P^*_W was defined as the natural logarithm of a weighted average of the European, US, and Japanese price levels, the weights being the theta estimates reported in Table 6.3.[13] The quarterly world inflation rate, defined as $\Pi_{t,3} \equiv P^*_{W,t} - P^*_{W,t-3}$, was converted to an annual rate, Π_t, and, as inflation may have lagged effects, the inflation components of $K^S(X_t)$ and $K^F(X_{t-3})$ were defined as $\gamma(L) \times \Pi$ and $\gamma(L) \times \Pi_{t-3}$. The inflation component of υ_{1t} is $\gamma(L) \times (\Pi_t - \Pi_{t-3})$, and was parameterized as $\gamma_0(\Pi_{t,3} - \Pi_{t-3,3}) + \gamma_1 \times (\Pi_{t-1,3} - \Pi_{t-4,3}) + \gamma_2 \times (\Pi_{t-2,3} - \Pi_{t-5,3})$. Moreover, using the property of any polynomial

$$A(L) = \sum_{i=0}^{N} a_i \cdot L_i$$

and any time series Y_t, that $A(L) \cdot Y_t$ can be reparameterized in error correction form as:

$$A(L) \cdot Y_t = \sum_{i=0}^{N-1} \left(\sum_{j=0}^{i} a_j \right) \cdot \Delta Y_{t-i} + A(1) \cdot Y_{t-N}$$

where the inflation term $\gamma(L) \times (\Pi_t - \Pi_{t-3})$ is expressed, in the case of two lags, as $\gamma_0 \times \Delta(\Pi_t - \Pi_{t-3}) + \gamma_1 \times \Delta(\Pi_{t-1} - \Pi_{t-4}) + \gamma(1) \times (\Pi_{t-2} - \Pi_{t-5})$, which permits a direct estimate of $\gamma(1)$, the long-term impact on the spot price of gold of a permanent change in the rate of world inflation. When the inflation variable was included, the no-cointegration null hypothesis was not rejected, nor was stationarity of the inflation variable rejected: the estimate of d for $\Pi_{t,3} - \Pi_{t-3,3}$ was 0.082. The results of an OLS estimate of equation (6.4) augmented by the inflation variable with two lags are summarized in Table 6.4; the estimates of θ_j are similar to those reported in Table 6.3, although the standard errors are smaller. The results show that world inflation, as a fundamental, is an anaemic one: a (permanent) rise in the (annual) rate of world inflation by one percentage point leads to a mere 0.78 per cent rise in the price of gold.

Table 6.4 OLS estimate of equation (6.4) with inflation variables: gold, January 1983 to December 1990 (Hansen–Hodrick standard errors)

(a) Unrestricted

Sum of θ_j coefficients	0.9718
Standard error of sum	0.0837
t-statistic (against unity)	–0.3365
P-value	0.7373

(b) Restricted

Parameter	Lag	Estimate	t-Statistic	P-value
θ_{DM}	—	0.5478	4.3817	0.0000
$\theta_{US\$}$	—	0.2521	3.5118	0.0007
θ_{Yen}	—	0.2001	2.2683	0.0257
$\gamma(1)$	2	0.7777	3.2081	0.0019

Note
$\bar{R}^2 = 0.4074$; SEE = 0.0587; D–W = 1.2521; Q(24) = 40.8280; P-value = 0.0174.

6.3.2   A more general formulation

The overlapping nature of the forecast error data results in strong serial correlation in the data and in the residuals of OLS estimates based on those data; indeed, the partial auto-correlations for the forecast error data are high for up to seven or eight lags and the Q statistics reported in Tables 6.3 and 6.4 are highly significant. This serial correlation suggests that lags may be useful even though weak market efficiency was not rejected. A more general specification of equation (6.4), which incorporate lags, is the following:

$$\alpha(L) \cdot Z_{1,t,n} = \mathrm{cons} \sum_{j=2}^{M} \Theta_j(L) \cdot Z_{E_{1j},t n} + \gamma(L)\left(\Pi - \Pi_{t-3}\right) + \upsilon_{1t} \qquad (6.4')$$

Experimentation indicated that lags on the independent variables became redundant (i.e. $\Theta_j(L) \equiv \Theta_j$) once lags on the dependent variable were introduced; accordingly, the final effect on the spot price of gold of a permanent shock to the jth exchange rate is ($j \equiv \Theta_j/\alpha(1)$, where $\alpha(1) = \Sigma^1_i = {}_0\alpha_i$ and $\alpha_0 = 1$, and the long-term reaction of the real spot price of gold to a permanent shock to world inflation is captured by the parameter $\Gamma \equiv \gamma(1)/\alpha(1)$.

With this modification, equation (6.4′) was estimated by OLS, with lags being added until the estimate of $\alpha(1)$ stabilized (which occurred after the eighth lag) and the standard errors were estimated by the H–H technique; the results appear in Table 6.5(a).[14] Since the unit-sum restriction on the θ_j was not rejected at the 70 per cent level of significance, equation (6.4) was re-estimated with that restriction imposed; the results for both the Θ_j and θ_j are reported in Table 6.5(b).

Table 6.5 OLS estimate of equation (6.4′) with inflation variables and nine lags on dependent variable: gold, January 1983 to December 1990 (Hansen–Hodrick standard errors)

(a) Unrestricted

Sum of θ_j coefficients	0.9654
Standard error of sum	0.0933
t-Statistic (against unity)	−0.3705
P-value	0.7120

(b) Restricted

Parameter	Lag	Estimate	t-Statistic	P-value
Θ_{DM}	0	0.4919	5.4858	0.0000
$\Theta_{US\$}$	0	0.1284	2.7900	0.0053
Θ_{Yen}	0	0.1327	2.3992	0.0164
$\alpha(1)$	9	−0.7531	−12.6609	0.0000
θ_{DM}	0	0.6532	5.2959	0.0000
$\theta_{US\$}$	0	0.1705	2.9334	0.0044
θ_{Yen}	0	0.1763	2.3580	0.0208
Γ	2	0.6446	2.8119	0.0062

Note
$\bar{R}^2 = 0.5105$; SEE $= 0.0507$.

Despite first differencing of the dependent variable, the new estimate of equation (6.4′) dominates those reported in Tables 6.3 and 6.4. The $\bar{R}^2$ increased by one-quarter to 0.51 and the standard error of estimate has declined to 0.051 from 0.059. The estimates of all thetas — both short and long run — are significant at the 2 per cent level, and the point estimate of θ_{DM}, which increased from 0.55 to 0.65, is nearly four times that of both $\theta_{US\$}$ and θ_{yen}. The estimate of Γ is also highly significant but declined from 0.78 to 0.64: a (permanent) rise of one point in the annual rate of world inflation rate leads to an increase in the *real* spot price of gold of only two-thirds of 1 per cent.

It is clear from Table 6.5 that the European countries heavily dominate the international market for gold, and hence movements in European exchange rates against the US dollar impact heavily on the dollar price of gold. While a 10 per cent appreciation of the DM (against all other currencies) increases the dollar price of gold by 6.5 per cent (and vice versa), the same appreciation of the yen increases the dollar price of gold by only 1.7 per cent. A 10 per cent appreciation of the dollar against both currencies depresses the dollar price of gold by about 8 per cent, and vice versa.

Three simulations, based on the restricted estimate of equation (6.4′), depicting the response of the US dollar price of gold to transitory and permanent depreciations of the US dollar *vis-à-vis* the DM, the yen and both currencies, are reported in Figure 6.1. The striking effect of the dollar/DM (i.e. US dollar/ECU) exchange rate on the dollar price of gold is readily evident.

6.4 Floating exchange rates and the stability of the gold market

There can be little doubt that floating exchange rates among the major currencies have contributed substantially to the variability of the price of gold during the 1980s. There is, of course, no way of divining the behaviour of the free-market price of gold had the Bretton Woods fixed exchange rate system endured (but without the link between the dollar and gold), but, to gain an idea of the degree to which the world gold market has been influenced by floating exchange rates, an experiment was conducted. Equation (6.4′) was parameterized in level form as:

$$Z_{1,t,n} = \text{constant} + \sum_{k=1}^{9} \alpha_k \cdot Z_{1,t-j,n} + \sum_{j=2}^{4} \theta_j \cdot Z_{E_{1,j},t\,n} + \upsilon_{1t}$$

and OLS estimates of the α_k and θ_j, with the unit-sum restriction (i.e. $\sum_{j=1}^{3} \hat{\theta}_j - \sum_{k=1}^{9}$ $\hat{\alpha}_k = \hat{\alpha}_0 = \alpha_0 = 1$) imposed on the long-run thetas were used to calculate the residuals of a reparameterized version of equation (6.3S):

$$\hat{u}_{1t} = P_{1,t}^S - \sum_{k=1}^{9} \hat{\alpha}_k \cdot P_{1,t-j}^S - \sum_{j=2}^{4} \hat{\theta}_j \cdot E_{1j,t}^S \qquad (6.3S')$$

Those residuals, which reflect all influences on the real spot price of gold *other than major currency exchange rates*, were taken as estimates of the fundamentals [the $K(X)$ term in equation (6.3)].

As all variables in equation (6.3S′) are in natural logs, the calculated residuals, $\hat{u}_{1t}$, were transformed into arithmetic values, to be dimensionally identical with the spot price of gold, and then converted into both nominal and real 'prices' in all four currencies. The coefficients of variation of the spot gold price and the transformed

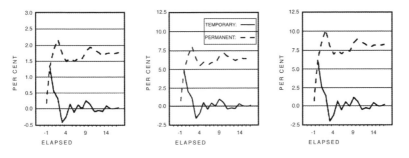

Figure 6.1 Simulated response of US dollar price of gold to 10 per cent depreciation of the dollar against the yen, the Deutschemark, both.

residuals appear in Table 6.6(a). For the period November 1982 to December 1990, the coefficients of variation of the actual spot prices of gold—both nominal and real—are approximately 80 per cent larger than those of the transformed residuals and, apart from the case of the pound sterling, the differences according to currency of denomination are very small.[15] Fluctuation in real exchange rates appear to account for nearly half of the variance in gold prices during the sample period.

It cannot be assumed that real exchange rates would have been constant had the Bretton Woods regime been preserved (again without the link between the dollar and gold), nor is it possible to know how they would have behaved under that system since 1973. Mussa (1986) and others, however, have shown that there is ample evidence that real exchange rates have been far less stable with floating exchange rates than under the Bretton Woods regime. To quantify the effect of the regime change, we calculated the standard deviations of quarterly first differences of the natural logarithms of the real exchange rates between the UK and the USA, Germany and Japan for the periods 1960–70 and 1973–90; price levels and exchange rates were defined as the natural logarithms of quarterly averages. The results, presented in Table 6.6(b), show that the variability in the UK real exchange rates with the USA and Japan have nearly tripled since 1973. Moreover, despite the growing monetary integration between the UK and Germany, the variability of that real exchange rate has more than doubled. While not definitive, these results support the proposition that floating exchange rates among the major currencies have exacerbated the instability of the free-market price of gold since 1973.

Table 6.6 The stability of the gold market and real exchange rates

(a) Sources of variation in gold prices: November 1982 to December 1990

Currency of denomination	Coefficient of variation of the nominal price of gold					
	Actual prices	$\hat{u}_{lt}$	Ratio	Actual prices	$\hat{u}_{lt}$	Ratio
Pound	5.11	2.43	2.10	5.40	2.53	2.14
DM	5.28	2.88	1.83	5.33	2.91	1.83
Dollar	4.92	2.78	1.77	5.04	2.83	1.78
Yen	5.68	3.15	1.80	5.63	3.10	1.82

(b) Standard deviations of quarterly first differences of logarithms of the UK real exchange rates with Germany, the USA and Japan, 1960–1970 and 1973–1990, in per cent

Real exchange rate defined on	Years	Germany	USA	Japan
Consumer prices	1960–70	2.1067	1.7755	2.1934
	1973–90	4.8402	5.4086	5.6491
Ratio		2.30	3.05	2.58
Producer prices	1960–70	2.0059	1.6974	2.1153
	1973–90	4.6049	5.3005	5.7939
Ratio		2.30	3.12	2.74

6.5　Summary of the main results

While we cannot claim that the empirical results for the case of gold can be generalized to other commodities, the main findings, based on an analysis of the gold and foreign exchange markets for the 1982–90 period, are:

1　The world gold market is dominated by the European currency bloc, which possesses about two-thirds of the 'market power' enjoyed by all participants in that market. Accordingly, real appreciations or depreciations of the European currencies have profound effects on the price of gold in all other currencies.
2　Although gold is usually denominated in US dollars, the dollar bloc has but a small influence on the dollar price of gold. Moreover, the major gold producers of the world (Australia, South Africa and the former USSR) appear to have no significant influence on the world price of gold.
3　Gold continues to be a store of value as 'world' inflation increases the demand for gold; it is estimated that the real price of gold rises by between two-thirds and three-quarters of 1 per cent in response to a one point increase in the world inflation rate.
4　The evidence strongly supports the market efficiency hypothesis for the international gold market for the 1982–90 period.
5　During the 1982–90 period, floating exchange rates among the major currencies contributed substantially to the instability of the world price of gold; indeed, fluctuations in the real exchange rates among the major currencies account for nearly half of the observed variance in the spot price of gold during that period.

Appendix

Fractional differencing

In Box–Jenkins (1976) terminology, time-series data are usually assumed to be integrated of either degree zero or one (and occasionally of degree two); when a variable X_t is integrated of degree zero [i.e. $X_t \sim I(0)$], its variance is finite and innovations have no lasting effect as the autocorrelation decays at an exponential rate for distant lags. However, if $X_t \sim I(1)$, the variance of X_t is not finite and, as X_t is the sum of all previous innovations, those innovations have a permanent effect.

A limitation of the conventional approach is that it only allows for discrete values for the degree of integration whereas there may exist a range of intermediate values that involve the so-called long memory models. These models stem from Granger (1966), who demonstrated that economic variables have a 'typical spectral shape', concluding that 'long term fluctuations in economic variables, if decomposed into frequency components, are such that the amplitudes of the components decrease smoothly with decreasing period'. In other words, the spectral density of economic time series is bounded at the origin and the autocorrelation function declines smoothly as the lag between observations increases. This means that variables tend to display long, irregular cycles or, stated differently, shocks are persistent.

The correct method for analysing economic time series, developed in the early 1980s, is known as fractional differencing. The intuition is rather straightforward. Standard time-series methodology considers only processes such as autoregressive integrated moving average (ARIMA) (p, d, q) where d, the order of differentiation, is assumed to be an integer. Granger and Joyeaux (1980) and Hosking (1981) argue, however, that d is not necessarily an integer; rather, it is a real number. They suggested a procedure by which d is estimated (which is closely related to unit-root tests) and then a filter based on the estimate of d is applied to preserve the information on persistence. The transformed series then can be analysed as an ARMA (p,q) process or by traditional time-series methods.

The simplest long memory process – the basic building block – is the fractional noise defined as:

$$(1-L)^d X_t = \sum_{j=0}^{\infty} a_j \cdot \varepsilon_{t-j} = A(L)\varepsilon_t$$

where d is a real number and ε_t is white noise. The process is stationary and invertible if $-0.5 < d < 0.5$ and the binomial expansion of $(1-L)^d$ allows one to express a_j, as:

$$a_j = \frac{\Gamma_{(j-d)}}{\Gamma_{(j+1)} \cdot \Gamma_{(-d)}}$$

which converges in mean square for $-0.5 < d < 0.5$. The fractional noise for $-0.5 < d < 0.5$ has an autoregressive representation:

$$\sum_{j=1}^{\infty} \left(\frac{\Gamma_{(j-d)}}{\Gamma_{(j+1)} \cdot \Gamma_{(-d)}} \right) L^j X_t = \varepsilon_t$$

and a moving average representation:

$$X_t = \sum_{j=1}^{\infty} \left(\frac{\Gamma_{(j-d)}}{\Gamma_{(j+1)} \cdot \Gamma_{(-d)}} \right) L^j \varepsilon_t$$

More general processes can be obtained from fractional noise; these are usually referred to as autoregressive fractionally integrated moving average (ARFIMA) and, in addition to the long memory component, they contain an ARMA component that determines the short-term movements:

$$(1 - L)^d B(L) X_t = C(L)\varepsilon_t$$

If d is in the open interval $(0, 0.5)$, the series X_t is stationary but displays non-periodic, irregular cycles. The auto-covariance of the series is positive and decays at a geometric rate (compared with the exponential rate of the standard ARIMA models). Alternatively, if $d \in (0.5, 1)$ the series is non-stationary; in either case, if d is significantly different from zero, a filter $(1 - L)^d$ is required to obtain a series integrated of degree zero.

Stationary tests on basic data

The first test to determine if the gold price and exchange rate data are random walks or (possibly non-stationary) long memory processes utilizes a procedure designed by Diebold (1989) and based on the variance-time function. With sample of size T and mean μ, the variance of the kth difference is:

$$\sigma_x^2(k) = \sum_{t=k}^{T} \left(X_t - X_{t-k} - k \cdot \mu\right)^2 \Big/ (T - k + 1)$$

and if X_t follows a random walk, $\sigma_x^2(k)$ is proportional to k:

$$\sigma_x^2(k) = k \cdot \sigma_x^2(1)$$

Under the null hypothesis that the series follows a random walk with drift, a simple scalar asymptotic test statistic, $R2(k)$, is calculated as:

$$R2(k) = k \cdot \sigma_x^2(1) / \sigma_x^2(k)$$

The fractiles of the $R2(k)$ statistic for $k = 1, 2, 4, 8, 16, 32$ corresponding to the (random-walk) null hypothesis that $R2(k) = 1$ and the fractiles of a *joint* test statistic, *J2*, under the null hypothesis that *all R2(k)* are equal unity have been calculated by Diebold (1989). The *R2* and *J2* tests statistics computed for all 108 overlapping observations on gold prices and exchange rates are reported in Table A6.1(a). The null hypothesis of random walk with drift is rejected only in the case of the Deutschemark, where the *J2* joint test statistics rejects it.

The results of stationarity tests using maximum likelihood estimates of the order of differentiation, d, based on all 108 *overlapping* observations on spot and forward gold prices and the original US dollar exchange rate data, are reported in Table A1(b). As none of the estimates of d differs significantly from unity, all series, both spot and forward, appear to be non-stationary; moreover, a model selection procedure based on the Akaike and the Schwarz information criteria indicates that the series have no ARMA component and hence can be treated as random walks.

Table 6A.1 Stationarity tests on gold price and exchange rate data

(a) Diebold random walk test on gold prices and exchange rates

Test	Gold		DM		Yen		Pound	
	Spot	Forward	Spot	Forward	Spot	Forward	Spot	Forward
R2(2)	0.98	0.91	1.17	1.19	1.10	1.11	0.90	0.80
R2(4)	0.86	0.76	0.93	0.95	0.87	0.90	0.96	0.93
R2(8)	1.84	2.30	0.65	0.65	0.58	0.61	1.11	1.14
R2(16)	1.42	1.85	0.47	0.45	0.81	0.82	0.81	0.85
R2(32)	1.95	2.06	0.20	0.20	0.34	0.34	0.33	0.34
J2	0.94	1.77	4.96	5.27	2.08	1.97	1.60	1.48

(b) Maximum likelihood estimates of d: gold and the exchange rates

Prices	Gold	DM	Yen	Pound
Spot	0.83	1.02	1.07	1.05
Forward	0.86	1.08	1.07	1.06

Acknowledgements

The authors are grateful for comments by participants in seminars at the Australian National University, Curtin University and the Universities of Chicago and Western Australia, and particularly for comments by Kenneth W. Clements, Michael McAleer, and anonymous referees; the usual disclaimer holds. The original version of this chapter appeared as Discussion Paper 92.05 of the Economic Research Centre and the Department of Economics of the University of Western Australia.

Notes

1 Of the currencies corresponding to the 150 members of the International Monetary Fund as of mid-1990, twelve were major currencies [ten of which made up the European Monetary System (the EMS)], leaving 138 minor currencies. Fifty-five minor currencies were tied to a single currency, forty-two to a currency basket and forty-one were floating.

2 To the best of the authors' knowledge, Ridler and Yandle (1972) were the first to use this approach to analyse the effect of exchange rate adjustments on commodity prices. The model presented here first appeared in Sjaastad (1985); a similar approach was developed by Dornbusch (1987).

3 *Global* fundamentals are defined as all factors *other than exchange rates and price levels* that influence the *global* demand for and supply of the commodity in question, including expectations.

4 See Frenkel (1981) concerning the large fluctuations in PPP, and hence in real exchange rates, experienced by the major currencies during the 1970s and Edwards (1989) for a massive compilation of real exchange rate data for smaller countries.

5 Lack of serial correlation in forecast errors also requires the absence of time-dependent risk premia; in what follows, that property is assumed to hold – and is subsequently tested – on forecast errors for exchange rates and the price of gold.

6 For the case at hand, the critical values for the *t*-statistics (two of which are reported in Table 6.1) are not the standard ones; for the correct critical values, see Hamilton (1994), p. 592 and his appendix tables.

7 While some *t*-lag statistics were significant for the pound/US dollar exchange rate, those forecast errors were never used in the actual estimation of equation (6.4). The rather voluminous details of these stationarity tests are available from the authors upon request.

8 The first subset contains all observations for the first month of each quarter, the second subset contains those on the second month, etc.

9 The cointegration tests were made using PCGIVE, version 8.0. The maximum likelihood estimates were made with a program kindly supplied by F. Sowell. Remaining estimation was by ESTIMA RATS 386 version 4.10c.

10 If equation (6.5) were estimated with a single lag on the independent variable, the expected value of the estimate of δ would be roughly 0.67 as two-thirds of the innovations in any observation on forecast errors tend to be common to adjoining observations. To avoid that bias, the independent variable was lagged three periods (i.e. one prediction period).

11 Since subsequent estimates of equation (6.5) using lags on the dependent variable reduce the regressions to the January 1983–December 1990 period, all estimates were made with data over that range to facilitate comparisons.

12 Because the observations are overlapping, the residuals are serially correlated and hence it is not possible to conduct the usual LM tests for autoregressive conditional heteroscedasticity (ARCH) or normality tests, as those tests assume the series to be independent and identically distributed.

13 The European price level was computed as a weighted average of German, UK and Italian producer prices and French consumer prices (producer prices are unavailable for France). The weights, 0.3142, 0.2594, 0.2109 and 0.2125, respectively, were based on relative real GDPs for the 1982–90 period.

14 An iterative procedure was used to set the weights in the world price level equal to the estimates of the thetas. Equation (6.4) was not parameterized to provide direct estimates of $\theta_j \equiv \Theta_j/\alpha(1)$ and $\Gamma \equiv \gamma(1)/\alpha(1)$ since the resulting non-linear equation would preclude using the Hansen–Hodrick (1980) method to estimate standard errors; instead, estimation was by OLS and the standard errors of θ_j and Γ were obtained by Taylor expansions.

15 Prior to calculating the standard deviations, the transformed residuals and spot prices were first differenced to remove negative trends, which are quite pronounced in the DM and yen series. The sample average spot price of gold was used to compute coefficients of variation.

References

Box, G.E. and Jenkins, G.M. (1976) *Time Series Analysis Forecasting and Control*, 2nd edn. San Francisco: Holden Day.

Clements, K. and Sjaastad, L. (1984) *How Protection Taxes Exporters*. Thames essay, Trade Policy Research Centre, Macmillan for the Trade Policy Research Centre, London.

Dickey, D.A. and Fuller, W.A. (1981) 'Likelihood ratio statistics for auto-regressive time series with a unit root', *Econometrica* 49: 1057–72.

Diebold, F.X. (1989) 'Random walks versus fractional integration' in B. Raj (ed.) *Advances in Econometrics and Modeling,* Dordrecht: Kluwer Academic Publishers.

Dornbusch, R. (1987) 'Exchange rate economics', *Economic Journal* 97: 1–18.

Edwards, S. (1989) *Real Exchange Rates, Devaluation, and Adjustment: Exchange Rate Policy in Developing Countries,* Cambridge, MA: MIT Press.

Engle, R.F. and Granger, C.W.J. (1987) 'Cointegration and error correction: representation, estimation and testing', *Econometrica* 55: 251–76.

Frenkel, J. (1981) 'The collapse of purchasing power parity during the 1970s', *European Economic Review* 16: 145–65.

Granger, C.W.J. (1966) 'The typical spectral shape of an economic variable', *Econometrica* 34: 151–61.

Granger, C.W.J. and Joyeaux, R. (1980) 'An introduction of long memory time series models'. *The Journal of Time Series Analysis* 4: 221–8.

Hamilton, J.D. (1994) *Time Series Analysis*, Princeton, NJ: Princeton University Press.

Hansen, L.P. and Hodrick, R.J. (1980) 'Forward exchange rates as optimal predictors of future spot rates: an ecnometric analysis', *The Journal of Political Economy* 88: 829–53.

Hosking, J.R.M. (1981) 'Fractional differencing', *Biometrika* 68: 165–76.

Mussa, M. (1986) 'Nominal exchange rate regimes and the behaviour of real exchange rates: evidence and implications'. *Carnegie-Rochester Conference Series on Public Policy*, Amsterdam: North-Holland Publishing Company, 25: 117–213.

Ridler, D. and Yandle, C.A. (1972) 'A simplified method for analyzing the effects of exchange rate changes on exports of a primary commodity', *IMF Staff Papers* 19.

Sjaastad, L.A. (1985) 'Exchange rate regimes and the real rate of interest', in M. Connolly and J. McDermott (eds) *The Economics of the Caribbean Basin*, New York: Praeger.

Sowell, F. (1991) *Maximum Likelihood Estimation of Stationary Univariate Fractionally Integrated Time Series Models* (mimeo), Pittsburgh: Graduate School of Industrial Administration. Carnegie Mellon University.

White, H. (1980) 'A heteroscedasticity-consistent covariance matrix estimator and a direct test for heteroscedasticity', *Econometria* 48: 817–38.

7 The determinants of gold price exposure

An Australian study

Izan H. Y. Izan and Jeffrey Wong

7.1 Introduction

Over the 3-year period from 1996 to 1999, the spot price of gold devalued by over 30 per cent. This devaluation was reflected in a drop in the gold companies' valuations in stock exchanges. In Australia, the share price of some gold mining companies decreased by 48–88 per cent over the same period.

Recently, various studies have assessed the impact of changes in the spot price of gold on the share price of gold companies. Some researchers state that the percentage change in the share price of a gold company should be greater than the percentage change in the value of gold, as gold mining stocks represent a levered investment in the gold price. Others argue that this should not be the case because there are other risks, uncorrelated with the price of gold, that are also being priced in the gold mining stocks.

The evidence shows that gold companies react differently to changes in the gold price. The question is 'Why are some companies more sensitive to changes in the gold price than others?' Intuitively, each company has its own characteristics, such as its production structure and financial leverage, which may influence the sensitivity of its share price to the fluctuations in the gold spot price. One would expect the gold mining companies' risk management policies, such as gold hedging,[1] to play an important role in determining the level of gold price exposure.

The purpose of this study is to address this research question. In particular, it examines the relationship between gold price exposure (the sensitivity of the share price to changes in the gold price) and the characteristics of gold companies. The analysis draws on the valuation models proposed by Tufano (1998) and uses data collected over the period of 1 July 1996 to 30 June 1999.

We observe that, using pooled data, the gold price exposure is greater than 1, but the size of the exposure for individual companies is not always greater than 1. We also find that the gold price, the firm's production costs and its financial leverage are the only significant determinants of the gold price exposure. Contrary to our expectation, the hedging quantity and the hedging contract price, variables that proxy for the companies' risk management policies, are not found to influence the gold price exposure of the company.

The remainder of this study is as follows: section 7.2 discusses the relevant empirical literature relating to gold price exposure; section 7.3 develops the hypotheses that will be tested in the empirical study; section 7.4 describes the data used and the methodology employed in this research; section 7.5 presents and interprets the results generated from the analysis; and, finallyy, section 7.6 concludes the chapter.

7.2 Literature review

Blose and Shieh (1995) took the view that gold mining stock represents a levered investment in gold. They developed their model for estimating the gold price elasticity of gold company shares on the assumptions that: (i) the forward gold prices are the market's unbiased expectations of future spot prices; and (ii) the value of a gold mine is a function of the return on gold, production costs, the level of gold reserves and the proportion of assets unrelated to gold price. They hypothesized that 'the stock price of firms engaged primarily in gold mining will have a gold price elasticity greater than one'. This has a practical implication for both investors and management of the firms. Firms with an elasticity that is greater than 1 will benefit investors when the gold market is bullish, but the opposite is true when the market is bearish.

Blose and Shieh (1995) used a sample of twenty-three companies that were primarily engaged in the gold mining industry during the period 1981 to 1990. The observed gold price elasticities of gold mining companies were calculated using a one-factor model and tested to determine if the elasticities are greater than 1. They also used a two-factor model to calculate the elasticities in order to account for the market risk as well as the gold price.

They found that the gold price elasticity for the entire sample is significantly greater than 1 (1.341), as predicted. This test was conducted for each stock individually and for all of the stocks combined. Even when they added market return as an additional explanatory variable, the remains unchanged. Based on their empirical findings, Blose and Shieh (1995) concluded that, if a company's primary business is gold mining, the price elasticity of the stock with respect to the price of gold should be greater than 1.

They acknowledged, however, that there was a potential bias in their results, arising from hedging activities of the mining companies. With the common use of futures, forwards, options and gold loans as part of the companies' risk management strategies, Blose and Shieh (1995) believed these activities could lower the gold price elasticity of the mining stock. This belief is consistent with the finding of Allayannis and Ofek (1997), who found that the use of foreign currency derivatives reduces the exchange rate exposure.

In a different industry research setting, Allayannis and Ofek (1997) examined the use of foreign currency derivatives by Standard & Poor's 500 non-financial firms during 1992–93 and their potential impact on exchange rate risk. They found that the extent to which firms use foreign currency derivatives is positively related to the ratios of foreign sales to total sales and total foreign trade to total production. Firms also use foreign debt as an alternative to, or in conjunction with, foreign currency derivatives, although to a lesser extent. Similarly, the level of foreign debt is positively related to the ratio of foreign sales to total sales. Consistent with a risk reduction motive for using foreign currency derivatives, they found that the use of foreign currency derivatives significantly reduces the exchange rate exposure faced by corporations.

Raston (1998), in an Australian study, used a multifactor model to examine the impact of risk management polices adopted by each Australian listed gold company on its stock return. Australia is one of the largest gold-producing countries in the world and Australian gold producers are known to have participated actively in gold hedging activities. Despite what appears to be widespread use of hedging activities by gold companies, large stock price changes were repeatedly observed following changes in the gold price.

He used the realized selling price[2] as a proxy for risk management policies and hypothesized that the realized selling price would be more significant in determining individual stock return than the spot price of gold. Quarterly data over the period April 1996 to March 1998 were used. He ran the multifactor model, using realized selling price and spot price of gold as independent variables separately.

Contrary to his expectation, he found the gold spot price to be the more significant variable, implying that investors do not incorporate the implicit value of risk management policies into their valuation. The result of Raston (1998) is consistent with those of Petersen and Thiagarajan (1996), who examined the practices of two firms and found that hedging has no effect on equity price exposures.

A limitation of Raston's research is the use of realized selling price for gold as a proxy for the risk management policies of the gold producers. This problem is acknowledged by Raston himself. He explained that the realized selling price reflects the current effects of a company's risk management strategy but does not account for the long-term price coverage which companies have. This proxy neglects the fact that the market views not only the current effect of the hedging policies, but also of the future benefits, and may explain why Raston's (1998) results did not match his expectations.

Another recent American paper by Tufano (1998) also examined the effect of risk management on firms' stock prices. His study is based on North American gold mining firms and the extent of the exposures to fluctuations in the gold price. Tufano (1998) was able to measure the size of these exposures, analytically establish their determinants, and empirically test how observed exposures corresponded to his predicted exposures. He also showed that the firm's exposure is determined jointly by market characteristics (the price of gold), exogenous firm characteristics (the firm's cost structure) and a company's financial policies (leverage and risk management policy).

Tufano's sample consisted of forty-eight North American gold mining companies over the period January 1990 to March 1994. Jorion's (1990) multifactor market model[3] was used to estimate gold price exposure, with individual stock returns being the dependent variable and returns on spot gold price and market returns being independent variables. Data on *gold spot prices* were collected from the COMEX (New York Commodity Exchange) and *market return* was calculated from the CRSP NYSE/AMEX/Nasdaq composite value-weighted index. Tufano

(1998) found gold mining firms have substantial gold price exposure at around two per cent, confirming Blose and Shieh's (1995) finding.

Tufano (1998) developed three models for the valuation of gold companies, namely the fixed production, flexible production and fixed production with hedging models to derive the determinants of gold price exposures. He expected that gold price, production quantity, volatility of gold returns, discount rate, fraction hedged and contract prices would have an inverse relationship with gold exposures, while production costs and gold lease rate would be positively related to gold price exposures.

The finding of Tufano (1998) generally confirmed his hypotheses. He found that the spot gold price is a significant determinant of the level of exposure faced by gold mining companies. As predicted, gold price exposure is lower in a higher gold price environment. The volatility of gold returns is found to be consistent with the hypothesis, which predicts an inverse relationship between volatility and gold price exposure. He also found that hedging has a material negative relationship with the gold price exposure. His results suggest that if we observe two identical companies, and one hedges all of its near-term production and the other hedges none, the gold price exposure of the company with hedging would be lower by at least 0.65 per cent. Contract prices of forwards are found to be negatively related to gold price exposure but the magnitude is quite small. Contrary to Tufano's expectation, the operating costs are not materially associated with the level of exposure. This result is quite unexpected because the firm's cost structure should have a material impact on its operating leverage and the degree to which this leverage amplifies price shocks. Also, both the gold lease rate and the interest rate are found to be inconsistent with his expectations. The gold lease rate is found to have a weak negative relationship with gold price exposure, while the interest rate does not appear to be a significant determinant of gold price exposure.

7.3 Hypothesis development

A number of analysts believe that investing in gold mining stock represents a levered investment in gold (Rolo, 1975; Ozanian, 1987; Schiffres, 1987; Panchapakesan, 1993). Panchapakesan (1993), for example, argued that the leverage stems from the fact that, as the price of gold rises, the earnings of the mining companies would rise even faster because the cost of mining remains fairly stable. There are others, however, who disagree with the conjecture that the gold price elasticity is greater than 1 because there are other non-gold price risks associated with the investment. They believed that these risks, such as unstable dividends, political risks, currency exchange risks and business risks (market conditions and mining technology), would influence the gold price risk in the return on the stocks (Train, 1978; Khoury, 1984). Although there was great debate about this issue, more current empirical research in general has provided support that the gold price exposure is greater than 1 (Blose and Shieh, 1995; Brimelow, 1996; Tufano, 1998; Faff and Chan, 1998; Raston, 1998). In this chapter, we will also attempt to measure the gold price elasticity, as part of our research, and to test if the elasticity is greater than 1. Therefore, the first alternative hypothesis is:

$H_{1,A}$: The gold price exposure is greater than 1

7.3.1 Establishing possible determinants of gold price exposure

In this section, we develop several hypotheses which relate the size of gold price exposure to company-specific characteristics, such as production quantity, production cost and hedging activities. We will use the valuation models developed by Tufano (1998) to form the basis to establish the determinants of gold price exposures.

7.3.1.1 Fixed production model

This production model assumes that a firm operates with a fixed production schedule, that its production profile cannot be altered and that it engages in no financial risk management. Blose and Shieh (1995) developed a model similar to this fixed production model.[4] Tufano (1998) assumed that this hypothetical firm owns a fixed quantity of gold reserves (R), which will be mined over N years at a rate of R/N, or Q. Fixed costs (Fc), such as overheads or financing costs, and variable costs (C), such as extraction and processing costs, will be incurred. Ultimately, the firm will sell its commodity output at the prevailing market price (P) and is a price taker. Hence, the market value of the gold mine is stated as:

$$V = \sum_{i=1}^{N} \frac{\left[Q(P-C)-Fc\right](1-\tau)}{(1+r)^i} \tag{7.1}$$

where V is the value of the gold mine, N is the number of years, Q is the fixed annual production $= R/N$ (total reserves/years of production), Fc is fixed costs such as general and administrative costs and financial fixed charges, r is the cost of capital/discount rate and τ is the corporate tax rate.

Assuming that the firm has no flexibility in its production schedule, then by arranging equation (7.1) mathematically, its gold price exposure (or gold beta), which is the percentage change in the firm's value for a one per cent permanent change in the gold price, would be:

$$\beta_{ig} = \frac{\partial V/V}{\partial P/P} = \frac{PQ(1-\tau)\sum_{i=1}^{n}\frac{1}{(1+r)^i}}{V} = \frac{PQ}{Q(P-C)-Fc} \tag{7.2}$$

From equation (7.2), we can see that the gold price exposure of the firm, β_{ig}, is sensitive to the factors stated in this model. Gold price exposure (β_{ig}) decreases as gold price (P) and production quantity (Q) increases. Therefore, the relevant hypotheses are:

H$_{2,A}$: Gold price exposure (β_{ig}) is inversely related to gold price (P)
H$_{3,A}$: Gold price exposure (β_{ig}) is inversely related to production quantity (Q)

In addition, we can also observe from equation (7.2) that the gold price exposure is an increasing function of both its variable (C) and fixed costs (Fc), as sensitivity to gold prices increases with the operating leverage. Therefore, the alternative hypotheses to be tested are:

H$_{4,A}$: Gold price exposure (β_{ig}) is positively related to marginal costs (C)
H$_{5,A}$: Gold price exposure (β_{ig}) is positively related to fixed costs (Fc)

7.3.1.2   Flexible production model

We believe that the fixed production model is a poorly specified model, which may not reflect all aspects of the operation of gold mines in real life. Gold mines have real options (Brennan and Schwartz, 1985; Brennan, 1990; Mardones, 1993; Davis, 1996) in the sense that they can choose to suspend mining (temporarily) or to cease (permanently) mining operations when the gold price falls below a particular level. In addition, mining firms can also choose to mine higher- or lower-grade ores, to stockpile ore or finished gold, and to change the rate of production. They argued that the flexibility in their operating decisions reduces their gold price exposure. If we ignore this flexibility, we will overstate the sensitivity of gold price shocks.

Brennan and Schwartz (1985) developed this real options model in which firms can open and shut mines, with the assumption that commodity prices are stochastic, and the firm incurs non-zero costs for closing and opening the mines. The option gives the firms a smaller gold price exposure than if the firms are locked into a fixed production schedule. This is parallel to the observation that the delta of a call (a right) is typically lower than the delta of a forward contract (a commitment). When gold prices are low, the firm is not committed to continuing to operate, and thus can suspend production and sales until later, when the gold price regains its position. Therefore, we can view it as if the firms hold a call option on gold, with the exercise price being their marginal production costs.

By using Brennan and Schwartz's (1985) model, we can show that the gold beta is a decreasing function of gold price volatility (σ). It behaves like a call option, in which past findings show that the elasticity of the value of a call option is a decreasing function of volatility. Hence, the testable alternative hypothesis is stated as:

H$_{6,A}$: Gold price exposure (β_{ig}) is inversely related to volatility of gold prices (σ)

Interest rates also affect the gold price exposure of the firms in the flexible production model. Any fluctuations in the standard corporate interest rate, which is used to discount the expenses, will change the valuation of the gold firms or mines. From equation (7.1), when this discount rate (r) increases, it is expected that the valuation of the firms will be lower. We can see from equation (7.2) that a lower valuation of firms will lead to a lower exposure to the gold price fluctuation.[5] If the discount rate decreases, the value of the firm will increase, to yield a higher gold beta. Therefore, the relationship between the discount rate and gold price exposure is expected to be negative. The alternative hypothesis is stated as:

$H_{7,A}$: Gold price exposure (β_{ig}) is inversely related to discount rate (r)

The other factor that can affect the gold price exposure of the firms is the gold lease rate (GLR). We can look at the influence of the lease rate from two different perspectives, namely from the lender's or borrower's. Firstly, if the gold firm is a lender of physical gold, this rate can be seen as 'the flow of services that accrues to an owner of the physical commodity but not to the owner of a contract for the future delivery of the commodity' (Brennan and Schwartz, 1985: 139). Therefore, the gold lease rate can be seen as interest received for owning a gold mine. If the gold lease rate increases, the value of the firm should increase too; hence, the gold price exposure of the firm will increase.

On the other hand, from the borrower's perspective, the gold lease rate can be seen as the cost of borrowing gold from the central banks by the producers. When the gold lease rate increases, this makes borrowing gold more expensive. The increase in the gold lease rate will translate to an increase in costs, which then increases the gold price exposure (similar to hypotheses 4 and 5).

Moreover, some producers will find it too expensive to borrow gold and tend not to see borrowing from the central bank as an option. This limits the operating flexibility of the firms, and, as we have explained earlier, operating flexibility reduces the gold price exposure of the firms. Therefore, regardless of whether the firm is a lender or borrower, an increase in the gold lease rate will lead to an increase in gold price exposure and vice versa. Hence, the alternative hypothesis is stated as:

$H_{8,A}$: Gold price exposure (β_{ig}) is positively related to gold lease rate (GLR)

Otherwise, this flexible production model will behave the same as the fixed production model in which the gold price exposure is inversely related to gold prices and the level of production, and directly related to the level of costs faced by the mine.

7.3.1.3   *Fixed production model with hedging*

As more and more innovation is being implemented into the financial sector, hedging has become an important strategy in helping to reduce a firm's commodity price risk. If it can forward sell its entire production profile, it can eliminate its exposure to the fluctuating gold prices, thereby pushing its gold price exposure towards zero. Therefore, a firm which hedges a greater proportion of its production profile should experience a lower gold price exposure.

Now, consider that the firm that sells forward a portion, α, of its future annual production, Q, with a forward contract which specifies that the firm will receive a payment of W per ounce of gold at the time of delivery. Thus, the gold beta is given by:

$$\beta_{ig} = \frac{\partial V/V}{\partial P/P} = \frac{(1-\alpha)PQ}{(1-\alpha)Q(P-C)+\alpha Q(W-C)-Fc}$$

$$= \frac{(1-\alpha)PQ}{Q[(P-C)-\alpha(P-W)]-Fc} \tag{7.3}$$

where α (fraction hedged) is the ounces of gold hedged expressed in fraction of total production or total reserves and W is the average forward contract price. If the fraction hedged is zero, then equation (7.3) will be reduced to equation (7.2). If the fraction hedged is 1, then the beta will be zero, which means that the firm will not have gold price exposure. Therefore, we can say that as the fraction hedged increases, the exposure to the gold price falls. Hence, the alternative hypothesis can be stated as:

$H_{9,A}$: Gold price exposure (β_{ig}) is inversely related to fraction hedged (α)

It can be seen from equation (7.3) that gold price exposure is also a function of the average contract price (W). If the average contract price increases, holding the fraction hedged constant, the gold beta will experience decreases, and vice versa. Therefore, the testable alternative hypothesis is stated as:

$H_{10,A}$: Gold price exposure (β_{ig}) is inversely related to contract price (W)

7.3.1.4   Financial leverage

Dolde (1995) found that highly leveraged firms are more likely to use derivatives to avoid the expected costs of financial distress. He explained that firms with higher leverage will have greater fixed obligations. So, whatever the firm earns from the proceeds of selling its gold production, it has to repay the fixed obligations, and the residual or free cash flow can be used for a distribution of dividend or invest in positive net present value (NPV) projects. If there is a fall in the price of gold, the free cash flow of the leveraged firm will be lower and, hence, the firm may have to seek costly external financing or forgo the positive NPV project, which in turn will lower the value of the firm. This is identified as the *underinvestment* problem (Froot *et al.*, 1993). On the other hand, a firm with no leverage and no fixed payments will tend not to face this underinvestment problem. Therefore, a leveraged firm is expected to have a larger stock price reaction to a change in the gold price.

$H_{11,A}$: Gold price exposure (β_{ig}) is positively related to financial leverage (F)

7.4 Data and methodology

Two separate tests are presented. First, a two-factor model is used to estimate the size of the gold price exposure. Next, the above hypotheses are tested using both univariate and multivariate models.

7.4.1 Data

This chapter examines the determinants of the gold price exposure of Australian gold mining companies over the period 1 July 1996 to 30 June 1999. These sample companies must be 'those made up of the ASX Gold Index as at 30 June 1999', which is the only selection criterion. A total of fifteen such companies are included in our sample (refer to the Appendix).

There are three reasons for having such a selection criterion. First, it means that they must be listed companies. Second, these gold index companies are the largest gold mining companies, and they represent a significant share of the gold mining industry in Australia. Third, the aim of this chapter is to examine *only* the gold price exposure. The selected gold index companies are chosen because their principal activity will primarily be gold related. In selecting in this way, we hope to minimize the price exposure of other commodities, such as silver and copper, and reduce the potential bias in the result.

This sample period is chosen because the Australian gold producers were quite active in their hedging activities over this sample period, providing a better research setting for examining the importance of hedging. In addition, disclosure of hedging activities by the individual companies is better over this recent period. There are more regulatory authorities or regulations, such as the ASX Listing Rules, Corporations Law Section 1001A and AASB 1033/AAS 33, which require mining entities to disclose their hedging activities over recent periods.

Share prices for the fifteen companies were obtained from the Department of Accounting and Finance. Company-specific data were collected manually from quarterly, half-yearly and annual reports. The following information was collected from these reports:

- production quantity;
- production costs – cash costs;
- total ounces of gold hedged;
- hedging contract exercise price;
- long- and short-term interest-bearing debts;
- macroeconomic data (ASX accumulation index, spot gold price, gold lease rate, interest rate and exchange rate), primarily collected from Datastream.

7.4.2   Measuring gold price exposures

The first step of our study is to estimate the size of the gold price exposure for each of the companies in our sample. These estimated gold price exposures over the whole 3-year period will then be used to test our first hypothesis above, namely whether it is significantly greater than 1.

We use MacDonald and Solnick's (1977) two-factor model to estimate the size of gold price exposure. This model has been used by other researchers, such as Faff and Chan (1998), Raston (1998) and Tufano (1998). The two-factor model is:

$$R_{it} = \alpha_i + \beta_{ig}R_{gt} + \beta_{im}R_{mt} + \epsilon_t \tag{7.4}$$

where R_{it} is the return on stock i at the period t, R_{gt} is the gold return from spot price, R_{mt} is the market return, β_{ig} is the gold beta and β_{im} is the market beta.

The variables used in equation (7.4) are measured on a daily basis. The continuous returns on stock i and the indexes over the time intervals are measured by taking the natural logarithm of today's price (or quote) divided by yesterday's price (or quote), adjusted for cash and stock dividends. Daily returns are used in this study.

This model will be applied on both pooled and individual company data sets. Examination of pooled data will give a general view of the gold price exposure of the whole industry while individual company data set will provide individual gold price exposure.

7.4.3   Determinants of gold price exposure

The second stage of the study investigates the determinants of gold price exposure. Based on our discussion in section 7.3, we estimate the following regression equation:

$$\begin{aligned}
GBETA_{ig,q} = {} & C + \phi GPRICE_q + \phi_2 PRDQTY_{i,q} + \phi_3 PRDCOST_{i,q} \\
& + \phi_4 VOLATILITY_q + \phi_5 DISCOUNT_q + \phi_6 LEASE_q \\
& + \phi_7 HDGQTY_{i,q} + \phi_8 HDGPRICE_{i,q} + \phi_9 LEVERAGE_{i,q} + \epsilon_{i,q}
\end{aligned} \tag{7.5}$$

where subscript q represents the quarter of the year

$GBETA_{ig,q}$	is the gold price exposure of company i for the quarter
C	is a constant
$GPRICE_q$	is the average US dollar gold spot price for the quarter
$PRDQTY_{i,q}$	is the production quantity of company i for the quarter
$PRDCOST_{i,q}$	is the production costs of company i for the quarter
$VOLATILITY_q$	is the volatility of gold price for the quarter
$DISCOUNT_q$	is the discount rate for the quarter
$LEASE_q$	is the gold lease rate for the quarter
$HDGQTY_{i,q}$	is the fractioned hedged of company i for the quarter
$HDGPRICE_{i,q}$	is the average contract price of company i for the quarter

$LEVERAGE_{i,q}$ is the financial leverage of company i for the quarter

7.4.3.1 Gold spot price

The first independent variable is the average gold spot price for the quarter. The daily gold price used in our study is the London AM Fix (in US dollars) collected from Datastream database, which is considered to be the world-wide benchmark for a gold price quote.[6] The other reason for choosing the London AM Fix is because the time that this quote is set in the morning is the closest to the closing time of the ASX eastern states time zone.

7.4.3.2 Volatility of gold price

The other variable derived from the return on gold spot price is the gold price volatility (σ), which is measured as the 90-day annualized volatility of gold price returns from historical gold price data in each quarter. This volatility is calculated from this formula:

$$\text{Volatility}(\sigma) = \frac{\text{standard deviation of daily gold return}}{\sqrt{\tau}}$$

where τ is the length of interval in a year.

7.4.3.4 Production quantity

Production quantity (Q) is quarterly production of gold measured in ounces. The data are collected from quarterly, half-yearly or annual reports.

7.4.3.5 Production costs

Both marginal and fixed costs will be combined and treated as production costs because of difficulties in segregating both costs. We believed that there is no effect on the expected result by doing so. Production costs (C) are normally reported in quarterly or annual reports as the cash costs of producing gold per ounce.[7] Cash costs represent the per ounce production costs, excluding non-cash items such as depreciation, depletion, amortization and financing costs, but including the royalty payments.

7.4.3.6 Discount rate

The discount rate used is the average 10-year domestic bond rate for the quarter. The data are collected from Datastream.

7.4.3.7   Gold lease rate

The gold lease rate is the convenience yield on gold (for a 1-year term), and is collected from Macquarie Equities.[8] The average of this rate for the quarter is then calculated.

7.4.3.8   Hedging quantity

This variable represents the hedging activities of the company. The main motivation for hedging is to limit the downside of the gold spot price, so that the company can sell its gold production at a higher price. Generally, most of the short selling positions, which includes forward, gold loan and put options, are in-the-money, therefore the company will normally go ahead with the short selling contract. On the other hand, its call options are usually out-of-the-money, which means that the company will let them lapse. Therefore, in this study, the total amount of forward, gold loan and puts is used to represent the overall hedging ounces.[9]

We have chosen not to use Tufano's (1998) method to measure the hedging quantity. Instead we will adopt a method similar to that used by MacDonald (1999a), which looked at the short selling position instead of the long position (call). The hedge ratio, delta of the call, is generally close to zero, and the call is generally out-of-the-money. Consistent with MacDonald, our measure of hedging quantity is the total of the forward, gold loan and the put amount.

7.4.3.9   Average contract price

Average hedging price (W_q) is calculated using the formula as follows:

$$W_q = \frac{\sum_q \left(Forward_q \times P_{Forward,q}\right) + \sum \left(Puts_q \times P_{Puts,q}\right) + \sum \left(Gold\,loan \times P_{Loan,q}\right)}{\sum_q Forward_q, Puts_q, and\,/\,or\,gold\,loan}$$

where $Forward_q$, $Puts_q$ and $Gold\,Loan_q$ are the amounts of forward, puts and gold loan ounces at quarter q respectively; $P_{Forward,\,q}$ is the forward price for the quarter q; $P_{Puts,\,q}$ is the exercise price for the quarter q; and $P_{Loan,\,q}$ is the contract price for the quarter q.

The information on these prices, the same as for hedging quantity, is collected from the quarterly reports and annual reports.

7.4.3.10   Financial leverage

Financial leverage (F) is the debt to equity ratio, which is calculated as year-end long-term debt plus current debt, divided by the market value of the firm at quarter *t*. It means that the total amount of debt for the year will be assumed to be constant throughout the whole year. These data can be collected from the ASX data disk and annual reports. As for the market value of the firm, it will be fluctuating quarter by quarter, depending on the market price of each share and the number of shares issued by the firm. These data are collected from Datastream.

7.5 Results

The results for the first part of the study on measuring the gold price exposure are presented in section 7.5.1, with the analysis of individual company data discussed first. Section 7.5.2 discusses the results for the second part of the study on the determinants of gold price exposure.

7.5.1   *Gold price exposure*

7.5.1.1   *Individual company data*

In Table 7.1, we present the results of the two-factor regression model using individual company data. The gold price exposure, which describes the relationship between the return on gold spot price and the return on share prices of the sample companies, varies from 0.622 to 1.579 per cent. If a gold mining company has a gold price exposure of 1.579, this implies that a 1 per cent increase in the return on gold spot price will lead to a 1.579 per cent increase in the return on the share of the company.

From the table, we can see that, of the fifteen companies in the sample, nine have a gold price exposure greater than 1. The *t*-statistic shows that, of these nine companies, eight have coefficients which are significantly different from 1 at a 10 per cent significance level (at least), supporting the first hypothesis that the gold price exposure is greater than 1. However, there are also companies that have a gold price exposure lower than 1, which is inconsistent with our hypothesis. Our findings here are not as significant as those of Blose and Shieh (1995), who reported that fifteen out of twenty-three of their sample companies had a gold price exposure significantly greater than 1, and only one had an exposure significantly less than 1.

The finding that the gold price exposure less than 1 for some companies could be because of other non-gold price related risks, such as unstable dividends, political risks and business risks, being incorporated in gold mining share prices (Train, 1978; Khoury, 1984). Another possible reason for the low gold price exposure could be high hedging activities by the company. As we have explained before, if a company can forward sell its entire production profile at a fixed price, this could eliminate most of its exposure to any fluctuation of the gold spot price, thus, reducing its measured gold price exposure. This factor will be discussed in detail in a later section.

Table 7.1 Regression results for two-factor model

Company	Gold price exposure	Significantly different from 1	Market beta		Adjusted R²	F-statistic		DW	
Pool	1.090	**	0.948	***	0.147	980.30	***	2.133	***
	(22.596)		(17.579)						
AAA	1.579	***	0.947	***	0.236	118.40	***	2.038	***
	(9.941)		(6.922)						
AUG	0.781		0.610	***	0.068	28.84	***	2.095	***
	(4.003)		(3.503)						
CNG	0.960		1.040	***	0.078	33.10	***	2.591	
	(3.756)		(2.929)						
CTR	1.086		1.379	***	0.157	71.60	***	1.956	***
	(4.377)		(4.884)						
DGD	1.257	*	1.325	***	0.208	100.80	***	2.117	***
	(6.121)		(5.684)						
GCM	0.759	**	0.732	***	0.135	59.75	***	1.849	***
	(5.448)		(6.596)						
GLDᵃ	0.633	**	0.914	***	0.071	30.18	***	2.277	***
	(3.747)		(6.705)						
LHG	1.324	**	0.974	***	0.235	117.50	***	1.970	***
	(8.202)		(9.856)						
NCM	1.562	***	1.076	***	0.214	104.20	***	1.938	***
	(8.183)		(8.309)						
NDY	1.197	*	0.893	***	0.234	116.70	***	2.079	***
	(8.432)		(6.819)						
NML	1.248	*	1.089	***	0.200	96.00	***	2.089	***
	(7.584)		(6.837)						
RGSᵃ	0.622	***	0.524	***	0.077	32.47	***	2.323	
	(5.506)		(5.737)						
RSG	1.360	**	1.144	***	0.211	102.40	***	1.908	***
	(7.642)		(6.201)						
RSM	1.235		1.008	***	0.141	63.28	***	2.184	***
	(5.552)		(2.942)						
SGWᵃ	0.748	***	0.560	***	0.141	63.32	***	1.871	***
	(8.139)		(7.554)						

Notes
*Coefficient significant at 0.1 level.
**Coefficient significant at 0.05 level.
***Coefficient significant at 0.01 level; *t*-statistics are shown in parentheses.
a White correction is *not* applied.

7.5.1.2   Pooled sample data

The two-factor model is also tested on the pooled sample data and the results are also reported in Table 7.1. The gold price exposure of all companies pooled together is 1.090, which is greater than 1. The coefficient is significantly different from 1 at a 5 per cent significance level. In contrast, Tufano (1998) found that the gold price exposure of his sample gold mining companies is a mean of 2, which is substantially greater than our findings.

There are three possible reasons to explain the difference between our findings and those of Tufano (1998). First, we have used a different measurement for the return on gold. Tufano (1998) used the *total return on gold*, which includes the return from buying gold, lending it temporarily and then selling it, while we use only the *return on gold spot price*. Second, our experiment samples are of different settings. Our finding of a lower gold price exposure than Tufano's (1998) could be that Australian gold producers are hedging more actively than their North American counterparts. Last but not least, Tufano (1998) has used Dimson's (1979) adjustment to correct the bias that may be introduced when daily data and infrequently traded stocks are involved.

7.5.2   Determinants of gold price exposure

The second part of the study involves an examination of the determinants of the gold price exposure of our sample of companies. The analysis is done by pooling all observations across the 3-year period.[10]

7.5.2.1   Univariate tests

The univariate results are presented in Table 7.2. As expected, the gold price exposure is inversely related to the gold price and significant at the 1 per cent level. This finding is consistent with our hypothesis 2 and Tufano's (1998) finding. From the valuation model, we expect that a company with a higher production quantity will have a lower gold price exposure. However, the production quantity is found to be positively related to the gold price exposure, which is similar to Tufano's (1998) finding and inconsistent with our hypothesis.

Tufano (1998) provided a possible explanation for such a finding. He explained that production quantity can be seen as an alternative measure for firm size and there is a systematic positive relationship between firm size and gold price exposure. This is due to information being impounded into the prices of larger firms faster than into smaller firms.

The finding of a positive relationship between gold price exposure and production quantity means that our third hypothesis is not accepted. However, this does not mean that our valuation model, from which we derived our hypothesis, is mis-specified. It could imply that the firm size effect is stronger than the valuation model, which then steers the coefficient of production quantity in a positive, instead of negative, direction.

Table 7.2 Regression results for univariate tests

	Direction	Coefficient	t-Statistic	R^2	Adjusted R^2	F-statistic
GPRICE	–	–0.006***	–4.434	0.099	0.094	19.662***
PRDQTY	–	0.001**	1.819	0.018	0.013	3.309*
PRDCOST	+	0.001	1.086	0.007	0.001	1.179
VOLATILITY	–	5.809***	4.013	0.083	0.078	16.104***
DISCOUNT	–	–0.175***	–3.588	0.067	0.062	12.874***
LEASE	+	0.025	0.137	0.000	–0.006	0.019
HDGQTY	–	0.027	1.042	0.007	0.001	1.086
HDGPRICE	–	0.0004	0.757	0.006	0.000	1.036
LEVERAGE	+	0.019	0.176	0.000	–0.005	0.031

Notes
*Coefficient significant at 10% level.
**Coefficient significant at 5% level.
***Coefficient significant at 1% level.

We had also expected the gold price exposure to be positively related to the production costs, and our results support this hypothesis. On average, we found that a A$1 increase in production costs will lead gold price exposure to be higher by 0.001. However, the relationship is not significant.

Under the flexible production model, theory suggests that companies should experience lower gold price exposure when the volatility of gold prices is high, which behaves like a call option. However, this negative relationship is not observed, which contradicts Tufano's (1998) finding. Instead, our regression result indicates a positive relationship between gold price exposure and volatility of gold prices and the relationship is significant. Thus, our sixth hypothesis is not accepted.

A possible explanation for this finding is that most of the Australian gold producers may be operating under the fixed production with hedging model.[11] It is not difficult to see that the gold producers operating under a fixed production model, with or without hedging, will face greater exposure to the fluctuations of gold price than those operating under a flexible production model. In fact, we would expect that a gold company without the production flexibility, in a more volatile environment, would have a greater exposure to fluctuations in that environment.

The results in Table 7.2 show that the relationship between the discount rate and the gold price exposure is significantly negative and is consistent with our hypothesis 7. The result implies that a one per cent increase in the discount rate will cause the gold price exposure to increase by 0.175 per cent.

We also expect a positive relationship between the gold price exposure and the gold lease rate, and this relationship is observed in all three models but is not statistically significant. Our result has provided some evidence to support the theory, which Tufano (1998) failed to support. He found a weak negative relationship between the gold lease rate and gold price exposure, which is inconsistent with predictions of the valuation model.

Both the hedging quantity and average contract price are also found to be inconsistent with the theory. It is expected that both factors would have a negative relationship with the gold price exposure, but this relationship is not observed. The positive coefficients found for both the hedging quantity and the average contract price means that our ninth and tenth hypotheses are rejected.

Interestingly, the positive coefficients of both the hedging quantity and the average contract price may indicate that some companies that forward sell their gold production may have done so for speculative rather than hedging purposes. These companies that engage in speculation may actually increase their exposure to the gold price fluctuations. MacDonald (1999b) stated:

> . . . the main value drivers for a gold company were exploration, mine operation, resource development and forward selling. The inclusion of forward selling in the selection of value drivers is no real surprise, but it does highlight the fact that for gold companies, the derivatives market is not about hedging or simple protection against falling prices. It is more about increasing shareholder's wealth, which mean speculation.

Financial leverage is found to be positively, but not significantly, related to the gold price exposure. This, however, provides a weak support for our tenth hypothesis that a high leveraged company will have a high gold price exposure.

7.5.2.2   *Multivariate tests*

Two separate models are estimated for over multivariate tests. Owing to the high correlation of 0.921 between gold price and discount rate, we re-estimated the original model without the 'discount rate' variable. We named the original model as Model 1 and the model without the discount rate variable as Model 2, and the results for these two models are presented in Table 7.3.

Table 7.3 shows that the spot gold price is negatively related to the gold price exposure of the gold mining companies and is a significant determinant. The coefficient for the gold price in Model 1 indicates that a unit (US$1) increase in the gold price causes the gold price exposure to decrease by 0.011. This significant negative relationship provides evidence for accepting our second hypothesis, that gold price exposure is inversely related to the gold price. This result is consistent with Tufano's (1998) finding.

Contrary to the prediction of the theory, we find that the coefficient for production quantity is positive. The coefficient is not significant in this multivariate regression though it is significant at a 5 per cent level in the univariate test. This finding is similar to Tufano's (1998), who found weak positive relationship between production quantity and gold price exposure. A possible reason for observing such a positive relationship is the firm size effect, which is discussed in the earlier section.

Consistent with the theory and the result of the univariate tests, the coefficient of production costs is found to be positive and is *only* significant at the 10 per cent level. This finding is robust across all three models. Therefore, we can conclude

Table 7.3 Regression results for multivariate tests

	Direction	Model 1		Model 2	
C	–	2.497	***	2.355	***
		(2.863)		(2.731)	
GPRICE	–	–0.011	***	–0.007	***
		(–2.615)		(–2.985)	
PRDQTY	–	0.001		0.001	
		(0.913)		(0.877)	
PRDCOST	+	0.001	*	0.001	*
		(1.397)		(1.434)	
VOLATILITY	–	1.882		1.587	
		(0.839)		(0.713)	
DISCOUNT	–	0.142		–	
		(1.063)			
LEASE	+	0.277		0.237	
		(1.235)		(1.071)	
HDGQTY	–	–0.026		–0.028	
		(–0.712)		(–0.756)	
HDGPRICE	–	0.0002		0.0002	
		(0.517)		(0.620)	
LEVERAGE	+	–0.198	*	–0.206	*
		(–1.602)		(–1.671)	
R^2		0.175		0.169	
Adjusted R^2		0.125		0.124	
DW statistic		1.482		1.487	
F-statistic		3.485	***	3.776	***
Prob(F-statistic)		0.001		0.000	

Notes
t-Statistic is shown in parentheses.
*Coefficient significant at 10% level.
**Coefficient significant at 5% level.
***Coefficient significant at 1% level.

that our fourth and fifth hypotheses, that gold price exposure is positively related to production costs, are accepted.

Our results provide the supporting evidence that Tufano (1998) could not find. He was puzzled by his finding that 'firms' operating costs, measured directly by cash costs, are not materially associated with the level of exposure'. He strongly believed that the firm's cost structure should have a material impact on its operating leverage and the degree to which this leverage amplifies price shocks.

The results in Table 7.3 provide weak evidence that the relationship between the volatility of gold prices and the gold price exposure is positive. Therefore, our sixth hypothesis is not accepted. This positive relationship between the volatility of gold prices and the gold price exposure is stronger in the univariate tests, implying that there is some interacting effect when more than one independent variable is used in the regression equation. A possible explanation for such a contradicting result to the hypothesis is provided in the earlier section.

The results from Model 1 display a positive but insignificant relationship between the gold price exposure and the discount rate, which is inconsistent with our seventh hypothesis. This is because of the high correlation between the discount rate and gold price.

Another possible reason for this finding is that the 10-year domestic bond rate may not be the appropriate rate to use as the discount rate. Probably a shorter-term bond rate should be used instead of the 10-year, because the intended investment horizon may be shorter than 10 years. Therefore, in a later section, we will re-estimate the relationship using 3-month and 5-year bond rate, one at a time, as independent variables. This can be served as a robustness check for the regression results.

Similar to the univariate tests, we find a positive relationship between the gold price exposure and the gold lease rate in all three models, but it is not statistically significant. We are unable to find supporting evidence for our eighth hypothesis, which is consistent with Tufano (1998).

The results also show that the amount (million ounces) of hedging undertaken by the companies is negatively, but not significantly, associated with the gold price exposures. We expect hedging to have a significant impact on the gold price exposure of the gold mining companies, but this is not observed. This result is inconsistent with the findings of Blose and Shieh (1995) and Tufano (1998), who found that the amount of hedging is a significant determinant of gold price exposure. This insignificant coefficient of hedging quantity can be interpreted as suggesting that there is no relationship between hedging and gold price exposure, which is consistent with the finding of Petersen and Thiagaranjan (1996). They studied two gold companies and found that hedging has no effect on the gold price exposure.

One possible reason for *not* finding hedging as a significant factor of gold price exposure is that the market is unable to see or appreciate the intrinsic value of the hedge book put in place by the gold mining company. This is consistent with Raston (1998), who does not find that the coefficient of realized selling price (proxy for hedging activities) is significant, implying that 'the market is valuing the gold stocks inefficiently'. This 'inefficient market perception' of hedging activities could be because of the quality of the data available to us. The other explanation could be that most of the quarterly reports normally are only available 1 month after the end of each quarter, causing a timing problem in capturing investor reaction.[12]

The result for the average contract price is similar to the result of the univariate tests. We find positive but insignificant relationship between the average contract price and the gold price exposure. The possible reason for such a relationship is discussed in an earlier section. Our finding is also inconsistent with our tenth hypothesis, that gold price exposure is inversely related to the average contract price.

Contrary to our eleventh hypothesis, that gold price exposure is positively related to financial leverage, we find that the coefficient of financial leverage is negative and significant *only* at a 10 per cent level. This result is constant throughout all three models. Therefore, we reject our hypothesis at a 10 per cent significance level.

The finding of a negative relationship between the financial leverage and the gold price exposure is inconsistent with Tufano (1998). One possible explanation is risk sharing. When a gold mining company finances its project through borrowing, it may in fact have transferred some of its investment risk from its shareholders to its debtholders (lenders and bankers). One of the risks that a gold mining company faces is the fluctuation of the gold spot price (gold price exposure). Generally, unless there is a substantial change in gold spot price, debtholders do not react frequently to the day-to-day fluctuations of gold prices than the shareholders do, which is because the term of a loan contract is normally very stable. Thus, in this sense, with more debtholders, the sensitivity of the gold mining company to gold price changes will be lesser. Therefore, we find that the gold price exposure is inversely related to the financial leverage.

7.5.3   *Robustness checks*

In an earlier section, we mentioned that a 10-year domestic bond rate may not be the appropriate discount rate for gold mining companies, and suggested the use of a shorter bond rate to re-estimate the relationship. Hence, we replace the 10-year bond rate with the 5-year bond rate to proxy the discount rate and run the OLS (ordinary least squares) regression. The results are reported in Table 7.4.

Generally, Table 7.4, column 1, shows that the results of regression using a 5-year rate do not differ from the results using the 10-year rate. The R^2, adjusted R^2 and F-statistic are just marginally higher than the 10-year rate, indicating that the 5-year bond rate may be a better proxy than the 10-year bond rate. The major difference is that the coefficient for the gold lease rate, which was previously found to be insignificant, is now significant at a 10 per cent level.

The second robustness check we use is replacing the volatility of gold price per annum, the 1-year gold lease rate and the 10-year bond rate with the volatility of gold price per quarter, the 3-month gold lease rate and the 3-month bill rate respectively. The regression is re-estimated. The result is shown in Table 7.4 and the inference remains unchanged.

In summary, when we use individual company data set, the result is mixed. The coefficients of gold return for some companies is less than 1, implying that some companies have gold price exposure lower than 1.

Using both univariate and multivariate tests, we find that gold price is negatively related to the gold price exposure at the 1 per cent significance level. Production cost and financial leverage are found to be positively related to exposure at the 10 per cent significance level. We failed to find evidence to support some of our hypotheses in regard to the determinants of gold price exposure. Especially, we expected the hedging quantity and the average contract price to have a significant negative effect on gold price exposure, but this relationship is not observed. We attribute the main reason of failure to support this relationship to market inefficiency in interpreting

Table 7.4 Results for robustness checks

	Model 1 with following changes	
	Five-year discount	*Three-month volatility* *Three-month discount* *Three-month lease*
C	2.518***	2.129**
	(2.887)	(2.156)
GPRICE	–0.011***	–0.003
	(–2.675)	(–0.451)
PRDQTY	0.001	0.001
	(0.910)	(0.890)
PRDCOST	0.001*	0.001*
	(1.394)	(1.326)
VOLATILITY	1.894	5.400
	(0.846)	(1.117)
DISCOUNT	0.174	–0.141
	(1.188)	(–0.527)
LEASE	0.294*	–0.043
	(1.303)	(–0.273)
HDGQTY	–0.026	–0.029
	(–0.707)	(–0.774)
HDGPRICE	0.0002	0.0002
	(0.526)	(0.598)
LEVERAGE	–0.198*	–0.199*
	(–1.606)	(–1.602)
R^2	0.176	0.165
Adjusted R^2	0.126	0.114
DW statistic	1.475	1.493
F-statistic	3.522***	3.254***
Prob(*F*-statistic)	0.001	0.001

Notes
t-Statistic is shown in parentheses.
*Coefficient significant at 10% level.
**Coefficient significant at 5% level.
***Coefficient significant at 1% level.

information on hedging activities. Some robustness checks have been conducted, but it seems that there is no significant difference in the result.

7.6 Conclusion

This study attempts to answer the question of whether gold price exposures of gold mining companies are greater than 1. There are two groups of argument. One group believes that the exposures of gold mining companies are greater than 1 while the other group believes otherwise. The latter argues that gold stocks also incorporate other risks, other than gold price risk. These risks include unstable dividends, political risks, foreign exchange risks, and business risks such as market conditions and technology changes. They also disrupt the influence of gold price risk in the returns of the gold stocks.

The result of OLS regression estimation using pooled sample data shows that, on average, the gold price exposure of the gold mining companies is greater than 1. However, using individual company data for the sample period, our results indicate the gold price exposures of the sample companies are not all greater than 1. Some companies have exposure to gold price changes as high as 1.579 per cent while the others can be as low as 0.622 per cent point.

The second stage of the research is to further elaborate our first conclusion. We attempt to investigate what factors influence the gold price exposure greater than 1. Using three valuation models, namely fixed, flexible and fixed with hedging production model, we list eight potential determinants that we believe will affect the exposure. A quarterly data set is run on a multifactor OLS regression model. Owing to the small number of observations, we pooled our sample across time and companies for the analysis of the determinants of the gold price exposure.

We conclude that the gold price, production costs and financial leverage are significant determinants of gold price exposure. The result indicates that the higher the level of gold prices, the lower the gold price exposure. Production costs are shown to have a positive relationship with gold price exposure. The negative relationship found between the gold price exposure and the financial leverage is inconsistent with our hypothesis. A possible explanation is that debtholders do not actively react with the change in gold prices, which, as a result, reduces the gold price exposure.

Unfortunately, the other factors are found to be insignificant in explaining gold price exposure. It is expected that hedging will reduce the gold price exposure and companies hedge because they believe that hedging can reduce their exposure. However, this effect is not found in this research. Raston (1998) also failed to find the significance of hedging in the stock return in Australia and attributed this finding to market inefficiency in interpreting information on hedging. We believe that the information on hedging activities reported on the quarterly reports does not capture the full extent of hedging because the new disclosure requirement introduced in 1996, may be recent enough and vague enough that its adoption is still very incomplete and inconsistent. Moreover, regardless of the disclosure requirements by the authorities, the companies still have great discretion in disclosure. Most of these hedgings are settled over-the-counter and the information on these transactions is confidential. In addition, most companies will not want to report because of competitive advantages. This may have some implications for further rectification of disclosure requirement by the authorities.

Appendix

Table 7A.1 List of the companies that made up the ASX Gold Index as at 30 June 1999

Company name	ASX Code
Acacia Resources	AAA
Aurora Gold	AUG
Central Norseman Gold Corp.	CNG
Centaur Mining & Exploration	CTR
Delta Gold	DGD
Great Central Mines[a]	GCM
Goldfields	GLD
Lihir Gold	LHG
Newcrest Mining	NCM
Normandy Mining	NDY
Niugini Mining	NML
Ranger Minerals	RGS
Resolute Resources	RSG
Ross Mining	RSM
Sons of Gwalia	SGW

Source: ASX Information Center.

Note
a Great Central Mines was suspended from 22 June 1999, but we still include it in our sample.

Acknowledgements

We would like to thank the World Gold Council, John Raston of the Resource Finance Corporation, John Braham of Macquarie Equities, John MacDonald of CIBC, Paul Heath of JB Were, Charles Crouch of the Australian Gold Council, Dennis Wilkins of Lynas Gold, Richard Borozdin of the Department of Minerals and Energy, and Professor Peter Tufano of the Harvard Business School for their assistance and other input, and Taylor Nelson Sofres Malaysia who provided the financial support for the review of this chapter.

Notes

1 Please note that risk management policies and gold hedging activities will be used interchangeably in the later sections.
2 Realized selling price is defined as the average selling price for gold reported by the company once their hedging has been taken into account. The data will come from the ASX Quarterly reports that the companies are required to submit.
3 Jorion (1990) multifactor model is:

$$R_{it} = \alpha_t + \beta_{ig} R_{gt} + \beta_{im} R_{mt} + \epsilon_t$$

where R_{it} = stock return, R_{gt} = return from gold spot price and R_{mt} = market return.
4 Blose and Shieh (1995) have theoretically shown that the firm's gold price elasticity is the market value of the gold reserves divided by the market value of the stock.

They further showed that higher production costs, higher debt levels, and lower level of non-gold assets will associate with higher elasticity. Their gold price elasticity equation is

$$e_s = \frac{P\sum q_t}{P\sum q_t - \sum C_t(1+r)^{-1} + V_{ng} - D}$$

where P is the price of gold, q_t is the quantity of gold extracted at time t, C is the cost of mining, V_{ng} is the value of non-gold assets and D is the debt.

5 Please note that, from equation (7.2), the value of gold mine is positively related to the gold beta.

6 The World Gold Council advised that London Fixes have the position of worldwide benchmark that other fixes do not enjoy. More information on London Fix can be found on this website: http://www.pamp.com/ff/fixing.html.

7 To ensure the comparability, cash costs per ounce, which are calculated according to Gold Institute Standard, will be collected.

8 Thanks to John Braham of Macquarie Equities for providing this information.

9 This does not include the calls because the delta of the calls are close to zero, which is considered worthless to the company.

10 Owing to the small number of observations for each individual company in our data, most of the diagnostic tests cannot be run, thus hampering the reliability of the regression results of these individual companies. Therefore, even though the regression model can be tested on the individual company sample, the results should be used with great caution and are not presented here.

11 As discussed in section 7.3, we believe that fixed production is unrealistic and does not reflect all aspect of the operation of gold mines. Therefore, it is more realistic to say that the gold producers are operating under fixed production with hedging.

12 This timing difference will be further discussed in section 7.6.

References

Allayannis, G. and Ofek, E. (1997) 'Exchange rate exposure, hedging and the use of foreign currency derivatives', *Social Science Research Network Electronic Library*. Online. Available at www ssrn.com

Blose, L.E. and Schwartz, E.S. (1985) 'Evaluating natural resources investments', *Journal of Business*, 58: 135–57.

Blose, L.E. and Shieh, J.P. (1995) 'The impact of gold price on the value of gold mining stock', *Review of Financial Economics*, 4(2): 125–39.

Brennan, M.J. (1990) 'Latent assets', *Journal of Finance,* 65: 709–30.

Brennan, M.J. and Schwarz, E.S. (1985) 'Evaluating natural resources investments', *Journal of Business*, 58: 135–57.

Brimelow, J. (1996) 'Gold: the hazards of hedging', *Forbes*, February 12: 180.

Davis, G. (1996) 'Option premiums in mineral asset pricing: are they important?', *Land Economics*, 72: 167–86.

Dimson, E. (1979) 'Risk measurement when shares are subject to infrequent trading', *Journal of Financial Economics*, 7: 197–220.

Dolde, W. (1995) 'Hedging, leverage, and primitive risk', *Journal of Financial Engineering*, 4: 187–216.

Faff, R. and Chan, H. (1998) 'A multifactor model of gold industry stock returns: evidence from the Australian equity market', *Applied Financial Economics*, 8: 21–8.

Froot, K.A., Scharfstein, D.S. and Stein, J.C. (1993) 'Risk management: coordinating investment and financing policies', *Journal of Finance*, 48: 1629–58.

Jorion, P. (1990) 'The exchange-rate exposure of US multinationals', *Journal of Business*, 63: 331–45.

Khoury, S.J. (1984) *Speculative Markets*, New York: Macmillan.

MacDonald, J. (1999a) 'Resource highlights: gold hedging in Australia', *CIBC World Markets Equity Research*, 8 October.

——(1999b) 'Resource highlights: gold hedging comparisons', *CIBC World Markets Equity Research*, 25 June.

—— and Solnik, B.H. (1977) 'Valuation and strategy for gold stocks', *Journal of Portfolio Management*, 4: 29–33.

Mardones, J.L. (1993) 'Option valuation of real assets: application to a copper mine with operating flexibility', *Resources Policy*, 19: 51–65.

Ozanian, M. (1987) 'Risky hedges', *Forbes*, May 18, 248.

Panchapakesan, M. (1993) 'The shining', *Financial World*, 193(3): 42–3.

Petersen, M. and Thiagarajan, S.M. (1996) 'Risk measurement and hedging', unpublished manuscript, Northwestern University.

Raston, J. (1998) 'Factors affecting Australian gold returns between 1988 and 1997', honours dissertation, the University of Western Australia.

Rolo, C. (1975) 'Gold stocks are not just for goldbugs', *Forbes*, April 1: 78–9.

Schiffres, M. (1987) 'Precious ways to hedge your bets', *US News and World Report*, April 27: 68.

Train, J. (1978) 'All the glitters', *Forbes*, December 25: 70.

Tufano, P. (1998) 'The determinants of stock price exposure: financial engineering and the gold mining industry', *The Journal of Finance*, LIII(3): 1015–52.

8 Output response to gold prices

More evidence for South Africa

Duane Rockerbie

Introduction

Studies of the price and world market for gold in past academic, financial and semipopular literature have neglected production technology and have concentrated primarily on how the price of gold influences gold production. With respect to gold production, classical theorists assumed gold supply to be completely elastic at the market price. Classical economists ignored the question of exhaustion, probably because of ever-increasing gold stocks during the nineteenth century (Rockoff, 1984). This implied that changes in non-monetary factors, such as real incomes and tastes, could not affect the price of gold in the long run. Supply was only a function of the real price of gold, with the nominal price set by the monetary authorities. Bordo and Ellison (1986) relaxed the assumption of constant costs for gold producers under a gold standard. Attempts to build forecasting models for the price of gold after the gold standard have had mixed results and have generally ignored supply considerations[1] (Salant and Henderson, 1978; Flood and Garber, 1980; Marsh, 1983; Baker and Van Tassel, 1985; Sherman, 1986).

A recent example studying gold production is Selvanathan and Selvanathan (1999). The authors estimate the short- and long-run response elasticities of gold production to changes in the world price of gold. The method is non-theoretical: gold production and the world price of gold are found not to be cointegrated. Thus, first differences are taken, then a simple Koyck lag specification is derived from a production function that is linear in the expected gold price. The model is estimated using data for Australia, and the long-term response elasticity is found to be slightly greater than 1. The approach may be flawed on two grounds. First, an instrumental variable for gold output was not constructed as the model contained only one apparently exogenous variable, the world price of gold. No other variables were included in the model and the basic principles of demand and supply identification were ignored. The resulting elasticity estimates are biased if the world price is endogenous to Australian production.[2]

Second, assuming that the variables in the model were exogenous may have affected the cointegration tests. Finding that the world price of gold and gold production for Australia are not cointegrated implies that there is no long-run equilibrium between the two. This seems counter-intuitive when price and quantity are the cointegrating variables. Australian production increased quickly from 1980 to 1993, although the world price of gold remained relatively flat. Despite the fact that the two time series were drifting apart, there should have been an equilibrium in the long term as demand and supply must intersect at some output level. If the world price of gold is exogenous for Australia, the demand curve it faces is completely elastic at the world price. Changes in production costs, technologies, quality of reserve deposits, taxation, etc. can shift the Australian gold supply curve, making it appear that the two series are drifting apart, when in fact they are still in equilibrium.

This chapter develops a model of gold production based on Rockerbie (1999) and estimates the model using South African production data. The discontinuous effect of grade depletion on extraction costs is explicitly modelled. South Africa is an interesting case for a number of reasons. The dramatic increase in the nominal and real price of gold during the 1970s generated incentives for new production throughout the world. The high price of gold, often in combination with new mining techniques, also permitted the re-opening of abandoned mines and the expansion of output in existing facilities. The result of this exploration has caused a dramatic increase in the annual production of gold by the world's major gold producers, except for the world's most dominant producer, South Africa.

In 1970, South Africa produced 1,000 tonnes of gold, or 83 per cent of the total world non-communist production of 1,250 tonnes (Jackson, 1988; *Gold 1988, Consolidated Gold Fields*). At this time, many mines were relatively new. Between 1970 and 1974, South African annual gold production fell to approximately 700 tonnes and remained near this level until 1986, when production fell further to approximately 600 tonnes. For the first time since 1954, annual South African gold production was less than the total gold produced by the rest of the world. In comparison, in non-communist countries, annual gold production rose from 300 tonnes to over 1,000 tonnes between 1981 and 1986. The average grade of ore mined in South Africa fell from 13 grams per tonne in 1970 to just 5 grams per tonne in 1995[3] and reached a historical low of only 4.6 grams per tonne by 1999. Since 1989, the gold industry in South Africa has responded to lower gold prices by cutting costs and launching unsuccessful attempts to mine higher average grades. Mines which have exhausted their profitable life have not been replaced by new mines. Other factors external to the mining industry (domestic price instability, political upheaval, etc.) have also contributed to the inflexible downward trend of the average grade. In fact, many South African gold mines have moved emphasis from mining tonnage of ore to quality mining in which all ore must be economically useful (Nattrass, 1995).

Unlike in the USA, reserve deposits are the property of the government of South Africa. Private mining concerns mine and extract the precious gold in exchange for paying taxes to the government and providing valuable employment to workers. Besides the usual types of taxes imposed, producers in South Africa also pay an additional tax if the average grade of mining operations rises above a threshold limit. This provides an incentive for mine producers to mine more than just the best-quality deposits, which otherwise would undergo rapid depletion. Although not modelled explicitly, the tax is an important feature of the production model to be developed in this paper as it forces producers to mine close to their average mill pay limit. Australia collects an *ad valorem* tax, or royalty, from its producers, based on total revenues. If the world price of gold rises above a threshold value, the tax is automatically imposed. Fraser (1999) argues that this type of tax encourages rapid depletion of the highest quality mines. When the price of gold is low, gold miners are unrestricted as to what deposits they choose to mine and they pay no tax. An increase in the price of gold above the threshold value may bring lower quality deposits into production, but the imposition of the revenue tax might also dampen this effect.

Despite the use of the average grade tax in South Africa to encourage responsible mining, gold production has become an increasingly low-profit enterprise. The *average mill pay limit* is the average grade of ore necessary to generate enough revenues to just cover production costs – a zero-profit grade of ore. Figure 8.1 plots the average grade of ore and the pay limit since 1970. Recently, the average grade of ore has dropped dangerously close to the average mill pay limit and, with grades falling further, production costs rising and the world price of gold relatively flat, the situation will worsen.

South Africa is also a useful test case since the Chamber of Mines of South

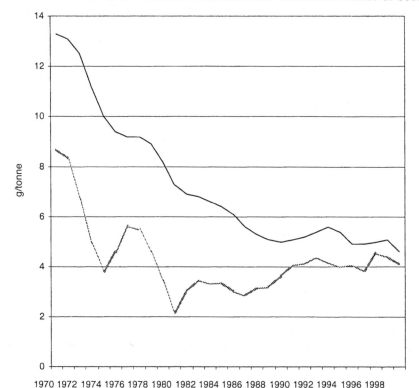

Figure 8.1 Average grade (—) (gram/tonne) vs. pay limit (---) for South Africa, 1970–99.
Sources: South African Mining Industry Statistical Tables 1999, Chamber of Miners of South Africa and own calculations.

Africa produces a rich annual statistical summary of revenues, costs, grades, etc. that is easily available and unique to South Africa.

The purpose of this paper is to develop a model of production that incorporates the special characteristics of the South African gold mining industry and which explicitly models the feedback effects of grade depletion. The model will show that the short-run supply curve should be negatively sloped. Keynes (1936), Paish (1938), Katzen (1964) and Marsh (1983) have noted that a negatively sloped gold supply curve is a distinct possibility for South Africa. Empirical testing will show that conditions do not exist for the long-run supply curve to be negatively sloped for South African gold production, as in Rockerbie (1999), but only just so.

A simple model of gold production

Define ore reserves (*orr*) as blocks of ore that have been made available for mining. Each ore block is evaluated to determine its average ore grade (*ag*), the number of grams of gold per tonne of ore. Payable ore reserves are those ore reserves which yield at least enough gold to cover production costs (*c*) at current market prices. Payable ore reserves are determined by the average mill pay limit (*pl*), which is formally defined as (let p_g = price of gold in rand per gram) the zero profit grade of ore.

$$pl\,(\text{gram/tonne}) = \frac{c\,(\text{rand/tonne})}{p_g\,(\text{rand/gram})} \tag{8.1}$$

Payable ore reserves (*porr*) are then those ore reserves with an average ore grade greater than or equal to the average mill pay limit [*porr* (tonnes) = *orr* (tonnes) with $ag \geq pl$]. The average grade of ore that a producer will find profitable (*ag**) is the total gold content of payable reserves as a percentage of payable reserves.

Total gold production (q_g) in grams is the average grade of ore of payable reserves multiplied by the quantity of ore milled (q_o).

$$q_g\,(\text{grams}) = ag\,(\text{grams/tonne}) \times q_o\,(\text{tonnes}) \tag{8.2}$$

Tonnes of ore milled, like the average mill pay limit, is dependent upon production costs and the price of gold. With higher gold prices and constant costs, the pay limit *pl* will fall from equation (8.1) as less productive deposits can now be processed profitably. The average grade above the average mill pay limit *ag** will fall as less productive deposits have lower grades. Mines in the short run will attempt to increase tonnage milled, q_o, from existing reserves. The extent of any increase will depend upon the accessibility of the ore. Where the gold is in alluvial deposits or shallow mines, the time needed for expansion may be quite short. Since 1994, some mines have been using low-grade surface materials to top up the amount of ore being processed through the mills in order to reach the point of economies of scale. Evidence for New Zealand (Cullen and Craw, 1990) suggests that producers still follow efficient extractions paths (Hotellings rule) in this case. In deep mines, such as those in South Africa, it may be a number of years before new ore can be accessed. In the long run, as more equipment, labour and capital are acquired, tonnage milled will increase. In general, the sensitivity of tonnage milled to cost and price changes will be determined by the elasticity of supply of labour and capital, the start-up time of mining investment and the degree of monopoly power.

The total amount of gold produced, q_g, may increase or decrease depending upon whether the increase in tonnage milled, q_o, outweighs the decrease in the average grade above the pay limit, ag^*. If the mine is relatively new and deposits are rich and easily accessible, the increase in q_o could easily outweigh the decrease in ag^* and q_g will rise. This may not be the case for South Africa, where most new deposits can only be found in deep mines, which may not be of high quality.[4]

The gold production model

The basic model is drawn in Figure 8.2. In quadrant I, it is assumed that the supply curve of tonnes of ore milled is inelastic in response to a change in the price of gold. This is justified by the fact that South African mines are extremely deep and new ore production is difficult to step up quickly in the short term. The curve does contain known deposits of ore of certain average grades that have not yet been mined but are easily obtainable. The elasticity is determined by the output elasticities of capital, labour and other factors, as well as the supply elasticities of these factors.

In quadrant II, the relationship between the price of gold and the average mill pay limit is inverse as higher gold prices reduce the pay limit pl, bringing less

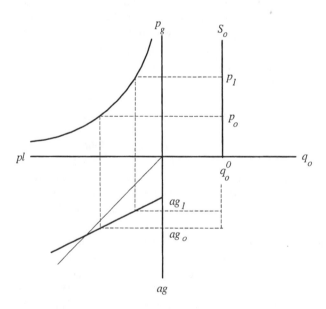

Figure 8.2 Short-run output response to an increase in the gold price.

profitable mines back into production. The curve shifts outwards to the left as a result of increases in production costs, c. The relationship is drawn as a hyperbola as a very high price of gold will reduce the pay limit to a value approaching zero and the mine will become totally depleted; for a very low gold price the pay limit approaches infinity and the mine will be shut down. Mining operators could mine to a point well above the average mill pay limit for a given price of gold, moving them to the left of the indicated average mill pay limit. This would mean that only high-quality mines are brought into production to insure that the average mill pay limit is exceeded. In South Africa, the previously discussed mining tax insures that producers mine close to *pl*. The formula allows for a 5 per cent gross profit margin before mines are taxed. To minimize their tax liability, producers will not mine too far above *pl*. The assumption here is that producers will mine just equal to the average mill pay limit.[5]

Quadrant III illustrates the relationship between the average mill pay limit, *pl*, and the average grade of profitable reserves, *ag**. The 45° line represents the zero profit position, at which the average grade is just equal to the pay limit. The slope of the curve is determined by quantities and proportions of low- and high-grade ore reserves. A mine with a high proportion of low-grade ores will have a flatter curve since increases in the average grade pay limit, owing to a higher price of gold, will have little effect on the average grade or ore above the pay limit. The curve is drawn as elastic to reflect the fact that many South African mines are now producing only low-grade ore. The producer will not operate beyond the point at which the curve intersects the zero profit line.

Given the price of gold, production costs, and the grade of ore being mined, gold production can be determined in quadrant IV. Assume the price of gold is p_o and the production capacity of ore milled is q_o^0. The average mill pay limit is given by pl_0 in quadrant II, resulting in an average grade of payable reserves of ag_o^* in quadrant III. The total amount of gold produced is given by $ag_o^* q_o^0$ in quadrant IV. One point on the gold supply curve is thus $(p_o, ag_o^* q_o^0)$. Assume that the price of gold increases to p_1 owing to a shift in ore demand in quadrant I. Given no change in cost conditions, the average mill pay limit is reduced to pl_1 and the the average grade of ore required of payable reserves is reduced to ag_1^*. A second point on the gold supply curve is given by $(p_1, ag_1^* q_o^0)$. The short-run gold supply curve will be downward sloping regardless of the elasticity of the *pl–ag* curve in quadrant III because of the inelasticity of ore supply.

It is more likely that an increase in gold production, in response to a higher world gold price, will also increase production costs. Higher costs shift the cost curve in quadrant II to the left and increase the pay limit. With higher production costs, producers will be forced to abandon less productive deposits and move factors into their higher grade deposits. As the average grade of ore of payable reserves is raised, total output of gold is increased. The gold supply curve is then upward sloping. More perversely, increases in production technologies which lower costs may serve to *lower* gold production in the short run. Conditions are derived in the next section which result in a downward-sloping gold supply curve in the short run.

Depletion of the average grade of ore is a significant factor in South African gold production.[6] In 1970, the average grade of ore above the pay limit $ag*$ was 15 g/tonne and fell to only 5 g/tonne by 1990. This occurred while the real price[7] of gold rose from US$14.50 to US$52.90. This, of course, ignores increases in technology which may have allowed for more profitable production, despite the drop in the average grade. In the production model in Figure 8.2, grade depletion is reflected in an upward shift in the average mill pay limit–average grade curve. Thus, at a given gold price and pay limit, the average grade of ore of profitable reserves falls and, eventually, the mine is shut down. The effect of significant grade depletion is to cause a reduction in gold output at the price of gold and cause a negatively sloped supply curve.

To summarize, the gold production model outlined above can generate a negatively sloped supply curve for gold if two conditions are met. First, the response of total ore milled to changes in the gold price must be inelastic; second, the curve relating the average mill pay limit and the average grade of ore above the pay limit must be relatively elastic, indicating a greater proportion of low-quality ore reserves. Depletion of the grade of ore over time magnifies the effect, causing the supply curve to become more negatively elastic. These conditions are explored further in the next section.

A condition for gold supply

The relationships in quadrants I, II and III in Figure 8.2 can be estimated to reveal whether the necessary conditions for the perverse negatively sloped gold supply curve exist for South Africa. In quadrant I, the supply curve of ore milled is combined with a derived demand curve for ore milled, derived from the demand for gold. The demand for gold has three components: the demand for gold for fabrication purposes (jewellery, electronics, etc.); official reserves demand; and the speculative and precautionary demands for gold. The fabrication demand for gold is the largest component of overall gold demand and is assumed to be a function of the price of gold (p_g) in rand and average world GDP growth (g) (Batchelor and Gulley, 1995). Official reserves demand is small and typically negative over the sample period, indicating official sales of gold reserves. The speculative and precautionary demands for gold are assumed to be a function of the price of gold, p_g, in rand, the 3-month London Interbank Offer Rate (LIBOR) (i), nominal exchange rates for the US dollar (e_{US}), Deutschemark (e_{DM}) and yen (e_Y) into South African rand, and a world inflation rate (π) computed from a weighted-average world GDP deflator. The choice of these variables is based on a gold pricing model developed by Sjaastad and Scacciavillani (1996).

The supply of ore milled is assumed to be a function of the price of gold, p_g, in rand, the LIBOR rate, i, the production costs in rand per tonne, c, and a lagged ore milled term to reflect partial adjustment [the speed of adjustment to the desired stock of ore milled = $(1 - \beta_3)$]. Inclusion of the LIBOR rate follows Hotelling's (1931) insight that rents from mining should rise and fall by the rate of interest in order to maximize rents over the expected lifetime of the mine. After 1989, the tonnage of ore milled in South Africa declined dramatically, yet production costs per tonne milled continued to climb. This vertical shift in the cost function may have been due to rising wage costs during and after the fall of apartheid. It has been noted that, during this period, labour productivity rose dramatically as a result of a substitution of labour for technology improvements. To capture this effect, an index of labour employment in the mining industry (*le*) was used as an inverse proxy for average wages. A detailed description of data sources is contained in the Appendix.

The ore supply curve is given by equation (8.3). All variables, except the LIBOR rate, *i*, are in natural logarithms.

$$q_o^s = \beta_1 + \beta_2 p_g + \beta_3 q_{t-1}^s + \beta_4 i + \beta_5 c + \beta_6 le \tag{8.3}$$

The expected signs are $\beta_2 > 0, \beta_3 > 0, \beta_4 > 0, \beta_5 < 0$. Owing to the partial adjustment assumption in equation (8.3), $\beta2 = \beta_2^* \lambda, \beta_3 = 1 - \lambda, \beta_4 = \beta_4^* \gamma, \beta_5 = \beta_5^* \lambda$, where an asterisk denotes the true value of the elasticity. The long run elasticities are the above elasticities divided by $1 - \lambda$.

The curve in quadrant II relates the pay limit to the price of gold and can shift outwards due to increases in production costs. The curve is modelled, in natural logarithms, as

$$pl = c(q_o) - p_g \tag{8.4}$$

In quadrant III, the linear relationship between the average grade of profitable reserves and the pay limit can shift upwards due to depletion of the mine. A time trend (*t*) is included to account for this. Both *ag* and *pl* are in natural logarithms. A dummy variable (*d*) taking on the value one after 1989 was included in equation (8.5) to reflect a detected shift in the average grade–pay limit relationship.

$$ag = \varphi_1 + \varphi_2 pl + \varphi_3 t \tag{8.5}$$

In quadrant IV, the model requires an identity between the average grade of ore of profitable reserves and the quantity of gold produced. All variables are in natural logs. Asterisks denote that these are equilibrium variables.

$$q_g = ag^*(p_g^*) + q_o^* \tag{8.6}$$

Assume a generalized Cobb–Douglas cost function of the form (in logs):

$$c = k + \frac{1}{\gamma} q_o = \theta_{ag} \tag{8.7}$$

where γ is the sum of the output elasticities of the factor inputs,[8] *k* is a constant and the cost function shifts upwards with reductions in the average grade of ore (< 0).

The simultaneous system is composed of the five equations (8.3–8.7). To further explore the conditions which may give rise to a downward-sloping gold supply curve, the solution for ag* can be found by inserting equation (8.4) into equation (8.5), then the result into equation (8.6).

$$q_g^* = \varphi_1 + \varphi_2(c(q_o^*) - p_g^*) + \varphi_3 t) + q_o^* \tag{8.8}$$

In equation (8.8) above, p_g^* and q_o^* are the reduced form solutions found from equation (8.3) and an unspecified demand curve,[9] ignoring error terms.

$$p_g^* = f(q_{o,t-1}, i, X) \tag{8.9}$$

$$q_o^* = \beta_1 + \beta_2 p_g + \beta_3 q_{t-1}^s + \beta_4 i + \beta_5 c^* + \beta_6 le \tag{8.10}$$

where X is a vector of exogenous variables in the demand function. In the short run, an increase in the price of gold causes a reduction in gold output if the elasticity of ore supply is completely inelastic. This was shown in Figure 8.2 of the last section. This is easily shown here by taking the derivative of equation (8.8) with respect to the price of gold p_g^*, holding ore output, q_o^*, constant [$\beta_2 = 0$ in equation (8.10)], gives:

$$\frac{\partial q_g^*}{\partial p_g^*} = -\varphi_2 \tag{8.11}$$

The larger the slope of the relationship between the pay limit and the average grade of ore (φ_2) the larger the reduction in gold output. This is an unlikely outcome in the long run as a change in the gold price changes the average mill pay limit and should bring forth a change in gold production and costs.

To derive the general effect of an increase in the gold price, the quantity of ore milled q_o and production costs c must be allowed to change. Because of the assumed endogeneity of the price of gold, it is importance to distinguish why the price is changing. Suppose a change in one of the logged exogenous variables in the vector X causes an outward shift in the derived demand for ore. Equation (8.8) is differentiated with respect to X which appears in the solutions for p_g^* and q_o^*.

$$\frac{\partial q_g^*}{\partial X} = \varphi_2 \left(\frac{\partial c^*}{\partial q_o^*} \frac{\partial q_o^*}{\partial p_g^*} \frac{\partial p_g^*}{\partial X} + \frac{\partial c^*}{\partial p_g^*} \frac{\partial p_g^*}{\partial X} - \frac{\partial p_g^*}{\partial X} \right) + \frac{\partial q_o^*}{\partial p_g^*} \frac{\partial p_g^*}{\partial X}$$

$$= \frac{\partial p_g^*}{\partial X} \left(\left(\varphi_2 \frac{\partial c^*}{\partial q_o^*} + 1 \right) \frac{\partial q_o^*}{\partial p_g^*} + \frac{\partial c^*}{\partial p_g^*} - 1 \right) \tag{8.12}$$

We need to solve for the explicit solutions for c and q_o. Working with equations (8.4) to (8.7) and (8.10), the solutions are:

$$q_o^* = \frac{\left(\beta_1 + \dfrac{\beta_5(k+\theta\varphi_1)}{1-\theta\varphi_2}\right) + \left(\beta_2 - \dfrac{\theta\varphi_2}{1-\theta\varphi_2}\right)p_g^* + \beta_3 q_{t-1} + \beta_4 i + \left(\dfrac{\beta_5\theta\varphi_3}{1-\theta\varphi_2}\right)t + \beta_6 le}{1 - \dfrac{\beta_5/\gamma}{1-\theta\varphi_2}}$$

(8.13)

$$c^* = \frac{(k+\theta\varphi_1) + \dfrac{1}{\gamma}q_o^* + \theta\varphi_3 t - \theta\varphi_2\, p_g^*}{1-\theta\varphi_2}$$

(8.14)

The derivatives in (8.12) can now be evaluated.

$$\frac{\partial q_o^*}{\partial X} = \frac{\beta_2 - (1+\beta_2)\theta\varphi_2}{1-\theta\varphi_2 - \beta_5/\gamma}$$

(8.15)

$$\frac{\partial c_o^*}{\partial q_o^*} = \frac{\gamma-1}{1-\theta\varphi_2}$$

(8.16)

$$\frac{\partial c^*}{\partial p_g^*} = \frac{-\theta\varphi_2}{1-\theta\varphi_2}$$

(8.17)

Inserting equations (8.15), (8.16) and (8.17) into (8.12) and simplifying gives:

$$\frac{\partial q_g^*}{\partial X} = \frac{\partial p_g^*}{\partial X}\left(\varphi_2\left(\left(\frac{1-\theta\gamma}{\gamma(1-\theta\varphi_2)}\right)+1\right)\left(\frac{\beta_2-(1+\beta_2)\theta\varphi_2}{1-\theta\varphi_2-\beta_5/\gamma}\right)-1\right)$$

(8.18)

The resulting product in equation (8.18) is positive so the condition for an upward sloping gold supply curve is given by:

$$\varphi_2\left(\left(\frac{1-\theta\gamma}{\gamma(1-\theta\varphi_2)}\right)+1\right)\left(\frac{\beta_2-(1+\beta_2)\theta\varphi_2}{1-\theta\varphi_2-\beta_5/\gamma}\right)>1$$

(8.19)

The condition in equation (8.19) is certainly not as intuitive as the condition derived in Rockerbie (1999), but that is because the model here considers the feedback from a declining average grade of ore to the cost function. The essence of equation (8.19) is that, when the price of gold increases, producers aim to step up gold production by milling more ore from deeper shafts or surface mining. This has several effects on the model which can lead to a reduction in gold produced.

The term γ is the inverse of the output elasticity of the production function and is also the marginal cost of ore milled. Increases in γ shift the cost function upward in quadrant II of Figure 8.2. For a given price of gold, the average mill pay limit will increase and the producer will respond by moving to higher grade deposits. This makes an upward-sloping supply curve of gold more likely.

The solution also depends on the value of ϕ_2, the elasticity of the average mill pay limit – the average grade curve in quadrant III of Figure 8.2, and the value of θ from the cost function. The larger this slope, the more the average grade of ore will fall given a decrease in the average mill pay limit caused by an increase in the price of gold. It is not clear what effect an increase in ϕ_2 or θ will have on equation (8.19).

A sufficiently inelastic supply curve of ore (small β_2) makes the adverse condition to equation (8.19) more likely, whereas a large value for the elasticity of ore supply to production costs, β_5, makes the condition in equation (8.19) more likely.

Econometric estimation and testing

The system of equations to estimate is given by equations (8.3), (8.5) and (8.7). Instrumental variables for the endogenous variables q_o^s, p_g, pl, ag, and deposits, were constructed using p_s, π_W, e_{US}, e_{DM}, e_Y, g, i, le and q_{t-1}^s as instruments. A generalized method of moments (GMM) technique, incorporating the Newey–West (Newey and West, 1987) autocorrelation consistent covariance matrix, was utilized. The sample period was 1970–99, using annual data. The results appear in Table 8.1.

The estimate of the Cobb–Douglas cost function in equation (8.7) shall be discussed first since its estimation was key to estimating values for equations (8.3) and (8.5). The estimation proved to be somewhat difficult as there was strong evidence to suggest that the cost function was not affected by changes in the average grade of ore until the average grade reached a low threshold level. At that point, costs increased dramatically despite a reduction in tonnage of ore milled. This effect can be seen by inspecting Figures 8.3 and 8.4. Figure 8.3 plots the real cost per tonne milled vs. the tonnage of ore milled. Average costs increase smoothly from 1970 to around 1992, after which costs increase despite a reduction in tonnage milled. The average grade of ore is plotted in Figure 8.4. The average grade falls continuously from 1970 to 1999. It appears that the threshold average grade was reached in 1992, when the average grade was only 5.6 grams per tonne. It has already been noted earlier in the chapter that South African producers began augmenting deep shaft mining output with low-grade surface deposits shortly after 1992.

The problem of the average grade not affecting costs significantly until the threshold average grade is reached was handled in an variable, but novel, way. The

Table 8.1 GMM estimates of equations (8.3), (8.5) and (8.14)

Variable	Equation (8.3)	Equation (8.5)	Equation (8.14)
q_{t-1}	0.731 (11.21)[a]		
p_g	0.128 (3.53)[a]		
i	0.004 (2.12)[a]		
le	0.148 (5.86)[a]		
c	−0.089 (1.66)		
β_0	1.005 (6.36)[a]		
pl		0.364 (8.00)[a]	
t		−0.032 (11.01)[a]	
d		0.017 (0.40)	
φ_0		1.895 (20.49)[a]	
q_t			4.080 (48.60)[a]
ag^a			−8.147 (15.86)[a]
K			−10.001 (26.10)[a]
System R^2 =0.9941			

Note
a   Statistical significance at 95 per cent confidence.

variable *ag* in the right-hand side of equation (8.7) was assigned the value zero up to 1992, after which *ag* = *ag* – 5.6 grams per tonne. The resulting estimate of the cost function in equation (8.7) proved very encouraging.

The equations fit the data well, with the system R^2 around the 0.99 range. A J-test[10] for overidentifying restrictions on the system yielded a value of 9.9485, not statistically significant. The adjustment speed of gold output was small at λ = 0.269, indicating that ore production takes approximately 4 years to adjust fully to shocks to the exogenous variables. The price elasticity of supply was estimated to be 0.128 (0.175 in the long run), quite inelastic as expected, but still significantly different from zero. The coefficient for the LIBOR (a semi-elasticity) was small at 0.004 (0.0055 in the long run), but statistically significant. The coefficient for *le* was small as well, at 0.148 (0.202 in the long run), and statistically significant. Production costs, *c*, proved to be statistically significant in shifting ore supply only at the 89.9 per cent confidence level.

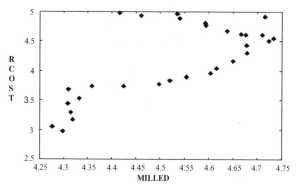

Figure 8.3 Gold production costs per tonne of ore milled vs. tonnes of ore milled (both in natural logs). RCOST, real cost per tonne milled; MILLED, tonnage of ore milled.

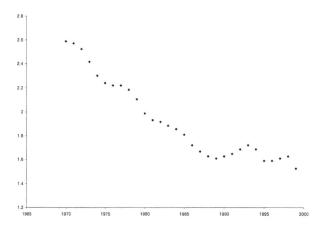

Figure 8.4 Average grade of ore milled (grams/tonne in natural logs), 1970–99.

The elasticity of the average grade (*ag*) of ore to changes in the average mill pay limit (*pl*) is small at only 0.364, but is statistically significant. In Figure 8.2 this would be represented by a steep linear relationship between the average grade and the pay limit, reflecting rapidly degrading deposits of mines operating over the sample period. The time trend variable is negative and highly significant, suggesting that, at 3.2 per cent annually, depletion is a significant factor in South African production over the sample period. The post-1989 dummy variable proved to be statistically insignificant.

The output elasticity of the cost function was estimated to be 4.08 and highly significant. This suggests that producers operated with decreasing returns to scale over the sample period. The threshold average grade indicator variable was negative and highly significant. As suspected, the cost function shifted upwards dramatically after 1992 owing to grade depletion of the milled ore.

The condition in equation (8.19) can be tested by inserting the necessary estimated elasticities.

$$\varphi_2\left(\left(\frac{1-\theta\gamma}{\gamma(1-\theta\varphi_2)}\right)+1\right)\left(\frac{\beta_2-(1+\beta_2)\theta\varphi_2}{1-\theta\varphi_2-\beta_5/\gamma}\right)>1$$

$$0.364\left(\left(\frac{1+(8.147)(0.245)}{(0.245)(1+(8.147)(0.364))}\right)+1\right)$$

$$\left(\frac{0.175+(1.175)(8.147)(0.364)}{1+(8.147)(0.364)+(0.089)/0.245)}\right)=1.2567$$

Equation (8.19) for an upward-sloping supply curve of gold in the long run is satisfied. Even with the addition of feedback effects from a declining average grade or ore to the cost function and the ore supply curve, the upward-sloping supply curve of gold result found in Rockerbie (1999) is confirmed here. It is difficult to determine if the condition is just satisfied or is overwhelmingly satisfied, owing to the complexity of equation (8.19). Simulations of equation (8.19) were performed in which each coefficient was allowed to vary between zero and 1 in increments of 0.01, with all other coefficients held constant to their estimated values. The results are summarized in Figure 8.5. They suggest that small changes in the coefficients from their estimate values could easily push values for equation (8.19) below 1. Hence, the upward-sloping gold supply curve result is quite tentative. This result differs from Rockerbie (1999), for which the evidence overwhelmingly supported the condition.

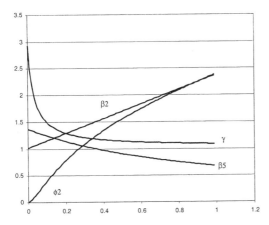

Figure 8.5 Sensitivity analysis of condition 8.19.

Concluding remarks

This paper has specified a model of gold production that makes use of the relationship between the price of gold and the average mill pay limit (the minimum grade of ore necessary to operate profitably), and between the average mill pay limit and the average grade of ore produced. Given an increase in the price of gold, with constant costs, the average mill pay limit will fall, which provides an incentive for producers to step up production and move into deeper shafts of possibly lower-quality ore. If the decrease in the average grade of ore outweighs the increase in the quantity of ore milled, the actual amount of gold produced will fall. The model also considered the feedback from falling average grades to higher extraction costs, which serves to slow the fall in the average grade in response to changes in gold prices.

The model was solved to give a necessary condition for an upward-sloping supply curve of gold which could have only been found by incorporating the average mill pay limit–average grade relationship. With constant ore output and costs in the short run, the model showed that an increase in gold price will produce the perverse result of a downward-sloping gold supply curve. Relaxing these restrictions in the long run produced a complicated condition for the normal gold supply curve which could only be evaluated empirically.

Using sample data for 1970–99 for South African gold production, the model was estimated as a simultaneous system of equations and was found to fit fairly well. Utilizing the estimated coefficients, the condition for a normal upward-sloping long-run gold supply curve was satisfied. A sensitivity analysis suggested that, with only small changes in the estimated coefficients, a downward-sloping gold supply curve result is possible.

Appendix

Data sources

q_o metric tonnes of ore milled
q_g metric tonnes of gold produced
c costs in rand per tonne or ore milled
ag average grade of ore milled, grams per metric tonne
Obtained from *Statistical Tables 1999*.
p_g price of gold per gram in rand converted from the US dollar price per ounce using the US dollar/rand exchange rate and the price of gold per ounce in US dollars deflated using a consumer price index for South Africa. All variables obtained from *International Financial Statistics*.
p_s price of silver per gram in rand converted from the US dollar price per ounce using the US$/rand exchange rate and the price of gold per ounce in US dollars. Deflated using a consumer price index for South Africa. All variables obtained from *International Financial Statistics*.
g an index of world GDP growth obtained from *International Financial Statistics*.

i   3-month London Interbank Offer Rate (LIBOR) obtained from *International Financial Statistics*.

π_w a world inflation rate computed from the percentage change in a weight average world GDP deflator, obtained from *International Financial Statistics*.

le   an index of labour employment in the mining industry in South Africa (1980 = 100), obtained from *International Financial Statistics*.

ex   an effective exchange rate for the South African rand (1980 = 100) obtained from *International Financial Statistics*.

Notes

1 All of these papers consider the long-term price of gold. Cai *et al.* (2001) consider forecasting the hourly price of gold on the COMEX division of the New York Mercantile Exchange, with fairly successful results. Since the supply of gold does not change significantly on an hourly basis, the approach used does not suffer the identification problems to be discussed shortly.

2 Australia is currently the world's third largest gold producer, accounting for 11.8 per cent of world gold production in 1999 (*South African Mining Industry Statistical Tables 1999*, Chamber of Mines of South Africa).

3 Obtained from *Statistical Tables 1994*, Publications Unit, Johannesburg: Chamber of Mines of South Africa, 1995. Supplemented with 1995 data from its annual table (www.bullion.org.za/statistics/min1.htm).

4 Deeper mines do not necessarily produce lower quality ore; however, they do have higher production costs, which through a higher average mill pay limit may be equivalent to lower grades. Of course, there is a limit to how deep mining can proceed profitably without new technologies. We assume that this point has not been reached yet.

5 Any deviation from this assumption should be picked up in the error terms of the regressions to follow.

6 This paper considers grade depletion, not payable ore deposit depletion. The effect of the latter would be to shift the curve in quadrant I to the left (see Hartwick, 1989). Our assumption of grade depletion follows Hotelling's (1931) result that the producer mines so that the average grade of ore declines over time.

7 Computed by deflating the world price of gold by the US Consumer Price Index.

8 This cost function has the property that if $g < 1$, the cost function exhibits decreasing returns to scale.

9 The unknown demand elasticities will not appear in the final condition for a downward-sloping supply curve, hence the demand curve need not be specified.

10 The *J*-test is distributed as a chi-squared random variable with degrees of freedom equal to $MK - P$ where *M* is the number of equations in the system, *K* is the number of instruments and *P* is the number of parameters to estimate. $MK - P = 14$ for the test (see Greene, 1997: 526).

References

Baker, S. and Van Tassel, R. (1985) 'Forecasting the price of gold: a fundamentalist approach', *Atlantic Economic Journal*, 43–51.

Batchelor, R. and Gulley, D. (1995) 'Jewellery demand and the price of gold', *Resources Policy*; 21(1): 37–42.

Bordo, M. and Ellison, R. (1986) *A Model of the Classical Gold Standard with Depletion*, Working Paper, University of South Carolina.

Cai, J., Cheung, Y.-L. and Wong, M. (2001) 'What moves the gold market?', *Journal of Futures Markets*, 21(3): 257–78.

Consolidated Gold Fields, London: PLC. (1988).

Cullen, R. and Craw, D. (1990) 'Gold mining, gold prices and technological change', *New Zealand Economic Papers*; 24: 42–56.

Flood, R. and Garber, P. (1980) 'Gold monetization and gold discipline', Cambridge, MA: NBER Working Paper Series.

Fraser, R. (1999) 'An analysis of the Western Australian gold royalty', *Australian Journal of Agricultural and Resource Economics*, 43(1): 5–50.

Greene, W. (1997) *Econometric Analysis*, 3rd edn, Upper Saddle River, NJ: Prentice-Hall.

Hartwick, J. (1989) *Non-Renewable Resources Extraction Programs and Markets*, New York: Harwood Academic Publishers.

Hotelling, H. (1931) 'The economics of exhaustable resources', *Journal of Political Economy* 39: 137–75.

International Financial Statistics CD-ROM 2001, Washington, DC: International Monetary Fund.

Jackson, R. (1988) *North American Gold Stocks*, Chicago: Probus Publishing.

Katzen, L. (1964) *Gold and the South African Economy*, Cape Town: A.A. Balkema.

Keynes, J. (1936) 'The supply of gold', *Economic Journal*, 412–18.

Mainardi, S. (1999) 'Supply determinants of mining companies: evidence for gold and other minerals in South Africa', *African Development Review*, 11(1): 31–53.

Marsh, B. (1983) 'Keynes on the supply of gold: A statistical test', *Eastern Economic Journal*: 7–12.

Nattrass, N. (1995) 'The crisis in South African gold mining', *World Development*; 23(5): 857–68.

Newey, W. and West, K. (1987) 'A simple, positive semi-definite, heteroskedasticity and autocorrelation consistent covariance matrix', *Econometrica*, 55: 703–8.

Paish, F. (1938) 'Causes of changes in gold supply', *Economica*, 379–409.

Rockerbie, D. (1999) 'Gold prices and gold production: evidence for South Africa', *Resources Policy*, 25: 69–76.

Rockoff, H. (1984) 'Some evidence on the real price of gold, its cost of production, and commodity prices' in M. Bordo and N. Schwartz (eds), *A Retrospective on the Classical Gold Standard, 1821 to 1931*, Chicago: University of Chicago Press.

Salant, S. and Henderson, D. (1978) 'Market anticipation of government policies and the price of gold', *Journal of Political Economy*, 227–49.

Selvanathan, S. and Selvanathan, E. (1999) 'The effect of the price of gold on its production: a time-series analysis', *Resources Policy*, 25(4): 265–75.

Sherman, E. (1986) *Gold Investment: Theory and Application*, New York: Institute of Finance.

Sjaastad, L. and Scacciavillani, F. (1996) 'The price of gold and the exchange rate', *Journal of International Money and Finance*, 15(6): 879–97.

Statistical Tables 1999, Publications Unit, Johannesburg: Chamber of Mines of South Africa, 1999. (http://www.bullion.org.za/).

9 Gold production in Western Australia

An econometric analysis

Saroja Selvanathan and Eliyathamby A. Selvanathan

Introduction

Production of gold in Australia has grown strongly in recent years. Australia is ranked the world's third largest gold producer, only South Africa and the USA producing more. Most of the Australian gold production comes from one state, Western Australia. In this chapter, we use recent developments in econometric time-series analysis to present an analysis of gold production and prices during the period 1948–94. The results show that, if the price of gold (relative to costs) increases by 10 per cent and the price (in levels) remains the same for the next 5 years, then in the first year gold production will rise by 0.3 per cent; in the second year by 2.2 per cent; in the third year by 7.4 per cent; in the fourth year by 8.9 per cent; and in the fifth year by 10.7 per cent. We also use Efron's bootstrap technique to forecast gold production and obtain its standard errors.

9.1 An overview

Mining takes place all over the world. The traditional mining countries, such as Australia, Canada, Chile, South Africa and the USA, are considered as leaders in mining as they progressively introduce new mineral exploration methods and technology. Australia contains 10 per cent of the world's mineral resources. In the last few decades, minerals such as gold, diamonds, base metal and platinum have become the most important commodities explored for and developed around the world.

In 2000, worldwide production of gold was 2,573 tonnes, whereas total demand for gold was 3,946 tonnes. Gold has been the ultimate symbol of wealth for thousands of years. Gold is mainly used for making jewellery and as an investment product. Currently, South Africa, USA and Australia are the major contributors to the production of gold in the world.

Gold is Australia's second largest export earner, after coal. Australia is also the world's third largest producer, producing 302 tonnes of gold in 2000 – which is 10 per cent of the world's gold production, after South Africa and the USA.

According to historians, gold search was initiated by Christopher Columbus in 1492, and the first gold discovery was made in California in 1848. In Australia, which is made up of six states: – New South Wales (NSW), Victoria, Queensland,

South Australia (SA), Western Australia (WA) and Tasmania – and two territories, Northern Territory and Australian Capital Territory (ACT), gold was discovered in various states and territories during different decades. The first gold discovery in Australia took place in 1851 at Hill End near Bathurst, NSW, and then in Bendigo and Ballarat, Victoria, in the same year. The discovery of gold continued at Charters Towers and Palmer River, Queensland, in 1870 and then at Halls Creek, WA, in 1885. The most significant discovery of gold in Australia was made in 1893 in Kargoolie, WA, and the biggest gold nugget, which weighed over 1136 oz (32.2 kg), was found in 1931 at Larkinville, WA, and, surprisingly, was found just 45 cm below the surface.

Table 9.1 shows how gold production has shifted across the various Australian states and territories over the last 150 years. In the initial phase, from 1850 to the turn of the century, Victoria was the leader in gold production in Australia, producing about six times that of NSW. From the early 1900s, WA became the dominant gold producer in Australia. From 1930 to 1979, gold production was on the decline. However, Australia experienced a gold boom during the 1980s, and production took off in all states and territories. Total Australian gold production jumped from 183.8 tonnes during the period 1970–79 to 701.5 tonnes during the period 1980–89 and then to 2,886.5 tonnes during the period 1990–2000. Currently, among all states and territories, gold production is dominated by WA, followed by Queensland, then Northern Territory, NSW, Victoria, Tasmania and SA. Total Australian gold production quadrupled between the 1980s and the 1990s. This increase resulted in gold becoming Australia's second largest export earner. Figure 9.1 shows the annual WA gold production and the total gold production of the rest of Australia for the years 1890–2000. This clearly shows the dominance of the WA gold production compared with all other states over the last century. While Australia, as the world's third largest gold producer, contributes about 12 per cent of the world gold production, 75 per cent of this gold is produced in WA.

In 2000–01, the value of gold exports from Western Australia totalled A$3.07 billion. Figure 9.2 shows the distribution of the WA gold exports across the major exporting markets. WA's major markets include Singapore (31 per cent), South Korea (18 per cent), the UK (14 per cent), Hong Kong (12 per cent), Japan (6 per cent) and Taiwan (6 per cent).

Although gold is important to Australia as a whole, it plays an especially significant role in the economy of WA as it is the largest export in WA. Currently, there are more than 200 gold mines in operation, out of which 80 per cent are open-cut mines. About 90 per cent of the gold produced in WA is exported.

Tables 9.2 and 9.3 show the significant contribution of gold to the Western Australian economy. Among the important mineral production, gold contributes about 17 per cent of the total mineral production, next to petroleum and iron ore. In terms of WA exports, in 1998, gold earned an export value of A$5,337m followed by iron ore (A$3,946m) and petroleum (A$1,839m).

In 1995–96, the gold industry in WA employed 13,838 people, representing about one-third of the total number employed in the mineral and energy industry in WA. As can be seen from all the above statistics, an investigation of the economic forces

Table 9.1 Gold production in Australia by states and territory, 1851–2000 (in tonnes)

Decade	NSW	Victoria	Queensland	SA	WA	Tasmania	NT	Total
1851–59	66.95	554.91	0.02	0.00	0.00	0.03	0.00	621.91
1860–69	93.34	451.83	10.50	0.00	0.00	0.06	0.00	555.73
1870–79	59.53	279.34	67.51	3.80	0.00	3.30	0.00	413.49
1880–89	28.18	192.96	82.80	1.48	0.60	10.77	4.67	321.48
1890–99	63.86	190.68	153.05	1.49	107.64	13.78	6.04	536.54
1900–09	64.62	203.26	160.33	1.95	494.63	17.90	3.39	946.09
1910–19	35.86	97.22	72.25	1.67	321.53	6.50	0.79	535.82
1920–29	6.70	20.14	15.10	0.30	132.73	1.26	0.09	176.31
1930–39	13.42	24.99	25.16	1.44	214.85	3.23	1.71	284.80
1940–49	17.33	25.47	22.02	0.37	202.69	4.46	3.79	276.13
1950–59	8.90	14.40	22.11	0.07	220.55	5.01	16.08	287.12
1960–69	2.71	5.32	21.62	0.01	181.18	8.29	21.02	240.15
1970–79	3.67	0.91	15.93	0.35	95.98	16.67	50.27	183.78
1980–89	24.29	7.46	67.82	0.29	521.67	19.91	60.04	701.53
1990–00	121.87	41.75	297.48	12.83	2,173.21	28.94	210.45	2,886.52

Source: T. Ferguson, 'Australia's Gold Production,' *Gold Net Australia Online Magazine*, January 2002.

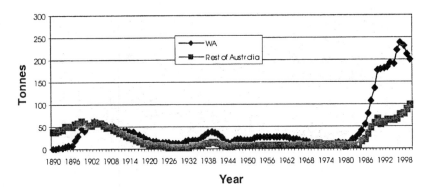

Figure 9.1 Gold production, 1890–1998, WA vs. rest of Australia.

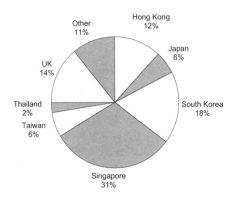

Figure 9.2 Gold exports, WA, 2000–01.

affecting the production of gold is of crucial importance for Australia, and WA in particular. As the ultimate aim in any economic production process is profitability, it is important to analyse the factors that influence and motivate such activity to continue. One of the major factors that drives the production of gold is its price. Worldwide, the gold market is very competitive with large supply and demand responses to changes in the price of gold. This was witnessed in 1995 when the gold price approached $US400/oz and there was a large influx of gold into the world market from non-traditional sources. A rise in the price of gold raises the present value of any discovered deposits and gives an incentive to increase efforts to discover new gold deposits. In the case of existing mines, an increase in the price of gold will possibly increase production by increasing the milling capacity and/or by expanding the gold mining activities near the mine site areas as long as gold price is higher than its variable production cost. A new mine will be opened if the present value of expected gold prices is higher than that of the total production cost. Therefore, in general, a rise in the price of gold will, over the long run, lead to

Table 9.2 Mineral production, WA, 1999

Commodity	Value ($million)	Percentage of state mineral production
Alumina	2,311	12
Coal	268	2
Diamonds	632	4
Gold	2,934	17
Heavy mineral sands	688	4
Iron ore	3,475	20
Nickel	1,135	7
Petroleum	4,806	28
Salt	186	1

Source: Western Australian Minerals Industry Statistics, *WA Chamber of Minerals and Energy Fact Sheets,* 1999.

Table 9.3 Exports, WA, 1998

Commodity	Value ($million)
Gold	5,337
Iron ore	3,946
Petroleum	1,839
LNG	1,551
Wheat	1,723
Wool	516
Nickel	583
Pigments and paints	386
Crustaceans	306

Source: Western Australian Minerals Industry Statistics, *WA Chamber of Minerals and Energy Fact Sheets*, 1999.

increased gold production and hence create more wealth, new jobs and an overall stimulation of the economy.

The declining trend of the gold price in US dollars over the last few years has prompted the Western Australian gold mining industry to take action to improve efficiency. This has resulted in a reduction in average production cost over the recent period, from an estimated A$350 an ounce in 1996 to A$318 an ounce in 2000.

Recently, Feltenstein (1997) analysed the implications of tax policies on the Australian gold mining industry and Sjaastad and Scacciavillani (1997) analysed the impact of exchange rates on the price of gold. A widely debated policy issue in WA is the level of royalty on gold. The Economic Research Centre at the University of Western Australia carried out a study on behalf of the gold mining industry to analyse the effects of the gold royalty on the gold mining industry (Greig, 1998a,b). From July 1998, a gold royalty has been introduced and is operational in WA. Furthermore, the numerical values of supply elasticities are crucial inputs into the economy-wide analysis based on various computable general equilibrium models or for the fiscal taxation issues on gold production (e.g. see Feltenstein, 1997).

Therefore, given the significance of gold to the WA economy and to Australia as a whole, a detailed analysis of gold price and gold production is very important and will be extremely useful to policy analysts in government and in the gold mining industry.

The main aim of this chapter is to analyse the effect of the price of gold on its production in Western Australia over the longer term by employing recent developments in econometric methodology for the analysis using aggregated gold mines production data. Further insights on the behaviour of gold producers can be analysed at the disaggregated level by considering the gold production level of individual mines against mine lifetimes and the cost structure of individual existing gold mines and gold deposits. However, such an analysis is not possible as the required disaggregated data are not available in the public domain and are confidential to individual mines. We also evaluate the supply elasticity of gold, which is used as an important tool/input into various policy analyses.

The organization of the chapter is as follows. In section 9.2, we present the basic data on gold prices and production for WA for the period 1948–94. In section 9.3, we examine the econometric issues concerning the price and production time series, namely stationarity, causality and cointegration, and estimate a gold production equation for WA. In section 9.4, we test the validity of the assumptions made about the model for the gold data. Section 9.5 utilizes Efron's (1979) bootstrap technique to assess the quality of the estimation results and, in section 9.6, we present the implied supply elasticities. Sections 9.7 and 9.8 present the gold production forecasts and the application of the bootstrap technique to obtain their standard errors. Finally, in section 9.9, we give our concluding comments.

9.2 The data

Table 9.4 presents the annual gold production (Q_t) and price data for the period 1948–94 for WA. In columns 2 and 3 of the table, we present the production and value of gold for each year obtained from various issues of the *Western Australian Yearbook,* Australian Bureau of Statistics (ABS). For example, in 1994, WA gold production was 193,599 kg, valued at A\$3,415m. Column 4 of Table 9.4 gives the annual nominal gold price obtained by dividing the value of gold in column 3 by the production in column 2. The retail consumer price index, obtained from the above source and various issues of the *WA Monthly Summary Statistics,* ABS, with base year 1981 (= 100), is given in column 5 of the same table. To obtain the real price (P_t) of gold, we deflate the implicit price in column 4 by the consumer price index[1] in column 5. Column 6 presents this real price, which shall be referred to as the price (P_t). Roughly speaking, this real price can be thought of as the gold price relative to production costs. The correlation coefficient between gold production and gold price is about 0.26 in level form. Here onwards, we use only the log-transformed production $q_t \, (= \ln Q_t)$ series and the log-transformed price $p_t \, (= \ln P_t)$ series for our analysis. We shall come back to columns 7 and 8 later.

In Figure 9.3, we plot the WA gold production and real gold price in log (natural logarithm) form for the years 1948–94. As can be seen from the figure, even though

Table 9.4 Production, value and prices of gold, and price indices: WA, 1948–94

Year	Production (kg)	Value ($'000)	Price	Real index[a]	Price	Log changes × 100	
						Quantity	Price
(1)	(2)	(3)	(4)	(5)	(6)	(7)	(8)
1948	20,684	14,314	692.0	12.6	54.9		
1949	20,155	15,926	790.2	14.1	56.0	−2.59	2.01
1950	18,973	18,933	997.9	15.4	64.8	−6.04	14.52
1951	19,533	19,451	995.8	17.2	57.9	2.91	−11.26
1952	22,706	23,696	1,043.6	21.0	49.7	15.05	−15.27
1953	25,629	26,598	1,037.8	23.2	44.7	12.11	−10.52
1954	26,469	26,627	1,006.0	23.9	42.1	3.22	−6.09
1955	26,189	26,749	1,021.4	24.4	41.9	−1.06	−0.55
1956	25,256	26,405	1,045.5	25.0	41.8	−3.63	−0.10
1957	27,900	29,102	1,043.1	26.2	39.8	9.96	−4.92
1958	26,967	28,357	1,051.5	26.4	39.8	−3.40	−0.05
1959	26,067	28,388	1,052.7	26.6	39.6	0.00	−0.65
1960	26,625	28,140	1,056.9	27.1	39.0	−1.28	−1.46
1961	27,122	28,584	1,053.9	28.1	37.5	1.85	−3.91
1962	26,717	28,115	1,052.3	28.2	37.3	−1.50	−0.51
1963	24,883	26,375	1,060.0	28.4	37.3	−7.11	0.02
1964	22,177	23,383	1,054.4	28.7	36.7	−11.51	−1.58
1965	20,497	22,381	1,091.9	29.6	36.9	−7.88	0.41
1966	19,564	23,316	1,191.8	30.7	38.8	−4.66	5.10
1967	17,916	21,690	1,210.6	32.0	37.8	−8.80	−2.58
1968	15,925	19,407	1,218.6	32.9	37.0	−11.78	−2.12
1969	14,961	19,040	1,272.6	33.7	37.8	−6.24	1.93
1970	12,310	15,811	1,284.4	35.0	36.7	−19.50	−2.87
1971	10,736	13,674	1,273.7	36.5	34.9	−13.68	−5.04
1972	10,848	14,835	1,367.5	38.6	35.4	1.04	1.52
1973	9,264	16,718	1,804.6	40.7	44.3	−15.78	22.44
1974	7,173	19,183	2,674.3	45.0	59.4	−25.58	29.29
1975	6,305	29,788	4,724.5	53.1	89.0	−12.90	40.35
1976	7,644	27,141	3,550.6	60.0	59.2	19.26	−41.78
1977	7,619	31,586	4,145.7	70.2	59.1	−0.33	0.79
1978	13,653	64,741	4,741.9	77.8	60.9	58.33	3.16
1979	12,231	78,313	6,402.8	84.0	76.2	−11.00	22.36
1980	11,598	158,253	13,644.9	91.9	148.5	−5.31	66.67
1981	10,532	165,376	15,702.2	100.0	157.0	−9.64	5.60
1982	16,135	178,566	11,067.0	111.2	99.5	42.66	−45.60
1983	22,992	334,802	14,561.7	122.5	116.9	35.42	17.76
1984	26,183	365,453	13,957.6	131.0	118.9	13.00	−10.95
1985	37,425	508,892	13,597.6	136.1	99.9	35.72	−6.43
1986	46,072	707,114	15,348.0	147.1	104.3	20.79	4.34
1987	64,911	1,300,079	20,028.6	161.8	123.8	34.28	17.09
1988	90,546	1,843,770	20,362.8	173.3	117.5	33.28	−5.21
1989	130,565	2,072,692	15,874.8	186.1	85.3	36.60	−32.02
1990	161,789	2,596,453	16,048.4	201.7	79.6	21.44	−6.96
1991	181,165	2,900,129	16,008.2	211.9	75.5	11.31	−5.18
1992	182,043	2,689,922	14,776.3	213.5	69.2	0.48	−8.76
1993	179,800	2,834,190	15,763.0	214.1	73.6	−1.24	6.18
1994	193,599	3,415,060	17,639.9	218.8	80.6	7.39	9.08

Note
a 1981 = 100.

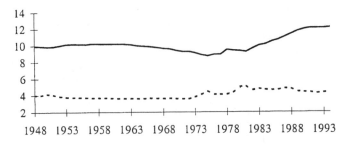

Figure 9.3 Gold production and prices, WA, 1948–94 (in natural logs). ---, Log(*P*); —, log(*Q*).

there are large fluctuations, production and prices tended to move together until the early 1980s and move apart from then on. Gold production increased during the 1950s. Then it declined from the early 1960s to mid-1970s. The decline in gold production during this period can be attributed to the mining boom resulting in the discovery of other mineral deposits such as bauxite etc. From the mid-1970s, again gold production mostly increased, and gold price mostly fluctuated. One reason for the increase in production and prices during the early 1980s is the floating exchange rate mechanism introduced in Australia during the early 1980s, combined with the introduction of new technologies in gold mining. The introduction of advanced technologies in the late 1980s also facilitated productivity improvements as well as new opportunities for mining developments that led to the discovery of new gold deposits and processing of low-grade gold deposits at a lower cost.

We define the production and price log changes as $DQ_t = q_t - q_{t-1}$ and $DP_t = p_t - p_{t-1}$, respectively, where $q_t = \ln Q_t$ and $p_t = \ln P_t$. These log changes, when multiplied by 100, presented in columns 7 and 8 of Table 9.4, are approximately equal to the percentage changes. As can be seen, during some periods, production and price growth rates are positive and very large, and in some other periods they are negative and very large. The average annual change in production (given by the average of all entries in column 7 of Table 9.4) is approximately 5 per cent. On average, prices increased by 0.8 per cent per annum (given by the average of all entries in column 8 of Table 9.4) during this period.

Figure 9.4 plots the production and price log changes given in columns 7 and 8 of Table 9.4. As can be seen from Figures 9.3 and 9.4, gold price was stable until the late 1970s and has become very volatile in the last 20 years. Gold production was also very stable in the early years and has surged suddenly to an all-time high in the last 20 years.

9.3 Are gold price and production series stationary?

A number of empirical studies have shown that many economic variables are either non-stationary or integrated of order 1. That is, their changes are stationary (Engle and Granger, 1987). In a regression model, to avoid spurious regression situations, the variables must be stationary or cointegrated (i.e. a linear combination of the

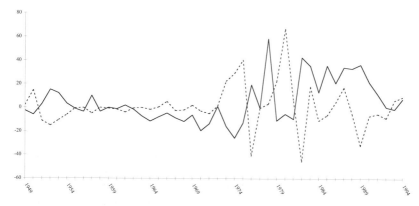

Figure 9.4 Gold production and real prices, WA, 1948–94 (in log changes × 100%). —, DQ; ---, DP.

variables are integrated of order 0). In this section, we investigate whether the gold price and production series are stationary.

As can be seen from Figure 9.3, the price and production series may be non-stationary as the mean is changing over time. The plot of the differenced series in Figure 9.4 suggests no evidence of changing means. This indicates that the price and production series may be integrated of order 1. Supporting evidence for this can also be found by looking at the correlograms of the original series and its first difference series. These plots (not presented here) show that the estimated autocorrelations die down only slowly for the original series (in logarithms) and for the first-differenced series die down to zero very quickly and then appear to fluctuate in a non-systematic way around and close to zero. Consequently, the conclusion is that, to achieve stationarity, we need to use at least the first-differenced series for both production and prices.

9.3.1   Test for stationarity

Now we formally confirm this by testing the two series for the presence of unit roots using the augmented Dickey–Fuller (Dickey and Fuller, 1981) test. In order to perform the 'augmented Dickey–Fuller' (ADF), test we first estimate the three regression equations for a time series Y_t:

$$\nabla Y_t = \alpha_1 Y_{t-1} + \sum_{j=1}^{p} \beta j \nabla Y_{t-j} + \varepsilon_t \tag{9.1}$$

$$\nabla Y_t = \alpha_0 \alpha_1 Y_{t-1} + \sum_{j=1}^{p} \beta j \nabla Y_{t-j} + \varepsilon_t \tag{9.2}$$

$$\nabla Y_t = \alpha_0 \alpha_1 Y_{t-1} + \alpha_2 t + \sum_{j=1}^{p} \beta j \nabla Y_{t-j} + \varepsilon_t \tag{9.3}$$

where ∇ is the difference operator and ε_t, for $t = 1, \ldots, T$, is assumed to be Gaussian white noise. Equation (9.2) includes a constant term but no trend term, and equation (9.3) includes a constant term and a trend term. The number of lagged terms, p, is chosen to ensure that the errors are uncorrelated. We follow the systematic procedure described in Enders (1995) to test the existence of unit roots for the production and price series using the econometric software package SHAZAM (White, 1997).

For the production series in level form, we found that two lags are required to eliminate serial correlation in the residuals. For the price series, this required number of lags is zero. The ADF test results for the gold production and price series in level form and first difference form using equations (9.1)–(9.3) are presented in Table 9.5. For the production series in level form, comparing the values of the test statistics in column 5 with the corresponding critical values in column 4 of the table, we can conclude that the production series in level form has a unit root but does not have a drift (constant) or a deterministic trend term. For the production series in first-difference form, comparing the values of the test statistics in column 7 with the corresponding critical values in column 4, we can conclude that the first-differenced production series is almost stationary. Similar test results for the price series (given in columns 9–12 of Table 9.5) also lead to the same conclusion that, while the price series in level form is non-stationary, in first-difference form it is stationary.

The overall conclusion is that both the production and price series have a unit root and are integrated of order 1 [I(1)]. Since the production and price series are both I(1), we will now investigate whether there exists a cointegrating relationship between the production and price variables. We use the Engle–Granger (1987) procedure, which is based on testing the residuals of the estimated equilibrium relationship for a unit root. Since the production and price series are I(1) with no deterministic trend, we consider the following cointegrating regression:

$$q_t = \beta_0 + \beta_1 p_t + u_t \qquad\qquad (9.4)$$

and test for cointegration by testing for a unit root in the estimated residuals u_t using the Dickey–Fuller (D–F) test. The above regression will not be spurious only when there is cointegration. For this to be true, given that the gold production and price series are I(1), we would require u_t to be I(0). We test the following null vs. alternative hypotheses:

H_0: The series u_t has a unit root (or u_t is non-stationary or non-cointegration between q and p)

H_A: The series u_t has no unit root (or u_t is stationary or cointegration exists between q and p).

The estimated cointegration model results showed $R^2 = 0.065$ and $DW = 0.074$. Usually, when the variables are cointegrated, the R^2 value will be quite high and the DW value will not be close to zero (e.g. Engle and Granger, 1987; White, 1997). The low value of R^2 and the DW statistic, being close to zero, would indicate that gold production and prices are not cointegrated. To confirm this result, we use the

Table 9.5 Augmented Dickey–Fuller test results for gold production and price series

Eqn	Null hypothesis	Test statistic	Critical value	Production				Price			
				Level		First difference		Level		First difference	
				Value of the test statistic	Conc.	Value of the test statistic	Conc.	Value of the test statistic	Conc.	Value of the test statistic	Conc.
(1)	(2)	(3)	(4)	(5)	(6)	(7)	(8)	(9)	(10)	(11)	(12)
(9.3)	H_0: $\alpha_1 = 0$	τ_τ	-3.13	-0.92	Do not rej H_0	-2.13	Do not rej H_0	-2.07	Do not rej H_0	-1.92	Do not rej H_0
(9.3)	H_0: $\alpha_1 = \alpha_2 = 0$	ϕ_3	5.34	1.10	Do not rej H_0	2.27	Do not rej H_0	2.22	Do not rej H_0	2.08	Do not rej H_0
(9.2)	H_0: $\alpha_1 = 0$	τ_μ	-2.57	-0.65	Do not rej H_0	-1.70	Do not rej H_0	-1.27	Do not rej H_0	-2.05	Do not rej H_0
(9.2)	H_0: $\alpha_0 = \alpha_1 = 0$	ϕ_1	3.78	0.63	Do not rej H_0	1.44	Do not rej H_0	0.86	Do not rej H_0	2.11	Do not rej H_0
(9.1)	H_0: $\alpha_1 = 0$	τ	-1.62	0.86	Do not rej H_0	-1.62	Reject H_0	0.18	Do not rej H_0	-2.03	Reject H_0
Conc.				Series is non-stationary		Series is almost stationary		Series is non-stationary		Series is stationary	

D–F unit root test on the residuals. The value of the D–F test statistic for the unit root test on the residuals is –2.98, which is larger than the critical value of –3.04. Therefore, we are unable to reject the null hypothesis of a unit root (or non-stationarity) of the residual series. Therefore, we confirm our earlier observation that the two variables are not cointegrated. As we found no cointegration, we continue the analysis using the first differences of the variables and test for causality (see Engle and Granger, 1987).

9.3.2   Test for causality

We now consider the following set of equations:

$$Dq_t = \sum_{j=1}^{r} b_j Dp_{t-j} + \sum_{j=1}^{s} c_j Dq_{t-j} + u_t \qquad (9.5)$$

$$Dp_t = \sum_{j=1}^{r} b_j^* Dq_{t-j} + \sum_{j=1}^{s} c_j^* Dp_{t-j} + u_t^* \qquad (9.6)$$

and determine the optimal lag length using the likelihood ratio test. The results show that $r = 3$ and $s = 3$ are the optimal lag lengths. Now we test for causality.

The variable Dp does not 'Granger' cause Dq if and only if the past values of Dp do not explain Dq (Granger, 1969). In terms of equation (9.5), this involves testing the null hypothesis H_0: $b_j = 0$ for all j against the alternative H_A: $b_j \neq 0$ for at least one j using standard F-tests. If the null hypothesis is rejected, then we can conclude that Dp causes Dq. Similarly, we can use equation (9.6) to test whether Dq 'Granger' causes Dp. When we tested Granger causality for gold prices and production using equation (9.5), the null hypothesis was rejected and for equation (9.6) the null hypothesis was not rejected. Therefore, we conclude that change in gold price causes change in gold production but change in gold production does not cause change in gold price, which can be interpreted as saying that prices are determined in the world market independent of the Australian production.[2]

Now we derive the supply function for gold. From the producers' point of view, there are a number of factors that will determine the amount of gold they supply. Expected future gold prices and the level of gold stocks, price of other minerals and gold exploration expenditure are some of these determinants. In the short run, as the stock level is almost fixed, gold producers may increase the price when there is a sudden increase in demand for gold. However, in the long run, as the price increase incentive brings new mines into production as well as increasing investment in the working of the existing mines, gold price will move to a lower level equilibrium price (lower than the short-run equilibrium price). This means that the supply elasticities will be substantially higher in the long run than in the short run.

The supply function we use in our analysis is an extended version of the usual adaptive expectation model (Koyck, 1954; Nerlove, 1958), which has been used by other studies in analysing the supply–price relationship of minerals (e.g. Fisher *et al.*, 1972; Eichengreen and McLean, 1994). Such a supply model is more suitable for our analysis since gold producers take a good deal of time to react to changes in gold prices and change their production level. As the adaptive expectation models fall into the class of distributed lag models, our supply equation explains the stock adjustment by expressing the current production of gold in terms of past production and prices. We demonstrate the derivation of the supply function in the simplest case as follows.

Suppose that the supply (q_t) adjustment in the long run can be made by assuming that supply linearly depends upon the long-run expected price (p^*_t):

$$q_t = \alpha + \beta p^*_t + u_t \tag{9.7}$$

with expectations being formed by an adaptive model as follows:

$$p^*_t - p^*_{t-1} = \mu(p^*_{t-1} - p^*_{t-1}) \qquad 0 < \mu < 1 \tag{9.8}$$

where μ is the speed of adjustment of price expectations and u_t is a stochastic disturbance term. Equation (9.8) means that the change in price expectations $(p^*_t - p^*_{t-1})$ are formed by revising earlier expectations in the direction of actual prices, i.e. by the difference between the actual price and the expected price in the last period, $(p_{t-1} - p^*_{t-1})$. If the gold price in period $t - 1$ exceeds expectations, we would expect the producers to revise their expectation upwards.

We rearrange equation (9.8) to give:

$$p^*_t = \mu p_{t-1} + (1 - \mu) p^*_{t-1} \tag{9.9}$$

From equation (9.7), we have

$$p^*_t = (q_t - \alpha - u_t)/\beta \tag{9.10}$$

Substituting for p^*_t and p^*_{t-1} from equation (9.10) in equation (9.9) and after solving for q_t using some algebraic manipulation, we get:

$$q_t = \lambda + \gamma_1 q_{t-1} + \kappa_1 p_{t-1} + v_t \tag{9.11}$$

where $\lambda = \mu\alpha$, $\gamma_1 = 1 - \mu$, $\kappa_1 = \mu\beta$ and $v_t = u_t - (1 - \mu)u_{t-1}$.

As the price and production variables, p_t and q_t, are non-stationary as well as not cointgrated, we consider the variables in equation (9.11) in their first-difference form. That is:

$$Dq_t = \lambda + \gamma_1 Dq_{t-1} + \kappa_1 Dp_{t-1} + v_t \tag{9.12}$$

From equation (9.12), we have the one-period short-run supply elasticity:

$$\frac{Dq_t}{Dp_{t-1}} = \kappa_1$$

To obtain the long-run supply elasticity, in equation (9.12), we set $u_t = 0$, $Dq_t = \tilde{q}$ and $Dp_t = D\tilde{p}_t$ for all t. This gives:

$$\frac{D\tilde{q}_t}{D\tilde{p}_{t-1}} = \frac{\kappa_1}{1-\gamma_1}$$

We shall use an extended version of equation (9.12) as our supply equation in the form:

$$Dq_t = \lambda + \delta D_t + \sum_{i=1}^{r} \gamma_i Dq_{t-1} + \sum_{i=1}^{s} \kappa_i Dp_{t-i} + \varepsilon_t \tag{9.13}$$

where λ is a constant, D_t is a dummy variable which takes value 1 if $t \geq 1985$ or 0 otherwise, γ_i and κ_i, respectively, are the ith lagged production and price coefficients and ε_t is a serially uncorrelated error term with zero mean and constant variance. The dummy variable, D_t, is included to take into account the surge in production during the period 1985–94. As the constant term is insignificant, we estimate the model without a constant term. We also checked the invertibility condition (see equation (9.2) in section 9.6). Using the likelihood ratio test, we determined the optimal lag lengths to be $r = 3$ and $s = 3$.

The estimation results of equation (9.13) without a constant term are presented in Table 9.6. As can be seen, the dummy variable coefficient, the second production lag coefficient and the third price lag coefficient are highly significant.

9.4 Model specification and stability tests

In equation (9.13), we expressed the supply of gold in terms of past prices and past gold production. Now we use the Ramsey's error specification test (RESET) to test the hypothesis that any relevant explanatory variables have been omitted from the supply function (equation 9.13). The RESET is an F-test that regresses the estimated residuals on various powers of the fitted dependent variable and tests whether or not the estimated coefficients are significant (see Ramsey, 1969; Kmenta, 1990: 452–5). If the estimation results in insignificant coefficients, this would indicate that the impact of the omitted variables is insignificant.

We used the fitted value of the dependent variable to the second, third and fourth powers. As can be seen from the table below, all three coefficients do not differ significantly from zero at the 5 per cent level of significance, which, in conjunction with the insignificant Durbin–Watson's value of –0.61, provides no support to suspect that the omitted variables (if any) are significant.

Table 9.6 Estimation results of production equation (9.13), 1948–94

Coefficient	Variable	Coefficient estimate	Standard error	t-Value
δ	D	0.145	0.067	2.17
γ_1	q_{t-1}	0.187	0.144	1.30
γ_2	q_{t-2}	0.296	0.143	2.07
γ_3	q_{t-3}	0.043	0.162	−0.26
κ_1	p_{t-1}	0.030	0.129	0.23
κ_2	p_{t-2}	0.181	0.121	1.50
κ_3	p_{t-3}	0.481	0.125	3.85

	F-calculated	*F*-critical
RESET(2)	1.40	4.08
RESET(3)	0.81	3.23
RESET(4)	0.52	2.84

When we estimated model (9.13), we also assumed that the parameters of the model are constant (i.e. stable over the sample period). Now we use Chow's (1960) predictive test to test the stability of the parameters. The Chow test, also essentially an *F*-test, gives a test for structural changes. The Chow test for structural changes estimates model (9.13) by dividing the whole sample period into two subsamples (for example, using the first thirty-one observations as one subsample and the remaining seventeen observations as the second subsample) and uses an *F*-test to test whether the coefficients of the model significantly differ under the two subsample periods. The results of the Chow test show that there is no evidence to conclude that the parameters vary over time. In other words, the assumption of constant parameters in model (9.13) is acceptable.

9.5 Assessing the quality of the estimates

In the last section, we used various statistical tests to test model specification and model stability for the gold production equation. Based on certain assumptions, the estimates of production equation (9.13) parameters we obtained in section 9.3 are BLUE (linear unbiased estimator). In this section, we use Efron's (1979) bootstrap simulation technique to evaluate the quality of these estimates and their standard errors. This technique has been extensively applied to econometric time series models in the last two decades. For the pioneering applications of the bootstrap technique, see Freedman and Peters (1984a,b) and Theil *et al.* (1984).

9.5.1   *The bootstrapping technique*

Basically, if we have a random sample $X = (X_1, X_2, \ldots, X_T)$ and its realization $x = (x_1, x_2, \ldots, x_T)$ such that X_is are identically independently distributed as F, the bootstrap gives us a way to estimate the sampling distribution of a specified random variable $R(X, F)$ depending on X and the unknown distribution F, on the basis of the observed data x. The bootstrap procedure for a single sample can be broken down into the following steps:

Step 1:   By assigning mass $1/T$ to each $x_1, x_2, \ldots, x_T$, we construct the sample probability distribution $\hat{F}$.

Step 2:   We draw a random sample of size T, $X^* = (X^*_1, X^*_2, \ldots X^*_T)$ and its realization $x^* = (x^*_1, x^*_2, \ldots x^*_T)$ from $\hat{F}$.

Step 3:   We approximate the sampling distribution of $R(X, F)$ by the bootstrap distribution $R^* = R(X^*, \hat{F})$.

We repeat steps 2 and 3 a number of times to obtain a number of random samples of realizations x^* and the bootstrap distribution of R^*.

9.5.1.2   Bootstrap estimates of the production model

Now we describe the application of the bootstrap simulation technique to the production model (9.13). Such a simulation can be used to assess the quality of the data-based estimates and their standard errors.

$E[\varepsilon_t] = 0, t = 1, \ldots, T$ (sample size)

and that the ε_ts are statistically independent and identically distributed in time. We use the estimates of the parameters given in Table 9.6 together with the observed values of the dependent and independent variables to evaluate the residuals:

$$e_t = Dq_t - \left(\delta D_t + \sum_{i=1}^{3} \gamma_i Dq_{t-1} + \sum_{i=1}^{3} \kappa_i Dp_{t-i} \right), t = 1, \ldots, T$$

We have T such residuals, which are identically independently distributed. Let $\hat{F} = \{e_t : t = 1, \ldots, T\}$ be the empirical distribution. We denote the bootstrap residuals, estimators and variables by '*'. We generate a new set of 'pseudo' dependent variables Dq^*_t for $t = 1, \ldots, T$ in the following manner:

Step 1:   Assign mass $1/T$ to each residual $e_t, t = 1, \ldots, T$. We draw T uniform random numbers We have assumed the stochastic disturbance terms in equation (9.13), that the ε_ts, are such that:with replacement in the range of 1 to T using SHAZAM routine UNI. Let the set of drawn random numbers be $\{t_1, t_2, \ldots t_T\}$, each of these ts is a number between 1 and T and they are in any order. As replacement is allowed they need not be distinct.

Step 2:   Define the new errors:

$\{e^*_1, e^*_2 \ldots e^*_T\} = \{e_{t1}, e_{t2} \ldots e_{tT}\}$

Step 3:   Generate the pseudo-dependent variable as:

$$Dq_t^* = \hat{\delta}D_t + \sum_{i=1}^{3}\hat{\gamma}_i Dq_{t-1} + \sum_{i=1}^{3}\hat{\kappa}_i Dp_{t-i} + \varepsilon_t^*, t = 1,\ldots,T$$

Using the D^*q_ts and the observed values of the independent variables, we re-estimate the model (9.13) to get the bootstrap parameter estimates δ^*, γ_i^* $\kappa_i^* = 1, 2, 3$. We repeat this procedure k times to get k sets of such bootstrap estimates.

Table 9.7 summarizes the results of a simulation involving $k = 1,000$ trials. For ease of comparison, we also present, in columns 2 and 3, the estimates and their standard errors given in Table 9.6. We call these the 'data-based' estimates to distinguish them from their bootstrap counterparts. The bootstrap estimates, given in column 4, are averaged over the 1,000 trials. Column 5 of the table gives the root mean square errors (RMSEs) and column 6 gives the root mean square standard errors (RMSSE)s. The RMSE corresponding to the estimate of a parameter θ is calculated as:

$$\text{RMSE}(\theta) = \sqrt{\frac{1}{1000}\sum_{k=1}^{1000}\left(\theta_k^* \overline{\theta}^*\right)^2}$$

and the RMSSE corresponding to the estimate of a parameter θ is calculated as:

$$\text{RMSE}(\theta) = \sqrt{\frac{1}{1000}\sum_{k=1}^{1000}Var\,\theta_k^*}$$

where θ_k^* is a bootstrap estimate of θ in the kth trial and

Table 9.7 Data-based and bootstrap simulation results for the production model

Parameter	Data-based		Bootstrap		
	Estimate	SE	Mean	RMSE	RMSSE
(1)	(2)	(3)	(4)	(5)	(6)
δ	0.145	0.067	0.133	0.062	0.063
γ_1	0.187	0.144	0.185	0.141	0.135
γ_2	0.296	0.143	0.298	0.137	0.134
γ_3	−0.043	0.162	−0.037	0.150	0.152
κ_1	0.030	0.129	0.021	0.122	0.121
κ_2	0.181	0.121	0.180	0.108	0.114
κ_3	0.481	0.125	0.472	0.116	0.117

$$\bar{\theta}^* = (1/1,000) \sum_{k=1}^{1000} \theta_k^*$$

is its average over the number of trials. As can be seen, the bootstrap estimates of all the parameters in column 4 are very close to the data-based estimates given in column 2, which means that the estimates are unbiased. A row-by-row comparison of the data-based standard errors in column 3 with the RMSEs in column 5 and with the RMSSEs in column 6 shows that the standard errors are also unbiased.

9.6 The implied supply elasticities

The gold price elasticity of supply refers to the responsiveness of gold production to changes in the price of gold. Many policy analysts in WA government who argue strongly for a gold royalty seem to believe that the supply elasticity of gold is highly inelastic, if not zero, so that the imposition of the royalty would have little or no effect on production. But the gold industry has argued that a gold royalty would have a severe impact on production, and hence on the WA economy. Consequently, the estimated value of the supply elasticity is crucial for this debate. In this section, we evaluate the implied gold price elasticity of supply using the equation estimated in the previous section.

Consider the estimated production equation (9.13) without the constant term:

$$Dq_t = \lambda + \hat{\delta} D_t + \sum_{i=1}^{3} \hat{\gamma}_i Dq_{t-i} + \sum_{i=1}^{3} \hat{\kappa}_i Dp_{t-i} \tag{9.14}$$

where $\hat{\delta}$, the $\hat{\gamma}_i$ values and the $\hat{\kappa}_i$ values are the coefficient estimates presented in Table 9.6.

Let

$$A(L) = \sum_{i=1}^{3} \hat{\gamma}_i L^i$$

and

$$B(L) = \sum_{i=1}^{3} \hat{\kappa}_i L^i$$

which are polynomials in the lag operator L. Then equation (9.14) can be written as:

$$Dq_t = [1 - A(L)]^{-1} \delta D_t + [1 - A(L)]^{-1} B(L) Dp_t \tag{9.15}$$

provided that $[1 - A(L)]$ is invertible. The term $[1 - A(L)]$ is invertible only if it satisfies the stability condition that the roots (ψ) of the equation $[1 - A(\psi)] = 0$ lie outside the unit circle. Based on the estimates $(\hat{\gamma}_i)$ presented in Table 9.6, we found that the stability condition is satisfied by the data.

In the Appendix, we show that the equation above, equation (9.15), can be expanded as an infinite series of past prices as:

$$Dq_t = [1 - A(L)]^{-1}\delta D_t + \sum_{i=1}^{\infty} v_i Dp_{t-i} \tag{9.16}$$

where

$$v_i = \sum_{j=1}^{3}\mu_{i-j}\hat{\kappa}_j, \mu_k = \sum_{j=1}^{3}\mu_{k-j}\hat{\gamma}_j, \mu_0 = 1 \text{ and } \mu_k = 0 \text{ for } k < 0$$

Recalling that $Dq_t = \ln Q_t - \ln Q_{t-1}$ and $Dp_t = \ln P_t - \ln P_{t-1}$, from equation (9.16), the coefficient v_i can be interpreted as the *implied supply elasticity* with respect to the ith lagged price. These supply elasticities are also referred to as the *impact elasticities*. Column 2 of Table 9.8 presents these elasticities for the first twenty lags. It also gives the asymptotic standard errors in parentheses. As can be seen,

Table 9.8 Implied supply elasticities (asymptotic standard errors are in parentheses)

Lag (years) (1)	Impact elasticity (2)	Dynamic elasticity (3)
1	0.030 (0.129)	0.030
2	0.187 (0.123)	0.217
3	0.525 (0.136)	0.741
4	0.152 (0.097)	0.894
5	0.176 (0.101)	1.069
6	0.056 (0.102)	1.125
7	0.056 (0.074)	1.181
8	0.020 (0.066)	1.201
9	0.018 (0.040)	1.219
10	0.007 (0.033)	1.225
11	0.006 (0.019)	1.231
12	0.002 (0.014)	1.233
13	0.002 (0.008)	1.235
14	0.003 (0.006)	1.236
15	0.001 (0.003)	1.237
16	0.000 (0.002)	1.237
17	0.000 (0.001)	1.237
18	0.000 (0.001)	1.237
19	0.000 (0.001)	1.237
20	0.000 (0.000)	1.237
Long run		1.237

the impact elasticities of lags 2, 3, 4 and 5 are larger in magnitude than the other elasticities.

The impact elasticity, v_i, measures the effect of a price change i lag periods ago on current production. As the change in price will affect production in more than just one period, we need to measure the *cumulative effect* of a number of price effects at lags 1, 2, . . . on the current production. These supply elasticities are referred to as the *dynamic elasticities*.

The τ-year cumulative elasticity (η_τ) is the response to an increase in price sustained over the past τ years:

$$\eta_\tau = \sum_{i=1}^{\tau} v_i$$

These cumulative elasticities (or dynamic elasticities) are presented in column 3 of Table 9.8. The dynamic elasticity reaches a steady state value of around 1.237 after fifteen lags.

The 1-year dynamic supply elasticity is 0.030 (see column 3, row 1, Table 9.8) which means that if, for example, the gold price increases by 10 per cent, this will lead to an increase in production by only 0.3 per cent in the following year. This small increase in production can be understood as showing that an increase in gold prices will take time to result in any major impact on production as new reserves have to be found to increase production. As is to be expected, if we allow a longer time horizon, an increase in gold price will have a larger accumulated effect on gold production. For example, a permanent 10 per cent increase in the price of gold will increase gold production by 10.7 per cent after 5 years, as indicated by the dynamic elasticity of 1.069 (row 5 of column 3 in Table 9.8).

To explain further the interpretation of the first five dynamic elasticities in column 3 of Table 9.8, in Table 9.9 we present the estimated effects (in percentages and levels) of a permanent 10 per cent increase in gold price on its production.

Consider a 10 per cent price increase in 1996, an increase which is permanent (in percentages), as shown in column 2 of Table 9.9. In turn, this will increase the price level from US$500/oz to US$550/oz in 1996 and it will remain the same for the next 5 years as shown (in levels) in column 3 of Table 9.9. The first five dynamic elasticities from Table 9.8 are reproduced in column 4 of Table 9.9. Columns 5 and 6 of the table present the expected increase in production in percentages and production levels in years 1997–2001 owing to the price increase in 1996. As can be seen, in the first year following the price rise, production will rise by 0.3 per cent (from 200,000 to 200,600 kg); in the second year production will rise by 2.17 per cent (from 200,000 to 204,300 kg); in the third year, production will rise by 7.41 per cent (from 200,000 to 214,800 kg); and so on. The corresponding cumulative increase in production levels will be 0.600 kg for 1997; 4,900 kg for 1998, 19,700 kg for 1999, 37,700 kg for 2000 and 59,100 kg for 2001. These are illustrated in Figures 9.5 and 9.6. Letting τ approach infinity gives the long-term (or steady-state) elasticity, called the long-run supply elasticity:

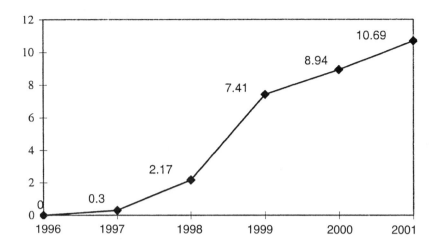

Figure 9.5 Estimated effects on WA gold production of a 10 per cent increase in its price.

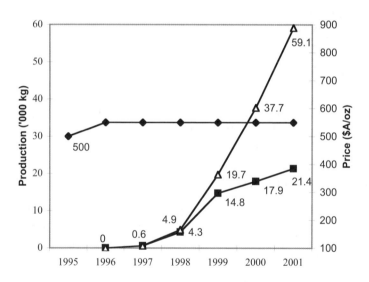

Figure 9.6 The effect of an increase in gold price in 1995 on gold production, WA, 1996–2001. ■, Annual additional production; Δ, cumulative additional production; ♦, price.

Table 9.9 Estimated effects on WA gold production due to a 10 per cent increase in price

Year	Price			Production		Increase in production (in '000 kg)	
	Increase (%)	Level (A$/oz)	Dynamic elasticity	Increase (%)	Level ('000 kg)	Annual	Cumulative
(1)	(2)	(3)	(4)	(5)	(6)	(7)	(8)
1995	–	500	–	–	200.0	–	–
1996	10	550	–	–	200.0	0	0
1997	0	550	0.030	0.30	200.6	0.6	0.6
1998	0	550	0.217	2.17	204.3	4.3	4.9
1999	0	550	0.741	7.41	214.8	14.8	19.7
2000	0	550	0.894	8.94	217.9	17.9	37.7
2001	0	550	1.069	10.69	221.4	21.4	59.1

Note
Production changes are relative to base-year production of 200 (thousand) kg in 1995.

$$\eta_L = \sum_{i=1}^{\infty} v_i = \frac{\sum_{i=1}^{3} \hat{\kappa}_i}{1 - \sum_{i=1}^{3} \hat{\lambda}_i} = 1.237$$

That is, in the long run, a 1 per cent sustained increase in prices would increase the supply of gold by 1.237 per cent. This long-run supply elasticity (also given in the last row of column 3 in Table 9.8) is the same as the converged value of the dynamic elasticities from lag 15 onwards given in column 3 of Table 9.8.

9.7 Forecasting gold production

In section 9.5, we used Efron's (1979) bootstrap technique to assess the quality of the production model estimates presented in Table 9.6. In this section, we set out the procedure to use the production model to predict the consumption for an out-of-sample year and show how the bootstrap techniques can be used to obtain the standard errors for our forecasts.

For the first out-of-sample year, 1995, we use the production model (9.13) to obtain the forecast value for Dq_{95}, using the observed values of Dq_{94}, Dq_{93}, Dq_{92}, Dp_{94}, Dp_{93} and Dp_{92}, and setting the error term to 0. We then obtain the forecast for the production for years 1995 using the relationship $Dq_t = \log(q_t/q_{t-1})$. That is:

$$q_{95} = q_{94}\exp(Dq_{95}).$$

To obtain Dq_{96} from equation (9.13), we need the values of Dq_{95}, Dq_{94}, Dq_{93}, Dp_{95}, Dp_{94} and Dp_{93}. Among the above six values, Dq_{95} and Dp_{95} are not observed while the other four values are observed. For Dq_{95}, we use the prediction obtained in the last step. To obtain the forecast value of Dp_{95}, we use a price model

$$Dp_t = \alpha + \beta t + \gamma \log p_{t-1} + u_t \tag{9.17}$$

which we found to be suitable to model the gold price. The data-based estimates and the bootstrap simulation results for this model are presented in Table 9.10. As can be seen, as before, the bootstrap estimates are very close to the data-based estimates given in column 2, which means that the estimates are unbiased. A row-by-row comparison of the data-based standard errors in column 3 with the RMSEs in column 5 and with the RMSSEs in column 6 shows that the standard errors are also unbiased.

We use the price model, equation (9.17), to obtain Dp_{95} and then use it in equation (9.13) to obtain Dq_{96}. As before, we then obtain the production for the year 1996 as $q_{96} = q_{95}\exp(Dq_{96})$.

For any other out-of-sample year, the same procedure can be used to obtain the forecast of gold production using equations (9.17) and (9.13). Column 2 of Table 9.11 gives the forecasts of gold production for the years 1995–8. For comparison, in column 3 of the table we also give the actual (published) gold productions. As can be seen, our production model forecasts the gold production reasonably well. In the next section, we show how to apply the bootstrapping procedure to obtain standard errors of our forecasts.

Table 9.10 Data-based and bootstrap simulation results for the price model (equation 9.17)

Parameter	Data-based		Bootstrap		
	Estimate	SE	Mean	RMSE	RMSSE
(1)	(2)	(3)	(4)	(5)	(6)
α	0.536	0.268	0.535	0.251	0.250
β	0.004	0.002	0.004	0.002	0.002
γ	–0.161	0.075	–0.160	0.070	0.070

Table 9.11 Actual and predicted gold production, 1995–8 (in kilograms)

Year	Data-based prediction	Observed actual
(1)	(2)	(3)
1995	190,100	189,479
1996	203,110	221,184
1997	214,530	238,335
1998	226,470	231,431

9.8 Standard errors for the forecasts

The application of bootstrapping procedure to forecasting involves four new concepts, namely (1) the simulated actual values of the independent variable; (2) the simulated actual values of the dependent variable; (3) the simulated predictions of the independent variable; and (4) the simulated predictions of the dependent variables. We now explain these concepts.

We start applying the bootstrap procedure to the exogenous variable Dp_t. We obtain the residuals from the price model as

$$\hat{u}_t = Dp_t - \hat{\alpha} - \hat{\beta} - \hat{\gamma}\log p_{t-1}, \; t = 1, \ldots, T \tag{9.18}$$

where $\hat{\alpha}, \hat{\beta}$ and $\hat{\gamma}$ are the parameter estimates of model (9.17) presented in column 2 of Table 9.10. Next, we assign mass $1/T$ to each $\hat{u}_t$, draw a residual from this distribution with replacement and write u^*_t for the tth draw. Then, for each t, taking successive out-of-sample years, we compute:

$$Dp^*_t = \hat{\alpha} + \hat{\beta}t + \hat{\gamma}\log p_{t-1} + u^*_t \tag{9.19}$$

These are the simulated actual values of the independent variable Dp_t.

Next, we replace Dp_t in equation (9.13) with its simulated (starred) counterpart defined in (9.18), the data-based parameter estimates in Table 9.6 and the bootstrap values of disturbance term to obtain the simulated value of Dq_t:

$$Dq^*_t = \sum_{i=1}^{3} \hat{\gamma}_i Dq^*_{t-1} + \sum_{i=1}^{3} \hat{\kappa}_i Dp^*_{t-i} + \varepsilon^*_t \tag{9.20}$$

This Dq^*_t involves two sets of residuals, u^*_t and ε^* the data-based estimates of the parameters of model (9.13) (the hatted values) and the simulated-actual values of Dp_t (i.e. Dp^*_t). The values of Dq^*_t given by equation (9.20) are called the *simulated actual values of the dependent variable Dq_t*. It is to be noted that these simulated actual values are the out-of-sample version of the pseudo-values of the dependent variable defined in step 3 of section 9.5.

To obtain the simulated predicted values of the independent variable Dp_t in equation (9.17), for each out-of-sample year we replace (1) the parameters with their bootstrap (starred) estimates and (2) the disturbances with their expected values of zero. That is:

$$D\hat{p}^*_t = \alpha^* + \beta^* t + \gamma^* \log p_{t-1} \tag{9.21}$$

This is the simulated predicted value of the independent variable.

To obtain the simulated predicted values of the dependent variable Dq_t in equation (9.13), for each out-of-sample year, we replace (1) the parameters with their bootstrap (starred) estimates, and (2) the disturbances with their expected values of zero. That is:

$$\hat{D}q_t^* = \sum_{i=1}^{3} \hat{\gamma}_i D\hat{q}_{t-1}^* + \sum_{i=1}^{3} \kappa_i^* D\hat{p}_{t-i}^*$$

(9.22)

This is the simulated predicted value of the dependent variable.

Comparing equations (9.20) and (9.22), we see that the difference between the simulated actual and simulated predictions of Dq_t is threefold. First, (9.20) uses the data-based parameter estimates ($\hat{\gamma}_i$ and $\hat{\kappa}_i$, $i = 1, 2, 3$), whereas equation (9.22) uses the bootstrap estimates ($\gamma*_i$ and $\kappa*_i$, $i = 1, 2, 3$). Second, for the exogenous variable, equation (9.20) uses the simulated actual values (Dq_{t-i}^* and Dp_{t-i}^*), which are obtained using the data-based estimates. By contrast, equation (9.22) uses the simulated predictions ($D\hat{q}_{t-i}^*$ and $D\hat{p}_{t-i}^*$) from the bootstrap estimates. Third, equation (9.20) has a disturbance term, whereas equation (9.22) does not.

For each out-of-sample year, t, we carried out 1,000 trials and obtained 1,000 bootstrap forecast errors, defined as the difference between the simulated actual and simulated predicted values of q_t.

Table 9.12 summarizes the results. In columns 2 and 3 of Table 9.12, we reproduce the predicted and the actual observed values of gold production from Table 9.11. Column 4 gives the means over 1,000 trials of the simulated predictions; and column 5 gives the means of the simulated actual values. In the last column, we give the root mean squared forecast errors. As can be seen, the difference between the data-based predictions, simulated predictions and simulated actual values are very small except in 1997. Root mean squared forecast errors have mostly increased as we proceed through the years, reflecting the greater uncertainty of the forecasts.

9.9 Conclusion

In this chapter, we have presented an analysis of gold production and prices in WA. We found that the evolution of production and prices can be represented by simple econometric models. The stationarity, cointegration and causality tests

Table 9.12 Actual and predicted gold production, 1995–8 (in kilograms)

| Year | Data-based prediction | Observed actual | Bootstrap means | | |
| | | | Simulated prediction | Simulated actual | Root-mean-square forecast errors |
(1)	(2)	(3)	(4)	(5)	(6)
1995	190,100	189,479	188,610	189,980	20,786
1996	203,110	221,184	202,680	202,730	21,223
1997	214,530	238,335	211,710	214,410	23,328
1998	226,470	231,431	224,120	226,150	24,168

were performed on the production and price time series. The results show that both price and production series are non-stationary, price and production are not cointegrated and that price causes production. Further analysis resulted in a model for the production in first difference with three lags of prices and production. We used the estimated model to evaluate the implied impact and dynamic gold supply elasticities and found that:

1   The impact elasticity at a lag of 3 years is about 0.5, reflecting that, for every 1 per cent increase (decrease) in gold price 3 years ago, gold production would increase (decrease) by 0.5 per cent in the current year and the impact of a price increase becomes negligibly small (less than 0.06 per cent) after 5 years.
2   The dynamic elasticity hits almost unity after 5 years, indicating that the total increase (decrease) in gold production is about 1 per cent for a 1 per cent increase (decrease) in prices during each of the previous 5 years. The long-run steady-state elasticity of value 1.24 is reached after 12 years.

We also used Efron's (1979) bootstrap technique to assess the quality of the estimated results and to assess the quality of our forecasts.

Appendix

Consider equation (9.15) from the text:

$$Dq_t = [1 - A(L)]^{-1} \delta D_t + [1 - A(L)]^{-1} B(L) Dp_t \tag{A1}$$

where $1 - A(L) = 1 - (\gamma_1 L + \gamma_2 L^2 + \gamma_3 L^3)$ and $B(L) = \kappa_1 L + \kappa_2 L^2 + \kappa_3 L^3$. We can write the expansion of $[1 - A(L)]^{-1}$ as the following infinite series:

$$[1 - A(L)]^{-1} = 1 + \mu_1 L + \mu_2 L^2 + \mu_3 L^3 + \mu_4 L^4 \cdots \tag{A2}$$

As $[1 - A(L)]^{-1}[1 - A(L)] = 1$, we have:

$$[1 + \mu_1 L + \mu_2 L^2 + \mu_3 L^3 + \mu_4 L^4 + \ldots][1 - - (\gamma_1 L + \gamma_2 L^2 + \gamma_3 L^3)] = 1$$

By equating the coefficients of $L, L^2, L^3, L^4, \ldots$ to zero, we obtain:

$$\mu_1 = \gamma_1 \tag{A3}$$
$$\mu_2 = \mu_1 \gamma_1 + \gamma_2$$
$$\mu_3 = \mu_2 \gamma_1 + \mu_1 \gamma_2 + \gamma_3$$
$$\mu_4 = \mu_3 \gamma_1 + \mu_2 \gamma_2 + \mu_1 \gamma_3$$
etc.

Substituting equation (A2) and the expansion of $B(L)$ in equation (A1), we obtain:

$$Dq_t = [1 - A(L)]^{-1} \delta D + [1 + \mu_1 L + \mu_2 L^2 + \mu_3 L^3 + \ldots](\kappa_1 L + \kappa_2 L^2 + \kappa_3 L^3) Dp_t$$

$$= [1 - A(L)]^{-1}\delta D + [v_1 L + v_2 L^2 + v_3 L^3 + \ldots]Dp_t$$

$$= [1 - A(L)]^{-1}\delta D + \sum_{i=1}^{\infty} v_i Dp_{t-i} \tag{A4}$$

where

$$v_i = \sum_{j=1}^{3} \mu_{i-j}\kappa_j, \mu_k = \sum_{j=1}^{3} \mu_{k-j}\gamma_j, \mu_0 = 1 \text{ and } \mu_k = 0 \text{ for } k < 0$$

Equation (A4) is the same as equation (9.16) given in the text.

Acknowledgements

The authors would like to thank Professor Kenneth W Clements, Dr Paul Crompton, Bob Greig, Dr H Ahammed, Peter Johnson, Dr Y Qiang and Wan Yang of The University of Western Australia for their valuable comments and suggestions on an earlier draft of this chapter. This chapter is an extended version of the paper, 'The effect of the price of gold on its production: A time series analysis', *Resource Policy* 25 (1999): 265–75.

Notes

1 A better index, which is commonly used to deflate the implicit price of gold, is the Whole Sale Price Index (WSPI). However, the Australian Bureau of Statistics does not compile a WSPI series. If sunk costs are taken into account, the CPI may not be the best approximation to the production cost.
2 We also investigated the impact of variables such as private gold exploration expenditure, private mineral exploration expenditure, the prices of other competing minerals such as iron ore and diamonds on the production of gold and found that none of these variables has a significant effect on gold production.

References

Chow, G.C. (1960) 'Tests of equality between sets of coefficients in two linear regressions', *Econometrica*, 28: 591–605.

Dickey, D.A. and Fuller, W.A. (1981) 'Likelihood ratio statistics for autoregressive time series with a unit root', *Econometrica*, 49: 1057–72.

Efron, B. (1979) 'Bootstrap methods: another look at the Jacknife', *Annals of Statistics*, 7(1): 1–26.

Eichengreen, B. and McLean, I.W. (1994) 'The supply of gold under the pre-1914 gold standard', *Economic History Review*, XLVII(2): 288–309.

Enders, W. (1995) *Applied Econometric Time Series*, New York: John Wiley and Sons.

Engle, R.E. and Granger, C.W.T.J. (1987) 'Cointegration and error correction: representations, estimation and testing', *Econometrica*, 55(2): 251–76.

Feltenstein, A. (1997) 'An analysis of the implications for the gold mining industry of alternative tax policies: a regional disaggregated model for Australia', *Economic Record*, 73(223): 305–14.

Fisher, F.M., Cootner, P.H. and Bailey, M.N. (1972) 'An econometric model of the world copper industry', *Bell Journal of Economics*, 3: 568–609.

Freedman, D.A. and Peters, S.C. (1984a) 'Bootstrapping a regression equation: some empirical results', *Journal of the American Statistical Association*, 79: 97–106.

—— (1984b) 'Bootstrapping an econometric model: some empirical results', *Journal of Business and Economic Statistics*, 2(2): 150–8.

Greig, R.A. (1998a) *The Western Australian Gold Study: Part I*, Discussion Paper No. 98.08, Department of Economics, the University of Western Australia.

—— (1998b) *The Western Australian Gold Study: Part II*, Discussion Paper No. 98.09, Department of Economics, the University of Western Australia.

Kmenta, J. (1990) *Elements of Econometrics,* 2nd edn, New York: Maxwell Macmillan International Editions.

Koyck, L.H. (1954) *Distributed Lags and Investment Analysis,* Amsterdam: North Holland Publishing Company.

Nerlove, H. (1958) 'Distributed lags and estimation of long-run supply and demand elasticities: theoretical considerations', *Journal of Farm Economics*, 40: 301–11.

Ramsey, J.B. (1969) 'Tests for specification errors in classical linear least squares regression analysis', *Journal of the Royal Statistical Society, Series* B, 31: 350–71.

Sjaasted, L. and Scacciavillano, F. (1997) 'The price of gold and the exchange rate', *Journal of International Money and Finance*, 15: 879–97.

Theil, H., Rosalsky, M.C. and Finke, R. (1984) 'A comparison of normal and discrete bootstraps for standard errors in equation systems', *Statistics and Probability Letters*, 2: 175–80.

WA Monthly Summary Statistics, Australian Bureau of Statistics, various issues.

Western Australian Yearbook, Australian Bureau of Statistics, various issues.

White, K.J. (1997). *SHAZAM,* Version 8.0, New York: McGraw-Hill.

10 An analysis of the implications for the gold mining industry of alternative tax policies

A regional disaggregated model for Australia

Andrew Feltenstein

Introduction

This chapter will analyse the implications for the Australian gold mining industry, as well as for the local and national economy, of a tax levy upon gold production. As mining in general, and gold mining in particular, are of special importance to the state of Western Australia (WA), we will also closely examine the macroeconomic impact of these tax policies upon the economy of WA.

We incorporate a regional model of WA as an integrated part of our national model, which consists of WA and the rest of Australia, RA. We permit economic impacts to run both from the national level to WA as well as in the opposite direction. The production structure of our model will incorporate considerable detail about the WA economy in general, and about the mining sector in particular.

The next section will briefly examine certain issues concerning the Australian gold mining industry. Following this, we will develop our model structure and carry out a series of numerical simulations. The final section will be a summary and conclusion.[1]

Issues in the Australian gold mining industry

Gold output has grown strongly in Australia in recent years. Production in WA rose by 4.7 per cent in 1994. This represented about 74 per cent of total Australian gold production, and about 8 per cent of total world output. Indeed, only South Africa and the USA produced more gold than Australia in 1994.

Gold has become especially important for the WA economy, and its current output value of A$3,257 million now makes it WA's highest valued mineral product. Almost 90 per cent of WA's gold output is exported, with the main importers being Japan and Singapore.

The WA government is currently considering enforcing a state royalty on gold production, primarily as a source of revenues. In particular, a 2.5 per cent tax is currently being proposed. Gold is currently exempted from any such royalty. The most common rationale for this tax is that, like all other minerals, gold mining should pay a fee for the purchase of the ore from the state. Another reason appears to be the belief that the tax would have little, if any, economic effects. In other words, the supply elasticity of gold is relatively low. Give the importance of gold to the WA economy, and to Australia as a whole, the imposition of a tax on gold should be carefully examined.

Model structure

Our model is a discrete time, perfect foresight general equilibrium system with an arbitrary number of time periods.[2] We will confine ourselves to two periods for the description of the model. There is production technology at both the state, WA, and national level, RA. There are also capital and labour that are specific to the two parts of the country.

Production

There are four factors of production and three types of financial assets. These are:

- RA capital;
- RA labour;
- money;
- domestic bonds;
- foreign currency;
- WA labour;
- WA capital.

Intuitively, capital is specific to the two parts of the country, but labour can migrate from one part of the country to the other in search of higher wages. Investors may create capital in either part of the country, based on rates of return in the two regions.

An input–output matrix, A, represents intermediate and final production. The technology of this matrix is also sector specific so that it has the form:

$$\begin{bmatrix} \mathbf{WA}_t & \mathbf{X}_{\mathbf{WA}_t} & 0 & 0 \\ \mathbf{M}_{\mathbf{WA}_t} & \mathbf{A}_t & 0 & 0 \\ 0 & 0 & \mathbf{WA}_{t+1} & \mathbf{X}_{\mathbf{WA}_{t+1}} \\ 0 & 0 & \mathbf{M}_{\mathbf{WA}_{t+1}} & \mathbf{A}_{t+1} \end{bmatrix} \tag{10.1}$$

Here we make the following definitions:

- **WA** denotes the WA input–output matrix
- **A** denotes the RA input–output matrix.
- $\mathbf{M}_{\mathbf{WA}}$ denotes imports to WA from RA.

- **X$_{WA}$** denotes exports to RA from WA.
- The subscripts **t, t + 1** denote time periods.

Thus, in each period both the RA and WA economies produce output, using sector-specific value-added. Trade takes place between the two parts of the economy, and the intermediate and final products of each part of the country are distinct, although they may be similar.

We have two data sources for the production technology. The Australian input–output matrix is derived from Australian Bureau of Statistics, *Australian National Accounts: Input–Output Tables* (1994). The WA matrix is taken from Clements and Qiang (1995), while interstate coefficients were derived from Lewis (1995) and *Australian Bureau of Statistics* (1990).

Value-added in the *j*th sector in time *I*, va_{ji}, is given by a constant elasticity of substitution (CES) production function that uses inputs of capital and labour from that period, as well as the existing stocks of infrastructure.[3] It is assumed that sector *j* cost-minimizes with respect to capital and labour. Each sector, *j*, pays value-added tax rates on inputs of capital and labour, given by t^j_{Ki}, t^j_{Li} respectively, in period *i*. Thus, if P_{Ki} and P_{Li} are the prices of capital and labour in period *i*, then the prices charged by enterprises, P_i are given by:

$$P_i = va(P, Y_{Gi1}, \ldots, Y_{Gim})(1 + t)(I - A)^{-1} \tag{10.2}$$

where $va(P, Y_{Gi1}, \ldots, Y_{Gim})$ is the vector of cost-minimizing nominal value-added per unit of output. Value-added is a function of the prices of capital and labour, $P = (P_{Ki}, P_{Li})$, as well as the vector of public infrastructure types, Y_{gi}, which augments the efficiency of value-added. The cost of value-added is, in turn, increased by capital and labour taxes, $t = (t_{Ki}, t_{Li})$, which are paid as withholding taxes by the firm. We use the term $(1 + t)$ to represent the vector $(1 + t_{Ki}, 1 + t_{Li})$. Hence, $va = va(P, Y_{Gi})(1 + t)$ represents the vector of total cost of value-added for each sector. The term $(I - A)^{-1}$ is the Leontief inverse, based on the input–output matrix, A.

The gold mining sector is treated differently from the other sectors in the economy. In particular, gold is not part of the input–output production. Rather, gold output is represented by a Cobb–Douglas production function.

There are two types of private investment, investment in WA capital, and investment in capital in the rest of Australia. In addition, the governments of both WA and RA invest in infrastructure that augments private production. Private investment is assumed to respond to anticipated future returns on capital, as well as future interest rates. Suppose that $H_i = H_i(Y_{Ki}, Y_{Li})$ is a neoclassical production function that produces capital using inputs of capital and labour, and which exhibits decreasing returns to scale. Let C_{Hi} be the cost-minimizing cost of producing the quantity H_i of capital. It is assumed that this capital does not begin to yield a return until the period after which it is produced. Accordingly, if P_{Ki} is the price of capital in period *i*, and r_i the nominal domestic interest rate, then we must have:

$$C_{Hi} = \frac{P_{K(i+1)}H_i}{1 + r_i} \qquad (10.3)$$

where r_i is the interest rate in period i, given by:

$$r_i = \frac{1}{P_{Bi}} \qquad (10.4)$$

where P_{Bi} is the price of a bond in period i. The price of capital is specific to each of the two parts of the country, so the rate of return to investment differs across the country.[4]

Consumption

There are two types of consumers, representing WA and RA labour. We suppose that both consumer classes have the same demand patterns for goods. The consumers differ, however, in their initial allocations of factors and financial assets.

The consumers maximize intertemporal utility functions. We permit RA–WA migration, which depends upon the relative wage rates in the two parts of the country.[5] The consumer has intertemporal budget constraints. He saves by holding money, domestic bonds, and possibly foreign currency. His money demand is interest sensitive. He receives income from factors, and from the interest payments on bonds.

Here, and in what follows, we will use x to denote a demand variable and y to denote a supply variable. The consumer's maximization problem is thus:

$$\max U(x), \, x = (x_1, x_{Lra1}, x_{Lwa1}, x_2, x_{Lra2}, x_{Lwa2}) \qquad (10.5)$$

subject to the following constraints:

(if the representative household is rural, otherwise labour holdings are constant)

$$(1 + t_i)P_i x_i + P_{Lrai} x_{rai} + P_{Lwai} x_{Lwai} + P_{mi} x_{mi} + P_{Bi} x_{Bi} + e_i P_{BFi} x_{BFi} = C_i$$

$$P_k K_0 + P_{A1} A_0 + P_{Lra1} x_{Lra1} + P_{Lwa1} X_{Lwa1} + P_{mi} M_0 + r_0 B_0 + P_{B1} B_0 +$$

$$e_1 P_{BF1} x_{BF0} + TR_1 = N_1$$

$$P_{k2}(1 - \delta)k_0 + P_{A2} A_0 + P_{Lra2} x_{Lra2} + P_{Lwa2} x_{Lwa2} + P_{M2} M_0 + r_1 x_{B1} +$$

$$P_{B2} B_1 + e_2 P_{BF2} x_{BF1} + T_{R2} = N_2$$

$$C_i = N_i \qquad (10.6a)$$

$$\log P_{Mi} x_{Mi} = a + b \log(1 + t_i) P_i x_i - c \log r_i \tag{10.6b}$$

$$\log P_{bi} - \log e_i P_{BFi} = \alpha + \beta \left(\log r_i - \log \frac{e_{i+1}}{e_i} \right) \tag{10.6c}$$

$$\log(L_{rai}/L_{wai}) = a_1 + a_2 \log \frac{P_{Lrai} - P_{Lwai}}{P_{Lrai} + P_{Lwai}} \tag{10.6d}$$

if $P_{Lrai} \geq P_{Lwai}$ otherwise $\log(L_{rai}/L_{wai})$

(if the representative household is rural, otherwise labour holdings are constant)

$$P_{B2} x B_2 = s(1 + t_2) P_2 x_2 \tag{10.6e}$$

where

P_i = price vector of consumption goods in period i.
x_i = vector of consumption in period i.
C = value of aggregate consumption in period i (including purchases of financial assets).
N_i = aggregate income in period i (including potential income from the sale of real and financial assets).
t_i = vector of sales tax rates in period i. Accordingly, the term,

$$(1 + t_i) = (1 + t_{1i,\dots,1+t_{Ni}})$$

where there are intermediate and final goods.
P_{lrai} = price of RA labour in period i.
L_{rai} = allocation of total labour to RA labour in period i.
xL_{rai} = demand for RA leisure in period i.
P_{lwai} = price of WA labour in period i.
L_{wai} = allocation of total labour to WA labour in period i.
x_{Lwai} = demand for WA leisure in period i.
a_2 = elasticity of WA/RA migration.
P_{Ki} = price of RA capital in period i.
K_0 = initial holding of RA capital.
P_{Ai} = price of WA capital in period i.
A_0 = initial holding of WA capital.
σ = rate of depreciation of capital.
P_{Mi} = price of money in period i. Money in period 1 is the numeraire and hence has a price of 1. A decline in the relative price of money from one period to the next represents inflation.
x_{Mi} = holdings of money in period i.
P_{Bi} = discount price of a domestic bond in period i.
r_i = domestic interest rate in period i.

x_{Bi} = quantity of domestic bonds purchased in period i.
e_i = the exchange rate in terms of units of domestic currency per unit of foreign currency in period i.
x_{BFi} = foreign currency price of foreign bonds in period i.
P_{BFi} = quantity of foreign bonds purchased in period i.
T_{Ri} = transfer payments from the government in period i.
s = the closure savings rate for the economy.
$a, b, c, a_1, a_2, \ldots, \beta$ are estimated constants.[6]

Thus, the left-hand side of the first of the four equations, denoted by equation (10.6a), in the consumer's constraint set represents the value of purchases. The next two equations contain the value of the consumer's holdings of capital and labour, as well as the principal and interest that he receives from the domestic and foreign financial assets that he held at the end of the previous period. The equation $C_i = N_i$ then imposes a budget constraint in each period. Equation (10.6b) is a standard money demand equation in which the demand for cash balances depends upon the domestic interest rate and the value of intended consumption. Equation (10.6c) says that the proportion of savings made up of domestic and foreign interest bearing assets depends upon relative domestic and foreign interest rates, deflated by the change in the exchange rate. Finally, equation (10.6d) is a migration equation that says that the change in the consumer's relative holdings of WA and RA labour depend on the relative wage rates.

In the final period of the model we impose an exogenous savings rate, s, on the consumers, as in equation (10.6e). This savings rate is incorporated to determine a closure rule for the economy. Without imposing this or some similar condition, there would be no demand for financial assets in the final period. In practice, we take s to be the long-run savings rate for the economy. Thus, savings rates are endogenously determined in period 1, but are fixed in period 2.

The government

There are two governments, one representing RA and the other WA. The RA government collects taxes and import duties, and pays for the production of public goods and subsidies. Also, the RA government covers both domestic and foreign interest obligations on public debt. The deficit of the RA government in period 1, D_1, is then:

$$D_1 = G_1 + S_1 + r_{F1} e_1 B_{F0} - T_1 \tag{10.7}$$

where S_1 represents subsidies given in period 1, G_1 is spending on goods and services, and the next two terms reflect domestic and foreign interest obligations of the government, based on its initial stocks of debt. Tax revenues are represented by T_1.

The resulting deficit is financed by a combination of monetization and domestic and foreign borrowing. If y_{BG1} represents the face value of domestic bonds sold by the government in period 1, and C_{F1} represents the dollar value of its foreign borrowing, then its budget deficit in period 2 is given by:

$$D_2 = G_2 + S_2 + r_2(\Delta y_{BG1} + B_0) + e_2 r_{F2}(C_{F1} + B_{F0}) - T_2 \tag{10.8}$$

where $r_2(y_{BG1} + B_0)$ represents the interest obligations on its initial domestic debt plus borrowing from period 1, and $e_2 r_{F2}(C_{F1} + B_{F0})$ is the interest payment on the initial stock of foreign debt plus period 1 foreign borrowing.

The government finances its budget deficit by a combination of monetization, domestic borrowing and foreign borrowing. As in Feltenstein (1992), we assume that foreign borrowing in period 1, C_{F1}, is exogenously determined by the lender. The government then determines the face value of its bond sales in period 1, y_{BG1}, and finances the remainder of the budget deficit by monetization.

The WA government spends on local infrastructure, but, unlike the federal government, receives only a portion of the taxes generated locally, as most tax collection is done by the federal government. We model the WA government as receiving all its revenues from revenue-sharing from the federal government. The WA government finances a deficit solely by domestic borrowing, rather than by the additional instruments of monetization and foreign borrowing. Accordingly, a WA deficit leads to debt, rather than monetary expansion.

The foreign sector and exchange rate determination

The foreign sector is represented by a simple export equation in which aggregate demand for exports is determined by domestic and foreign price indices, as well as world income. The specific form of the non-mining export equation is:

$$\Delta X_{noi} = \sigma_1 \left[\frac{\Pi_i}{\Delta e_i + \Pi_{Fi}} \right] + \sigma_2 \Delta y_{wi} \tag{10.9}$$

where the left-hand side of the equation represents the change in the dollar value of Australian non-mining exports in period i, Π_i is inflation in the domestic price index, Δe_i is the percentage change in the exchange rate, and Π_{Fi} is the foreign rate of inflation. Also, Δy_{wi} represents the percentage change in world income, denominated in dollars. Finally, σ_1 and σ_2 are corresponding elasticities.

Gold exports are determined separately. We take supply elasticities from Selvanathan (1986) and use them to derive export response. We use Selvanathan's 1-year 'dynamic elasticity' estimates (Table 4.1) to derive a medium-term supply response elasticity. Thus the export response of WA gold is endogenously determined based on the domestic currency price change and the assumed supply elasticities.

Demand for imports is endogenous; foreign lending is exogenous. Thus, gross capital inflows are exogenous, but the overall change in reserves is endogenous.

The RA government also attempts to adjust the exchange rate. The supply of foreign reserves available to the government in period i is given by:

$$yFGi = yFG(i-1) + X_i - M_{fti-1)} + - x_{Fi} + C_{Fi} \qquad (10.10)$$

Here x_{Fi} represents the demand for foreign assets by citizens of RA, so $x_{F(I-1)} - x_{Fi}$ represents private capital flows. The current account is determined by x_i exports and M_i imports. Finally, C_{Fi} denotes exogenous foreign borrowing by the home government. As before, the subscripts $i = 1, 2$ denote the time period.

The RA government has a demand for foreign assets which, we suppose, is determined by an exchange rate rule. Let y_{Fi} represent whatever the government feels to be the critical level of foreign reserves in period i. The government wishes to peg the exchange rate in period i, e_{i-1} at its level of the previous period, e_{i-1}. It will, however, adjust the exchange rate if its stock of reserves, y_{FGi} deviates from its target, y_{Fi}. When reserves exceed the government's target, the government leaves the exchange rate as it is, or revalues it only slightly. When reserves are below the government's target, the government devalues the exchange rate substantially.

Numerical results

As our model does not permit an analytical solution, we will use a numerical solution method to derive certain qualitative conclusions about government policies.[7] We then derive a fixed point that corresponds to an intertemporal equilibrium. Our numerical algorithm determines the prices and quantities that constitute this fixed point, and that, in turn, are the market clearing equilibrium for our model.

Calibration and data sources

In order to simulate our model we have used parameter estimates that are derived from a variety of Australian sources. The Australian input–output matrix is taken from Clements and Qiang (CQ) (1995). We have created a 7×7 matrix, based on their 42×42 dimensional matrix by adding corresponding rows and columns. The WA input–output matrix was also derived from Clements and Qiang (1995) in a similar manner. The inputs of real value-added are taken to be equal to employment in each sector in both the WA and RA matrices. These, in turn, are taken from CQ Table 2.2. The coefficients of capital and labour in the WA and RA production functions are derived by aggregating shares in the RA input–output matrix given in Table 11 of *Australian National Accounts – Input–Output Tables 1989–90* (IO-90) and by a similar aggregation in Table 4.2 in CQ.[8]

Finally, we need to derive coefficients for inter-state trade. We use Lewis (1995), Table 9, to derive inputs into RA from WA by assuming that all exports from WA to RA are used as intermediate inputs to RA production. Import coefficients into WA are derived from Australian Bureau of Statistics (1990), Table 7.

Tax rates are assumed to be the same in both parts of the country. Sales tax rates are derived by taking the total commodity and indirect taxes paid by sector, divided by the value of final demand for the sector. These, in turn, are taken from Table 11 (IO-90). Corporate and personal income tax rates are derived from Reserve Bank of Australia (RBA) (December 1992), Table E.1. The corresponding income from capital and labour is taken from Table 11 (IO-90). We assume the same income tax rates for WA and RA.

Federal government spending as a share of GDP is taken from *Australian National Accounts – Input–Output Tables 1989–90*, Tables E.1 and G.6. In the government's production function, we have assumed that factor shares are the same for the RA service sector. Factor shares in the investment functions are taken to be the same as their shares in the RA construction sector.

The demand side of the economy is developed in the following way. We assume that both the WA and RA representative consumers have the same demand parameters. These parameters are then taken to be expenditure shares. We derive these shares from *Australian National Accounts – Input–Output Tables 1989–90*, Table 11. Initial allocations are derived from several sources. The allocations of capital and labour are taken as the 1989–90 value of the returns to capital and labour from IO-90, Table 11. The initial holdings of money are taken as the 1989–90 end of year stock of M1. We divide the holdings of money between the two consumer classes according to the relative sizes of RA vs. WA incomes. These stocks are taken from RBA (December 1992), Table D1. The stocks of debt are taken to be the outstanding Treasure notes at the end of 1989–90, taken from RBA (December 1992), Table E.3. Finally, initial holdings of foreign assets by domestic citizens is given by non-official foreign borrowing, taken from RBA (June 1994), Table H.6. We also need certain behavioural parameters.

These are those in the money demand equation (10.6b), the portfolio balance equation (10.6c) and the migration equation (10.6d). These parameters were estimated in Feltenstein (1986).

We have incorporated the various estimated parameters described above and have then run the macroeconomic model for the years 1990–91 to 1991–92, taking 1989–90 as the base year. In order to specify an exchange rate regime, we have said that, if the level of foreign reserves falls below a target level equal to 3 months of reserves, then the slope of the central bank's devaluation is set equal to –2.0. If the level of reserves rises above the target level, then the bank revalues with a slope of –0.5. Clearly, these numbers are for illustrative purposes only. Table 10.1 gives the results of our base simulation.

We accurately project the rate of growth of real GDP. However, we underestimate tax revenues. This discrepancy is due to our inclusion of only a limited number of taxes. Our simulated values for the tax revenues of the RA government and for WA state income are reasonably accurate. We are accurate in simulating the national rate of inflation. Our prediction of national exports is accurate, although imports are low. Interest rates are reasonably accurately predicted.

Table 10.1 Base simulation (the numbers in parentheses are historical values)

	1990/91		1991/92	
Nominal GDP[a]	378.1	(378.1)	407.2	(384.7)
Real GDP[b]	257.1	(257.1)	257.1	(257.9)
Government spending[c]	24.5	(27.2)	25.8	(28.5)
Revenues[c]	16.7	(24.7)	20.3	(24.7)
Government budget surplus[c]	−7.8	(−2.5)	−5.5	(−3.8)
WA state income[a]	40.7	(34.3)	41.6	(36.7)
RA/WA migration (per cent)[d]	NA		0.2	
WA gold output (gross)[e]	100.0	(NA)	104.9	(NA)
WA budget surplus[f]	4.5	(NA)	9.6	(NA)
Exports[c]	13.4	(13.8)	13.2	(14.3)
Imports[c]	9.1	(13.0)	11.2	(13.3)
Trade balance[c]	4.3	(0.8)	2.0	(1.0)
Inflation rate[g]	8.1	(8.1)	7.7	(5.2)
Interest rate[h]	11.2	(11.2)	10.1	(8.9)
Real interest rate	2.8	(2.8)	2.2	(3.5)
Exchange rate[i]	1.30	(1.30)	1.35	(1.34)

Notes
a In billions of dollars.
b In billions of 1984–85 dollars.
c As a percentage of GDP.
d This is the percentage of the RA work force that moves to WA after the first year. A (−) sign would indicate migration from WA to RA.
e This is an index number based on 1990–91.
f As a percentage of WA state income.
g In per cent.
h The historical interest rate is the 10-year treasury bond rate, taken from Reserve Bank of Australia, *Bulletin* (December 1992), Table F2.
i In A$ per US$.
NA, not available.

A gold tax

Suppose we now impose a tax on the exports of gold. We will introduce a 2.5 per cent tax on gold, paid by producers. The results of this simulation are given in Table 10.2.

We observe some interesting changes. Real national income has declined by 0.08 per cent by the second year, as compared with the benchmark case. The government budget deficit has remained roughly constant in both years. WA State income has declined, along with moderate drops in gold output of 0.5 per cent in the first year and 1.1 per cent by the second year. The trade balance has deteriorated by 0.1 per cent of GDP in both years, compared with the base case. The WA budget surplus has increased.

Table 10.3 presents the results of Table 10.2 in a slightly different fashion. Here we calculate the percentage change in the relevant variable from the base simulation to the simulation with a tax increase.

Table 10.2 A tax of 2.5 per cent on gold

	1990/91	*1991/92*
Nominal GDP[a]	377.3	405.8
Real GDP[b]	257.1	256.9
Government spending[c]	24.4	25.8
Revenues[c]	16.6	20.3
Government budget surplus[c]	–7.8	–5.5
WA state income[a]	40.6	41.4
RA/WA migration (per cent)[d]	NA	0.2
WA gold output (gross)[e]	99.5	103.7
WA budget surplus[f]	4.6	9.7
Exports[c]	13.3	13.2
Imports[c]	9.1	11.3
Trade balance[c]	4.2	1.9
Inflation rate[g]	7.9	7.6
Interest rate	11.1	10.1
Real interest rate	3.0	2.3
Exchange rate[h]	1.30	1.35

Notes
a In billions of dollars.
b In billions of 1984–85 dollars.
c As a per cent of GDP.
d This is the per cent of the RA work force that moves to WA after the first year. A (–) sign would indicate migration from WA to RA.
e This is an index number base on 1990–91 of the Table 10.1 simulation.
f As a per cent of WA state income.
g In per cent.
h In A$ per US$.
NA, not available.

As a further analysis of our results, Table 10.4 reports percentage changes in gross real output for each of the WA sectors, when Table 10.2 is compared with Table 10.1. This thus gives a disaggregated view of the impact of the tax increase on the real state economy.

The tax change has had a small and relatively uniform effect upon sectoral output in WA. Sectoral changes are largely generated by changes in factor prices, which are, in turn, uniform across sectors. Accordingly, the only sectoral differences come from the different structure of costs. Imports from RA decline because of the slight decline in WA state income. We notice that WA sectoral gross (real) outputs decline less than does WA nominal income, as shown in Table 10.3. The reason for this is that the WA rate of inflation declines as a result of the tax change, just as does the RA inflation rate. Accordingly, the decline in nominal WA income is greater than the real decline, which would essentially correspond to the sectoral changes of Table 10.4.

We thus see that the gold tax has had a slight, but largely negative, impact upon both the national and WA economies. Indeed, the expected national budgetary

Table 10.3 Percentage changes caused by tax implementation[a]

	1990/91	*1991/92*
Nominal GDP	–0.2	–0.3
Real GDP	0.0	–0.08
Government spending	–0.4	0.0
Revenues	–0.6	0.0
Government budget surplus	0.0	0.0
WA state income	–0.2	–0.5
RA/WA migration (per cent)	NA	0.0
WA gold output (gross)	–0.5	–1.1
WA budget surplus	2.2	1.0
Exports	–0.7	0.0
Imports	0.0	0.9
Trade balance	–2.3	–0.5
Inflation rate	–2.5	–1.3
Interest rate	–0.9	0.0
Real interest rate	7.1	4.5
Exchange rate	0.0	0.0

Note

a   The numbers represent the percentage changes from Table 10.1 to Table 10.2, thus some of these percentages differences, such as changes in GDP, or shares of GDP. Others are second differences, such as changes in rates of inflation or interest rates.

Table 10.4 Sectoral changes caused by 2.5 per cent gold tax[a] in WA

Sector	*1990/91*	*1991/92*
Agriculture	–0.1	–0.1
Mining	–0.1	–0.2
Manufacturing	–0.1	–0.1
Electricity	0.0	–0.1
Construction	–0.2	0.0
Commerce and services	–0.1	–0.1
Imports from RA	–0.1	–0.1

Note

a   These represent the percentage change in real gross output of each of the seven WA production sectors when the gold tax is implemented.

improvements have not materialized, and both RA and WA real incomes have declined. Real interest rates have increased, presumably stifling future investment, and the trade balance has deteriorated.

Summary and conclusion

We have constructed a dynamic model of the Australian economy that has a regional subsection representing Western Australia. Each part of the economy is represented by distinct technologies, consumer groups and governments. Within the West Australia subeconomy, we have a technology for the gold mining industry as a subset of the aggregate mining industry.

We use estimated behavioural parameters from a variety of sources to implement our model. As a first step, we show that the estimated model generates a reasonably accurate approximation to actual Australian outcomes for the years 1990–92. We then carry out a simulation in which gold exports are subject to a 2.5 per cent tax. The resulting outcome indicates that there is no fiscal improvement at the national level, although the WA budget improves. At the same time, however, real income falls both nationally and in WA, as reduced gold sales cause the trade balance to deteriorate, and an increased real interest rate causes investment to fall.

We conclude that the taxation of gold exports may appear to be a promising source of revenues. However, our results indicate that such taxation leads to few measurable benefits, and, in fact, may have quite negative consequences.

Acknowledgements

This chapter was written as part of an analysis of the gold mining industry in Australia. Most of the underlying work was carried out while I was visiting the Economic Research Centre of the University of Western Australia. I would like to thank Kenneth Clements and Robert Greig for many suggestions. I would also like to thank Eleanor Lewis and Ye Qiang for assistance.

Notes

1 Much of this section is taken from Department of Minerals and Energy (1994).
2 In our applications, the length of a period is 1 year.
3 Here and in all subsequent equations, the subscript i, referring to a time period, has, unless otherwise specified, the values $i = 1, 2$.
4 Here, p_k differs from WA to RA. We use the same notation for both parts of the country to avoid unreadable subscripts.
5 This approach is motivated by the Harris and Todaro (1970) model. Feltenstein (1992) estimates such a model for Mexico.
6 The first three of these constraints are the coefficients of equation (10.6b), money demand. The next two are the coefficients of migration (the subscripts do not refer to time periods). The last two are the coefficients for the portfolio balance equation.
7 In our numerical implementation, we use values from Feltenstein (1986) for these behavioural coefficients.
8 We use an iterative algorithm based upon Merrill (1972).

References

Australian Bureau of Statistics (various issues) *State Accounts: Australian National Accounts*.

Australian Bureau of Statistics (1990*) Interstate and Foreign Trade: Western Australia 1988–9*, Western Australia.

Australian Bureau of Statistics (1994) *Labour Force Estimates*.

Clements, K.W. and Qiang, Y. (1995) *A New Input–Output Table for Western Australia*, Economic Research Centre Monograph, Perth: Department of Economics, the University of Western Australia.

Department of Minerals and Energy (1994*) Mineral and Petroleum Production: Statistics Digest*, Western Australia: Policy and Planning Division.

Feltenstein, A. (1986) 'An inter-temporal general equilibrium analysis of financial crowding out: a policy model and an application to Australia', *Journal of Public Economics*, 31: 79–104.

Feltenstein, A. (1992) 'Oil prices and rural migration: the Dutch disease goes south', *Journal of International Money and Finance*, 11: 273–91.

Harris, J.R. and Todaro, M. (1970) 'Migration, unemployment and development: a two sector model', *American Economic Review*, 40: 126–42.

Lewis, E. (1995) 'Western Australian interstate and overseas exports by industry', Economic Research Centre Discussion Paper, Perth: Department of Economics, University of Western Australia.

Merrill, O.H. (1972) 'Application and extensions of an algorithm that computes fixed points of certain non-empty convex upper semi-continuous point to set mappings', Doctoral dissertation of Ann Arbor, MI, University of Michigan.

Reserve Bank of Australia (various issues) *Bulletin*, Australia, Sydney.

Selvanathan, S. (1986) 'An econometric study of gold production and prices', Discussion Paper No. 86.07, Perth: Department of Economics, the University of Western Australia.

Index